What This Book Will Do for You

IT WILL:

1. Tell you how to give your life a new purpose, a new meaning, a new importance.
2. Show you how to make new friendships quickly and easily.
3. Bring you a new way to cultivate self-confidence, inner peace and spiritual strength.
4. Tell you how to overcome the worries that burden your life.
5. Give you the secret of feeling youthful indefinitely.
6. Provide you with a tested formula for marital happiness in your retirement years.
7. Give you the inspiring stories of more than one hundred everyday people who refused to grow old.
8. Tell you how to make younger people like you instantly.
9. Give you twelve reasons why the rest of your life can be the best of your life.

How to Make
the Rest of Your Life
the Best of Your Life

BY

HENRY LEGLER

SIMON AND SCHUSTER
NEW YORK

LIBRARY OF CONGRESS CATALOG CARD NUMBER: 67–25383
DESIGNED BY EVE METZ
MANUFACTURED IN THE UNITED STATES OF AMERICA
BY AMERICAN BOOK–STRATFORD PRESS, INC., NEW YORK

For permission to include excerpted material, grateful thanks must go to the authors and publishers listed below. Any omissions are accidental and will be corrected in future printings upon notification to the editor or publisher.

Bell-McClure Syndicate for quotations by Dorothy Dix, from her newspaper column.

The Bobbs-Merrill Company, Inc., for quotations from *How Never to Be Tired*, copyright 1944, 1954 by Marie Beynon Ray, reprinted by permission of the publishers.

Thomas Collins for anecdote excerpt from *The Golden Years*.

Doubleday & Company, Inc., for permission to reprint the passage from *Adventures in Friendship* by David Grayson.

William H. Dreier for permission to use quotation which appeared in *Modern Maturity*, the magazine of the A.A.R.P. (American Association of Retired Persons).

Emerson Books, Inc., for permission to use quotation from *A Woman's Best Years* by W. Beran Wolfe.

Encyclopedia of Mental Health, Division of Frank Watts, Inc., for permission to use quotation by Felix von Mendelsohn in *The Encyclopedia of Mental Health*.

Fort Lauderdale *News*, for permission to reprint the article of December 9, 1964, on Mr. Orra O. Bishop.

Harper & Row, Publishers, Inc., for permission to use quotation from *On Being a Real Person* by Harry Emerson Fosdick, copyright 1943; and from *This I Do Believe* by David E. Lilienthal, copyright 1949.

The John Day Company, Inc., for permission to use quotation from *The Importance of Living* by Lin Yutang, copyright 1937 by The John Day Company, Inc.

Helen Keller for excerpt from her writings in chapter entitled, "Something to Cling To."

Donald P. Kent, former Director of the Office of Aging of the Welfare Administration, U.S. Department of Health, Education and Welfare, for

Dedicated to
LEON SHIMKIN
who inspired me,
guided me,
aided me,
humored me,
coaxed me,
cajoled me,
and encouraged me
to write and to
FINISH
this book.

How This Book Was Written—and Why

Not long ago I rented a "drive yourself" automobile at New York's Kennedy International Airport. It was a brand-new model. I remember commenting to the uniformed attendant, "I'm lucky to get a new one." She said, *"All* our cars are new, sir."

I was curious. "What do you do with your last year's models?"

"We dispose of them, sir."

"Do you mean to say your cars are worn out after one year of service?"

"Oh no, sir," she said. "But you see, our customers insist on the latest models."

As I drove off in my brand-new rented car, I wondered what her answer might have been if I had asked, "What do you do with the president of your company when he reaches sixty-five?" And with a grim sense of humor I imagined her saying, "We dispose of him, sir!"

So completely has the cult of contrived obsolescence taken over in today's competitive world that even human beings are tagged for discard long before their usefulness is over.

It is not the purpose of this book to editorialize on the defects of compulsory retirement. The practice of dumping out personnel, willy-nilly, at age sixty-five or even earlier is sweeping American business and industry like a contagion.

And nothing can stop it. The best that can be said for this
senseless custom is that it plays no favorites. Presidents,
treasurers, general managers, factory workers—each and every
one feels the sharp blade of the guillotine at three-score years
and five.

My own retirement, I am happy to say, was voluntary.
Perhaps as a result I can be more objective in writing a book
entitled *How to Make the Rest of Your Life the Best of Your
Life*. Before I left the advertising agency where I had spent
twenty-five years of my life, I asked my partner, H. Paul War-
wick, an earnest favor. "Please don't give me a farewell
luncheon," I said. "And don't announce that I am moving to
Florida. I'm just . . . taking a vacation. If they begin to ask
questions after a few weeks, tell them I'm on a leave of
absence. Or a sabbatical year. Explain it any way you like—
but don't say 'Henry has retired.' " Paul respected my wishes,
and late one afternoon when the office had closed for the day
I cleaned out my desk and quietly slipped away.

Looking back, I feel sure that my clandestine departure
after a quarter of a century with the same company must
have seemed to my associates a callous and cowardly exit. I
rationalized my rudeness with the excuse that I hated to say
"goodbyes." But I knew in my heart that I could not face the
agonizing ceremonial which the world of business has devised, mistakenly, to flatter its outgoing retirees but which
more often deflates and debases their egos.

I had sat through several of these "Luncheons in Honor of
Our Retiring Vice-President" with a sickening sadness at the
sight of intelligent, well-meaning men indulging in bathos.
How many times I had risen to my feet at luncheon tables to
applaud long-winded eulogies, sticky with fulsome praise.
One in particular I shall never forget. It was a dinner in

honor of a whip-cracking sales manager whose retirement was covertly regarded by his associates as a real occasion for rejoicing. There was much mirth, laughter and goodwill as the chairman presented their sacrificial leader with a tissue-wrapped gift from "the boys in the sales department."

It was a rocking chair! This was his reward, a token of doubtful esteem after twenty-seven years of faithful service to his company. Eloquently it said, "You're finished, old boy!" He got the message. I talked with him later and he told me how he had suffered through that farewell dinner. "I realize," he said, "that the rocking chair was just a gimmick, but it was too meaningful a symbol for comfort."

I have seen at close range the devastating effects of compulsory retirement on the minds and bodies of men. The frustration. The loss of self-respect. The shocking realization that their days of importance are over. I have watched a retired neighbor, once the comptroller of a huge network of companies, puttering in his garage, painting a kitchen chair, mending a screen, polishing some old golf clubs—desperately seeking ways to pass the time. Every day, it seemed to me, he stooped a little lower and walked a little slower.

And so in many ways I was forewarned that retirement could be a bleak and barren existence. I vowed that when my turn came, I would reverse the process. Instead of docilely accepting the wistful philosophy of the late Douglas MacArthur ("old soldiers fade away") I would prove by precept and example that *the rest of your life can be the best of your life.*

As a long-time student of semantics, I have always been intrigued by the hopeful sound of the word *rejuvenescence.* I looked it up one day in a biological dictionary and found this definition:

re-ju' ve-nes cence   1. A renewing of youth. 2. A method of cell formation in which the entire protoplasm of an *old* cell escapes by rupture of the cell wall, and develops a *new* cell wall.

Translated into people-talk, this could mean: trade in your old life for a new one—just as you do your automobile. An inspiring thought. Who wants to be scientific?

In a carefully cultivated frenzy of enthusiasm, I decided to escape from my old cell wall—to trade in my life for a new one. I would *never* retire—but simply exchange one activity for another. I would publish a book about Florida. It would be the most informative book, the most beautifully illustrated book on Florida that ever rolled off a printing press. I mailed letters in a hundred different directions—seeking answers to a thousand questions—on houses and homes, taxes and title insurance, landscaping and lawns, pools and patios, co-ops and condominiums—every phase of Florida living.

The book, *Living in Florida Year Round,* is now in its twelfth printing, with sales mounting toward a half million copies, a gratifying success by every professional standard. But far more important, something miraculous happened to me. A metamorphosis—a *rejuvenescence.* I found myself living in a perpetual state of euphoria. Too busy to be tired. Too excited to be bored. Too engrossed with the challenge of each day to notice the passage of time.

Convinced that I had found the elixir of life, I felt a great urge to share my discovery. But nobody would listen. Most of my friends and neighbors have felt the chopping block of compulsory retirement and are living, comfortably but miserably, in a state of suspended animation. Bored with bridge. Fed up with fishing. Too tired to take up golf. And totally disinterested in a contrived activity such as mine.

When I have the temerity to suggest starting a small business, "not necessarily for income but just for kicks," they look at me as if to say, "Are you crazy?"

I see them everywhere in this city of retired people. Slouching on street-corner benches. Aimlessly trudging the beaches. But mostly in the supermarkets, pushing their shopping carts with a shuffling gait and a bewildered look in their eyes. Getting, every day, a little grayer, a little balder, a little more bandy-legged in their Madras shorts.

The old fogies! They are my age—but I am twenty years younger. Why won't they listen? It's too late! They are a lost generation. What a shameful waste of human life.

Perhaps if I wrote a book? No, they wouldn't read it! Let them shuffle off to their rocking chairs. *But what about the next generation? And the next?* I'll concentrate on them. I'll sound my warning to men—and to women, too—in their forties and fifties. I'll point out the pitfalls of bungling into retirement unprepared. I'll prove that it takes ten years, or even fifteen years, of careful education to be ready for that fateful day when full-time work is replaced by full-time leisure. I'll call my book *How to Make the Rest of Your Life the Best of Your Life.* I'll show them in simple everyday language how to make their lives at 40, or 50, or 60, rich, fruitful, meaningful, secure and rewarding. I'll tell them the secret of eternal youth—and extend their lease on life by twenty years. I'll give them a philosophy that will shock the living daylights out of them. I'll prescribe a medicine that will cure their tired blood in one dose. I'll teach them a new religion, a curious new way to pray that produces guaranteed results, even for non-believers. I'll show them how to repair a worn-out marriage—and make it shine like new. I'll tell them how to banish boredom, how to sleep all night every night and how to wake up in the morning, glad to be alive.

Do these sound like extravagant promises? Read the book! Read it from cover to cover with an open mind! Try sincerely to practice what it preaches and I will guarantee—you won't be quite the same person when you finish the last page that you were when you started the first.

H. L.

Contents

Part 3

HOW YOU CAN FEEL THIRTY-NINE THE REST OF YOUR LIFE

Part 4

HOW TO FIND INNER PEACE AND CONTENTMENT IN THE YEARS
AHEAD

Part 5
HOW TO MAKE NEW FRIENDS AND KEEP YOUR OLD ONES

Part 6
HOW TO FACE UP TO THE INEVITABLE WITH CALMNESS
AND COURAGE

Part 7

HOW TO GIVE YOUR LIFE A NEW PURPOSE
AND A NEW MEANING

PART 1

Funda-Mental Attitudes You Should Cultivate in Later Years

CHAPTER 1

What the Doctor Didn't Learn at Medical School

We must so plan our pattern of life that the golden period lies ahead.
—Lin Yutang

I was teeing up my ball for a solo round of golf one Sunday morning when a voice behind me said, "Mind if we make it a twosome?"

"Sure thing," I said, "if you'll share my electric cart."

Conversation comes easy when you are quietly rolling along the fairway, and I soon learned that my companion was Dr. Harvey Haddon, general practitioner, with offices in the local professional building.

"I suppose you're retired," he said.

"Definitely *not!* 'Retirement' is a word that should be banned from the English language—along with 'senior citizen.' "

"You really mean it, don't you!" Dr. Haddon smiled. "You know, I can't wait for the day when I can put aside my practice and play golf four days a week."

"I would like to comment on that—but first let me whack my ball out of this sand trap!"

Back in the cart, I said, "Doctor, do you mind telling me your age?"

"Fifty-two."

"So you're thinking about retiring. What are you doing to prepare for it?"

"Well, I'm building up a nice portfolio of municipal bonds. Some good sound stocks, A. T. & T., General Motors . . ."

"I don't mean *financially*. How are you preparing yourself *psychologically?*"

"My patients do that for me—with phone calls in the middle of the night and imaginary illnesses."

"That's not what I mean. You went to medical school, of course. How many years?"

"Eight, including pre-med."

"And you had your internship?"

"Of course. And I was a resident physician at Broward General for two years," said Dr. Haddon. "Why do you ask?"

"Ten years before you had a steady practice! Suppose I were to tell you it takes ten years to prepare for retirement, what would you say?"

"I'd say it was a slight exaggeration. And I certainly don't mean to be rude—because I am enjoying your company—but, tell me, how did you become an expert on retirement if you are so opposed to the whole idea?"

"I'm opposed to the whole idea of men quitting their life's work at fifty-five, or sixty, or sixty-five—under the grand delusion that retirement is a bed of roses. For most men it's hell on earth—boredom, disillusionment, frustration—a devastating blow to their egos."

"You've got a point," said Dr. Haddon. "Some of my patients are men in their sixties, retired men, rapidly falling apart. Heart attacks, hardening of the arteries, embolisms; of course, you can't say those things are due to retirement."

"Why not? You know, a friend of mine, Aaron Sussman,

owns an electric organ which he finds very relaxing. Recently
he had it overhauled after some of the keys stopped working.
When the mechanic had it in perfect working order Aaron
asked him, 'Is there anything I can do to prevent this deterioration?' The mechanic smiled and said, 'Yes, there is. But the
cure is so simple that no one takes it seriously. All you have
to do to keep the organ in top condition is to *use it!* Yes, just
use it! The parts can't corrode if they're in motion!' "

Dr. Haddon let loose with a roaring laugh. "Very, very
good!" he said. "Let's putt this hole out and continue this
conversation. I've got a question I want to ask you."

We both took double bogeys on the 4-par hole. Perhaps it
was my fault; obviously our minds were not on the game.

Gliding along on the 603-yard second hole, Dr. Haddon
said, "Tell me what you had in mind by 'preparing for
retirement.' How do you go about it?"

"You said you would like to fold up your practice in a few
years—while you are still vigorous. Where would you like to
live?"

"I haven't given it much thought," said the doctor. "I read
an article in *Holiday* magazine once about a beautiful spot in
Mexico. Cuernavaca—lot of retired professional people are
living there. Or possibly the Bahamas. Or maybe I'll just buy
a condominium apartment right here in Fort Lauderdale and
spend part of each year traveling. Mrs. Haddon will have
something to say about it."

"Why not take a three-months' leave of absence and spend
it in Cuernavaca—or the Bahamas. It might save you a costly
mistake a few years from now."

"Sounds like it makes sense. I'll think about it!"

"You mentioned Mrs. Haddon," I said. "One of the tragic
mistakes that most men make when they retire is to contem-

plate the luxury of sitting around their homes day after day with not a care in the world. Watching television in the afternoon. Or snoozing on the living-room couch. And they are bitterly shocked and hurt when they discover that their wives resent having them *underfoot*. Matter of fact, retirement brings an entirely new relationship between husband and wife that can be positively explosive unless you're prepared to handle it with kid gloves."

"How so? I'm interested."

"Well, for example, when the husband left home every morning to go to his office, he was the knight in shining armor—the breadwinner, the big executive whom people looked up to and respected and consulted for advice. With no place to go, except home, you suddenly become a lazy bum hanging around the house all day long—the house which, until now, had always been your wife's castle."

Dr. Haddon was silent for several minutes. Later, on the fifth hole, I said, "I hope I haven't been boring you with all this mishmash about retirement."

"On the contrary," said the doctor. "I'm fascinated. I'm also curious. How do you know so much if you aren't retired?"

"Who said I didn't retire? I just call it by a different name. I gave up doing *what I had to do* to do *what I want to do*. And it took me ten years to get the answers."

"Are you a consultant?"

"You might call it that. I wrote a course of twelve lessons entitled 'Preparing for Retirement.' Some of the big companies, like Magnavox and Allis-Chalmers and General Electric—asked me if they could use it to help their employees get adjusted, before they went off the payroll, automatically, at sixty, or sixty-five."

"I'd like to see it."

"Better still, I'm in the process of writing a book called *How to Make the Rest of Your Life the Best of Your Life*. In fact, the conversation we have had this morning might very well occupy a conspicuous place in the manuscript. That is, with your permission."

"Good Lord, you wouldn't use my name."

"Not unless you say it's O.K."

"I'm afraid not. The Medical Association takes a rather dim view of doctors who appear in public print. Change my name and you have my permission to reproduce every word. Frankly, I think it will do a lot of good. You've given me food for thought about my own retirement."

"We've barely touched the surface! It's like trying to go through medical school on a golf cart. There's a lot more to it. Remember, I said it takes *ten years!*"

"Well, I hope it doesn't take you ten years to write your book. I want an autographed copy!"

"You'll get it! Now, let's settle down and play the next nine holes like a couple of golfers instead of like professors at a seminar."

"You've got a deal! Dollar a hole!"

Later, on my way home, I thought, Why are doctors, who are so skilled in the healing arts, so unaware of the great need for pre-retirement education? Perhaps this blind spot in their training stems from the general public apathy toward preventive medicine. Or perhaps they accept the physical deterioration that often accompanies retirement as a natural and regrettable phenomenon of our social system.

Companies, too, have shied away from the responsibility of preparing their employees, psychologically, for that grim day when they are lopped off the payroll. Much is done to ease the financial burden, through pensions and benefits, but little or nothing is done to cushion the emotional aftermath of retirement.

The indifferent attitude of most employers was brought to light in a recent study of the retirement programs of 284 companies by the Dartnell Corporation of Chicago. Only 28 per cent believe it is their obligation to educate their employees through seminars, discussion programs or the distribution of effective literature on the subject.

The comment most frequently made was "We provide an adequate pension, but we do not feel that we should intrude on the private lives of our employees. We believe they are perfectly capable of making their own plans and adjustments." Of course, there are some enlightened corporation retirement programs, but the Dartnell survey shows how pitifully few are bothering to provide more than a pension plan.

Unhappily, most individuals in their late thirties, forties and fifties lack the initiative to prepare themselves for a happier retirement. A New York advertising agency (Batten, Barton, Durstine & Osborne) recently questioned 2,000 men and 2,000 women of varying ages to determine what period— past, present or future—they regarded as their best time of life. Only the young and expectant (eighteen to twenty-four) look ahead to the future for their happiest days. All the others, from twenty-five on, yearn for the years gone by. Those under thirty-four believe their mid-twenties were their balmiest times. The older types (fifty and up) think of their late thirties as their best days.

What a sorry world this would be if nostalgia for yesterday closed the door on future hopes and dreams. The purpose of this book is to shake loose the tendency of human beings to look backward—and to point the way to a better and brighter tomorrow. Whether you are forty, fifty or sixty, you can make the rest of your life the best of your life.

But it will take a monumental preparation on your part— and a realistic understanding of the human problems you will be facing in the future, especially at retirement. It will take a sincere resolve to meet these problems, methodically, systematically and diligently.

If you are to avoid that frightening state which Bob Considine calls "Modern Society's Scrap Pile of Obsolete People," you would do well to heed the warning signals while there is still plenty of time. To start you off, here is a "Twenty Questions" game, a catechism, a guide to self-analysis which will show you some of the areas that require careful thought and study.

If You're Thirty-five to Forty-five, Ask Yourself These Questions

1. Have you started an annuity investment program that will someday pay you dividends over and above the bare necessities you will have with Social Security?

2. Will your insurance policies be "paid up" before you retire, so you will no longer have annual premiums to worry about when your income has tapered off?

3. In your investment program, have you allowed for inflationary trends that are almost certain to lessen the buying power of the dollar fifteen or twenty years hence?

4. Now that you are approaching your "middle years," are you beginning to put on weight, to become sedentary, to develop a paunch?

5. Are you a little more careful in your eating habits,

avoiding rich foods, sauces, gravies; watching your cholesterol intake?

6. Are you becoming too dependent on that second martini?

7. Are you pushing so hard to get ahead in business that you don't take time off for golf, or fishing, or sailing, or some other relaxing exercise?

8. Are you so busy that you no longer have time to read a book?

9. Do you find good literature stimulating—or is your reading confined to trashy novels?

10. Do you enjoy "do-it-yourself" activities such as building kitchen cabinets, antiquing furniture, tending a rose garden, growing camellias, or using power tools? Or do you call in a plumber when a faucet needs a washer?

11. Do you dance with your wife (not necessarily the watusi) when other couples take the floor?

12. Have you a consuming interest outside your business—a hobby that you practice with enthusiasm?

13. With passing years, have you become more adaptable, more agreeable—or more intransigent and opinionated in your conversations with others?

14. Do you play bridge? Poker? Scrabble? Chess? Or don't you have time for such diversions?

15. Do you take an active interest in civic activities—United Fund, Rotary, Kiwanis, church committees?

16. Do you live on a pre-planned budget, or according to the balance in your checkbook?

17. Do you maintain a lively interest in current events—political, intellectual, cultural—or is your horizon limited to sports events on TV?

18. Do you like to travel—and if so, do you enjoy acquiring information about the places you visit?

19. Do you enjoy meeting people, making new friends—or are you inclined to be shy and introspective?

20. Do you ever think about eventual retirement and wonder what you might like to do, or is it too remote and far in the future to concern you?

If You're Forty-five to Fifty-five, Ask Yourself These Questions

1. Are you beginning to feel the pressures of competition from younger men in your business or occupation?

2. Do you dream of the day when you can quit your job and take life easy?

3. Have you acquainted yourself thoroughly with the pension plan offered by your company?

4. Do you hesitate to discuss such matters with your personnel manager or boss for fear he may get the impression you are planning to leave?

5. Even though retirement may seem a long way off, have you put on paper a detailed outline of the income you will have from dividends, pension, income from investments and Social Security?

6. Have you collected and read all the literature on the subject?

7. Are you maintaining a faithful program of physical exercise—not too strenuous, but enough to keep you in good health?

8. Are you watching your waistline?

9. Do you visit your doctor regularly for a physical checkup?

10. Do you visit your dentist every six months and have all necessary dental work done to prevent abscessed teeth, impacted teeth, unhealthy gums and other mouth troubles that may cause eventual loss of your teeth?

11. Do you make a sincere effort to practice moderation—or does your social drinking get a little out of hand?

12. Have you learned the rewarding technique of deliberately building your wife's ego by commenting only on her virtues, never on her faults?

13. Have you maintained a boyish curiosity about life—always seeking, probing, exploring new and interesting activities and events?

14. Have you thought about places where you might someday like to retire—and have you confirmed your dreams by an actual visit to these places?

15. Have you vigorously pursued a hobby that absorbs your interest—or have the demands of business and raising a family relegated such activities to the attic?

16. Have you come to realize that your children are now adults, or about to be, and will soon be taking on the responsibilities of a life and a family of their own?

17. Are you ready to relinquish your paternal and protective attitude?

18. Are you consciously beginning to develop activities outside of your business which may someday supplant the routine of your workaday world?

19. Are you dreaming of the day when you can give up *doing what you have to do—to do what you want to do?*

20. Do you know what you want to do?

If You're Fifty-five to Sixty-five, Ask Yourself These Questions

1. Have you a fixed date, either voluntary or mandatory, for your retirement?

2. Are your financial affairs in good order? Insurance premiums paid up to date? No outstanding loans? House mortgage paid off?

3. Have you checked recently on the current value of your stock certificates and other assets?

4. Have you verified with your insurance company the exact date when your annuities start paying off? Amount? Frequency? Duration?

5. Have you checked with your Social Security office so you are thoroughly familiar with the benefits due you and your wife? Due dates? Amount? Medicare? Extent of coverage? Major medical expenses?

6. Have you filled out the necessary papers? Applications?

7. Are you adjusted mentally to the expectation of a sudden or gradual letdown you are bound to feel when you are no longer a salaried executive or employee?

8. Are you prepared to abandon altogether the business ties that hold you sentimentally to your company or your job? Prepared, also, to see little or nothing of your associates, who will no longer have the time, or inclination, to enjoy (or tolerate) your companionship?

9. Are you ready, psychologically, to make a clean break with the past; to start life all over again; to sell your home, if it seems desirable or necessary; to move to a new location—possibly a retirement community in Florida, California, Arizona, New England or any other place that appeals to you?

10. Have you made a thorough investigation of the place you have chosen to live so there will be no unpleasant surprises awaiting you?

11. Are you looking forward with enthusiasm to the pursuit of a hobby for which you have planned eagerly, intelligently and expectantly?

12. Are you aware of the new relationship that is bound to develop between you and your wife when you are no longer the breadwinner but are "underfoot" in *her* house all day long?

13. Are you prepared to spend time away from home during the day, in an office, possibly with a full-time job, or an activity that keeps you busy and occupied?

14. Have you a thorough understanding with your children so there will be no guilt feelings, or hurt feelings, on their part or yours if you should decide to move your home to a new location?

15. Have you planned a transition to some constructive activity which will give you a feeling of self-importance? Possibly to some kind of community service?

16. Have you familiarized yourself with the scope of community activities so you will know where to offer your services, and the kind of work that will be expected of you?

17. Have you practiced living on a lower budget, so that you will be able to abandon accustomed extravagances without feeling their loss?

18. Have you acquired a backlog of good habits and accomplishments so you will be able to spend your leisure time enjoyably—at bridge, golf, reading, adult education, writing, gardening, or a thousand and one activities?

19. Have you guarded your health through the years, with moderate habits, mild exercise, plenty of rest, and periodic checkups with your doctor, so that the sudden change in your environment will not bring about a decline in your physical condition?

20. Are you looking forward eagerly—but realistically—to your retirement, fully aware of all the problems you may encounter? And are you ready to meet them as they appear?

CHAPTER 2

The Two Words That Will Bring You the Secret of Happiness Throughout Your Life

Thank God when you get up in the morning that you have something to do.
—JAMES RUSSELL LOWELL

In the fall of 1922 a young man tucked a square of cardboard into the glassine envelope of his wallet, where he could see it every time he reached for his money. On it, in big letters, were two words that were destined to become the driving force of his life. He had just accepted a job as a riveter with the Bethlehem Steel Company. Lacking a college education, he was determined to make good the hard way.

The two words, backed by his enormous energy and his grim desire to be successful in life, substituted for a diploma in engineering and helped him rise up the ranks to become one of the great builders of twentieth-century America. His achievements are prodigious. As superintendent in charge of construction, he built the famous sixty-story Chase Manhattan Bank Building. He built Rockefeller Center with its towering skyscrapers. He built the long span of Throgs Neck Bridge over the lower end of Long Island Sound. His crowning achievement was the giant Triborough Bridge between Manhattan, Queens and Bronx. As he modestly says: "I only

built half of it. Another fellow built the other side. We had
to meet in the middle with only a quarter of an inch to
spare."

When Brazil decided to move its capital from Rio de
Janeiro to a wilderness plateau six hundred miles inland, he
was selected to clear the jungle and to create a vast new city
of marble buildings, to be known throughout the world as
Brasilia.

The name of this great unsung engineer is John Stuart.
And the two words that are still his motivating force are
simply

KEEP BUSY.

In 1962, forty years after he took his first job, John Stuart
was called into the office of the general manager of Bethlehem Steel. He was prepared. This was it, the day he had
dreaded. For months he had known about the new company
policy of compulsory retirement at age sixty-five. As he followed the brisk secretary into the mahogany-paneled sanctum
of Mr. John Wagner, he pictured with embarrassed anticipation the warm handclasps and platinum watch that were part
of the ritual. But instead Mr. Wagner said: "John, we want
to ask a favor of you. If any man has earned the privilege of
retiring, you have. But we need you for one more job. The
government has just given us the contract for the missile
base at Minot, North Dakota. Underground silos. An enormous construction—biggest we've ever had, I suppose—and
there's only one man who can do it. You're elected, John!"

So company rules were set aside and John Stuart's retirement was delayed for a whole year. But the day finally came
when the steel helmet was replaced with a sun-visored cap,
the familiar headpiece of the Florida retiree. John had

earned at last the doubtful privilege of relaxing under a palm tree at a luxury seaside hotel.

That is where I first met John Stuart, the man whose career was carved out of the two words *Keep Busy*. He was at a cocktail party, clumsily trying to balance a delicate-stemmed martini glass and a plate of hors d'oeuvres in one hand as he shook hands with the other. John was surrounded with newly made friends, idle retirees like himself. Never have I seen a man so miserable, so totally out of place in his new environment.

We talked about his new status. John is a rugged personality. "Retirement," he said, "is for the birds!"

"Why don't you do something?"

"Me? At sixty-seven? Who wants me? They think I'm too old, but I've got news for you. I know more about construction today than I ever knew before. And, so help me, I've got more energy. It's crazy, I tell you. Real crazy!"

Two months later I was driving along Florida's Gold Coast, impressed with the fabulous new skyline of high-rise apartments. Co-ops and condominiums. Eighteen stories high. Twenty-two stories. Building after building. And as I skirted a parked trailer that was being used as an engineering office, I saw a familiar figure, a commanding figure, definitely in charge of operations. It was John Stuart, with steel helmet and open shirt, a roll of blueprints in his hand.

"John!" I said. "You old son of a gun! You did it, didn't you?"

John grinned. "A fella's gotta keep busy—or go nuts!" How bluntly he put it. And how true. The big secret of happiness after sixty-five—"keep busy or go nuts!" That's a pretty good rule to follow all through life—but it is even more important during the years of enforced idleness when company policy lops you off the payroll and puts you out to pasture for a "well-earned rest." A long time ago Benjamin Disraeli said: "Action may not always bring happiness; but there is no happiness without action."

When I was a freshman at the University of Wisconsin nearly fifty years ago, my roommate at the fraternity house where I lived was a serious-minded and exceptionally well-informed student named Jack Bickel. He was a straight-"A" student, and I remember how I envied him for the gold Phi Beta Kappa scholarship key that dangled from the watch chain on his vest. I lost track of Jack through the years but heard that he had become an executive with the world-famous Carrier Corporation, the air-conditioning firm in Syracuse, New York. A few days ago I ran into an old classmate from college days, and as we reminisced I asked him, "Whatever became of Jack Bickel?"

"Jack," he said, "is the happiest man in the world. Carrier retired him at sixty-five and for a couple of years he was really lost. Didn't know what to do with himself. He was disconsolate and depressed. One day he was asked to give a talk before a civic group—on merchandising or something connected with his old job. It was a smash hit. That was when he really found himself. Today Jack has more than 150 speaking engagements a year at big corporations all over the United States. He's one of the most popular lecturers in the country."

So Jack Bickel found the secret—the two little words that bring happiness after sixty-five—*Keep Busy*. I wonder if his triumph wasn't even more satisfying for another reason. You see, Jack Bickel is the older brother of Fredric March, two-time winner of Hollywood's Oscar award. And perhaps, for the first time, *his own talent as an actor* is winning applause.

Coincidentally, Fredric (Bickel) March, at sixty-six, is still one of the great actors of all time. His role as President of the United States in the motion picture *Seven Days in May* was portrayed with such heroic stature and able statesmanship that some editorial writers suggested seriously (quote), "The country would be fortunate to have a man like March in the White House."

Other stars of the motion-picture and television world who have quietly observed their sixty-fifth birthdays without taking a final curtain call are Groucho Marx, Raymond Massey, George Burns, and Jack Benny. Their determination to *keep busy,* to keep in the stream of life, is the key to their perennial popularity and continuing happiness.

There is nothing new in this philosophy of keeping active beyond the normal years of achievement. At seventy-eight, Paderewski played the piano superbly before large audiences. Grandma Moses, who began painting at seventy-nine, was the most outstanding primitive artist of our time. At ninety, Mary Baker Eddy founded the world-famous *Christian Science Monitor*. Stradivarius made his finest violins between sixty and seventy and continued making them up to his ninety-third year. Michelangelo painted the ceiling of the Sistine Chapel in his late eighties. But these were people with outstanding talents. People who had tasted the fruits of success. What about the everyday people? The bookkeeper. The barber. The shoe clerk. The schoolteacher. The man at the factory lathe. What sort of satisfactions will reward their efforts to *keep busy* in their sixties and seventies?

Let's take the case of Orra O. Bishop, who began teaching school in 1895.

"I was twenty years old then," he says. "My classes consisted of twenty-three pupils in five separate grades. I taught all subjects and also served as janitor. For these services I received the sum of one dollar a day."

After forty-seven years as a teacher and chemical engineer, Bishop moved from Michigan to Fort Lauderdale and retired.

"I thought I'd take life easy, just playing golf and cards. But I couldn't stand it. So I began tutoring at the Pine Crest School. Then I decided to go to college. I had never received a degree in education and I wanted one."

Bishop earned his bachelor's degree from the University of Miami at seventy-six, his master's at seventy-eight. Today he is back at Pine Crest instructing winter students in the ABCs of chemistry and physics. He is now eighty-nine years old. Bishop's secret of youth is a fairly simple one and his own words are a remarkable parallel to the philosophy of John Stuart. "I try to keep busy," he says. "I always have two or three irons in the fire because that way I don't have time to worry about myself."

Bishop sets aside at least two hours a day for good, hard physical work. He is proud of the fact that his arms retain their firmness of youth. "You don't have to get flabby," he says, "just because you are over sixty-five. Exercise a little. Trim the shrubbery. Just do something to keep up the muscle tone." At his present pace, Orra Bishop doesn't have time to be old.

The theme of *Keep Busy* has been put forth in a variety of forms. Justice Oliver Wendell Holmes put it bluntly: "To live is to function. That is all there is to living." Long before Holmes's time, Thomas Carlyle also stressed the keep-busy theme when he said, "Blessed is he who has found his work; let him ask no other blessedness."

But not all people in their sixties and seventies can apply

their skills to useful work. The desire to keep busy requires compromise and imagination. Compromise comes into the picture when someone is confronted with a limited situation. It may be a case of limited funds, limited talents, or even being "stuck" in one location. The first step is to take stock. If the situation is really unchangeable, then instead of giving it up as hopeless, call on imagination for aid.

There are many people who have carefully recognized their limits and proceeded to use their imagination to find ways to keep busy, to function, to live. During visiting hours at a hospital recently, I was sitting at the bedside of a friend who was convalescing from an operation. The door was partly open and I noticed an elderly man peering into the room, his face radiating a cheerful smile. "May I come in?" he said. Obviously he was a stranger, for my friend looked puzzled. "I've brought you a little token of happiness," the man said, and as he walked toward the bedside he held out a single red rose wrapped in tissue paper. "It's from my own garden," he said. "I hope you'll be well soon." And without another word he backed out of the room with a pathetic little wave of his hand.

"Well, how about that," said my friend.

"Do you know him?" I asked.

"Never saw him before. What a nice old guy."

I learned later from the nurse on the floor that this donor of roses was a daily visitor at the hospital. He had found a simple and a satisfying way to *keep busy,* a way that must have gladdened the hearts of many people as well as his own. In the words of an old Chinese proverb: "A bit of fragrance always clings to the hand that gives you roses."

There is nothing quite so tragic as the man in his middle sixties who spurns the thought of participating in a useful activity. Dale Carnegie may have supplied the clue to much hostility toward work of any kind when he wrote, "Millions of people have never discovered the kind of work they could love and do well. Instead, they seethe with inner rebellion because they spend their lives doing work they despise." And so, in retirement, the very thought of keeping busy, to such people, is anathema.

Too bad they never read or remembered *The Adventures of Tom Sawyer*. It was Samuel Langhorne Clemens, better known as Mark Twain, who wrote, with a deep understanding of human nature, "Work consists of whatever a body is obliged to do—and play consists of whatever a body is not obliged to do." Perhaps this explains why *keeping busy,* when there is no longer a need to earn a living, can be one of the most joyous experiences in life. It is no longer *work*. It is *play*.

Karl Scoglund serves as an illuminating illustration of an "ordinary guy" who found that out. He came to this country from Norway when he was in his teens. He spent his life in hard work as a longshoreman, truck driver, auto repairman, and lumberjack. He worked long hours and during the depression years he barely managed to survive. At the age of sixty-eight he knew nothing but work. It was then that the doctor told him that his heart couldn't take it any more, that although his body looked as powerful as ever, he couldn't endure the eight-hour physical labor he was still putting in.

He was offered the job of caretaker at an isolated summer camp. He was to live there virtually alone, all winter, making minor repairs and keeping the place open and in shape. He had his room, food, and a small union pension payment that brought him adequate pin money. But for Karl it was like a death sentence. He was used to other workers around him—

used to bull sessions after work over a glass of beer. Lonely and bored to distraction, he sized up his situation.

Carefully he laid out his plan. He suggested to the managers that they should advertise for groups of young people to come up for winter weekends and school breaks at Christmas and Easter. He offered to shop for the food and let the youngsters do their own cooking. In that way, a kitchen staff wouldn't be necessary and the cost could be easily kept within the slim budgets of most students. The scheme was tried, and within a few months the camp was crowded every weekend, all year round. The real secret of the successful venture was Karl. Being with the young people made all his abilities suddenly important. He couldn't do much heavy work himself, but he designed and directed the building of an outdoor dance pavilion that the kids wanted for the summer. He showed the boys how to cut down the timber, how to strip it down for boards, and on bitter days Karl was out in the clearing in his old flannel lumberjack shirt directing the construction.

The girls told him their love troubles, and many a time he played cupid in a most discreet and helpful way. He baby-sat for young couples so that they could join the others for a Saturday-night movie, umpired ball games, diagnosed the diseases of many a sick car and told the owners how to get them running again, played chess and Scrabble and cards with the students, always making a lively and competitive fourth. Young history majors got valuable information by asking him for stories of the early trade-union movement, of job conditions in the "old days." Novice fishermen asked his advice on the local streams.

In short, all the "work" that Karl had done during his early days became the "play" that he had never had. He became a living legend. The "few more years" that the doctors had offered him stretched to over twenty. In his twentieth winter at the camp, he was talking with a new batch of students around the old fireplace in the camp recreation room. His drink was balanced on the chair arm and his pipe was smoking in the ashtray. His young friends thought he had dozed off, a smile still on his face, as he often did. Karl was dead at eighty-seven, but those last twenty years had been the happiest of his life. Many young couples are still showing pictures of Karl to their children, talking about him with love and affection.

So, to find, for yourself, the secret of happiness after sixty-five, remember the two words that inspired John Stuart, the engineer, to a lifetime of achievements:

Keep Busy

**If you are in your middle sixties,
why not ask yourself these questions
before you read the next chapter:**

1. Am I content to drift along from day to day without any real purpose in life?

2. Am I making a sincere effort to *keep busy* doing something I really like to do?

3. Do I wake up in the morning eagerly anticipating some task or activity I have planned for the day? Or is tomorrow just another day?

4. Am I finding a useful outlet for my talents and experience?

5. Am I keeping alert and informed, *au courant*, as they say, or am I "going to seed" mentally because I lack an incentive?

An unknown author wrote this little poem that perhaps can sum up this chapter:

> *Age is a quality of mind.*
> *If you have left your dreams behind,*
> *If hope is cold,*
> *If you no longer look ahead,*
> *If your ambitions' fires are dead—*
> *Then you are old.*
>
> *But if from life you take the best,*
> *And if in life you keep the jest,*
> *If love you hold;*
> *No matter how the years go by,*
> *No matter how the birthdays fly—*
> *You are not old.*

CHAPTER 3

When They Put You Out to Pasture, Romp Like a Colt

*For those who will fight bravely and not
yield, there is triumphant victory over all
the dark things of life.*

—JAMES ALLEN

I spent an exciting evening recently at the beautiful new Pompano Park Harness Track, watching the trotters and pacers under the lights. I congratulated Fred Van Lennep on the magnificent establishment into which he and his associates have poured an investment, I understand, of some twenty million dollars.

"Tell me, Fred," I asked, "what happens to these beautiful horses when their racing days are over? Do you retire them or, as the saying goes, put them out to pasture?"

"Strangely enough," said Mr. Van Lennep, "only about one per cent of the horses are retired to graze in the meadows. The champion mares, of course, are foaled in the hope of producing future trotters, but the great majority are sold as saddle horses. They are still strong and vigorous and they give their new owners many years of satisfactory pleasure."

Which proves, I suppose, that maturing horses are treated with more horse sense than human beings. The practice of retiring men and women at an arbitrary age of sixty-two or sixty-five implies an end to their days of usefulness. Unhappily there are millions who accept this bitter mandate as the inexorable law of nature, and, like the retired horses that are put out to pasture, they spend the rest of their lives nibbling grass, sagging a little more in their middle, and getting a little bonier every day.

Some never survive the self-debasement that often accompanies retirement, the corrosive feeling that life, for them, is finished. Others regard their new freedom as a God-given opportunity to do the things they have always wanted to do. To write a book. To travel around the world. To go into politics. To study languages.

About a year ago I received a telephone call from a former client of my business days, John S. Hewitt, once president of the Home Products Division of Warner-Lambert, the pharmaceutical house in New Jersey. "Peggy and I are in town for a few hours. Would you like to have dinner with us?"

"Delighted! But what are you doing in Fort Lauderdale?"

"I'm going to buy a boat. We're planning to ship it over to Genoa. We're going to cruise the Greek Islands. I'm retired, you know."

I gasped. "Jack," I said, "where do you get all your energy? I heard you were over in Austria, mountain-skiing."

He laughed. "Oh, that was last year. When I got back from the safari in Africa, we went over to Innsbruck for a few months. My daughter, Jackie, broke her leg skiing and we stayed with her until she was O.K."

It was a delightful evening. As a raconteur, Jack Hewitt painted a fascinating story of his adventures.

Perhaps you are thinking, No wonder Hewitt is enjoying his retirement. With his income, who wouldn't? Yet just the other day my doctor told me about a millionaire friend of his, a patient who had recently died of a stroke. "Three months before his retirement," said the doctor, "he developed a skin condition that was difficult to diagnose. It was what we call a neuro-dermatitis. He was intensely disturbed over his pending retirement. Like so many men, his business had become his entire life. In fact, he became so depressed, I was concerned that he might destroy himself. Four months later he had a fatal stroke."

These two cases represent extremes. In between there are thousands who have made the adjustment to a retired status successfully and just as many thousands who have failed. The purpose of this book is to tilt the odds, if possible, in favor of those who have found the secret of a satisfying life after sixty-five.

I suspect that perhaps there are hundreds of other anonymous retirees, tucked away in small towns all over the country, who could do what the fellow did in a story told to me by a young New York couple. They were vacationing in New England one summer, cruising around the sea-coast towns, trying out the beaches and sightseeing. At last, tired of tourist traps, high prices and crowds, they steered off the course of the tourist brochures into a small, untouted town.

Night was approaching, and there were no hotels or motels in sight. They parked on a small street and stepped out of their car, trying to get their bearings and make a decision. From an adjoining parking lot an elderly man walked briskly toward them, greeting them cheerfully. He seemed almost to know their problem, and within minutes he had steered them into the parking lot, pointed out a quiet beach for a sundown swim and promised them that he'd "line them up a berth for the night." Then he disappeared as quickly as he had appeared.

Within minutes he was back, offering them a choice of

three rooms at three different prices in local homes and suggesting to them that they eat in a restaurant a few blocks away that specialized in reasonably priced dinners and also offered a small dance band and a lively dance floor for an evening's fun. He reeled off the program at the local movie, just in case dancing didn't appeal to them.

The young pair told me that they had the best evening of their whole vacation. The beach was lovely and almost deserted. The room they chose was clean and comfortable; the lady who owned the house was warm and helpful. She offered them the use of her iron and ironing board to freshen up their clothes and served them breakfast so they wouldn't have to go out looking for a cup of coffee. The restaurant was a haven for young married couples and they danced until two in the morning. In fact, they liked it so much they stayed for two more days.

They didn't see their guide again, but they found out from their landlady that on his own initiative he had taken the job of keeping the little town alive. He was a retired factory worker, living on his Social Security. He owned a house in the neighborhood and he was determined not to end his days in a ghost town.

Often the homeowners and restaurant people would pay him small sums for his help in steering customers to them. But the people who drifted into the town were the ones who never forgot him. To them he was nameless, anonymous; but each summer hundreds remembered him whenever they reminisced fondly about their vacations.

Thomas Collins, author of *The Golden Years*, tells the true story of a watchmaker who was facing retirement. He wanted a little more than his pension promised, and he wanted to live in Florida. Yet the only trade he had ever known was the manufacture of watches. He went to the front office of the plant where he worked and obtained the names of major jewelry stores in Jacksonville, Tampa, St. Petersburg and Miami. One by one he wrote them a personal letter:

> DEAR SIR:
>
> For nearly thirty years, I have been employed in the plant of the _____ Company. I am a skilled watchmaker with enough general knowledge of timepieces to be an expert in repairing all of them.
>
> I am now retiring from my company on a modest pension and wish to make your city my home. But I do not want to stop work, nor am I averse to adding a few dollars to my income.
>
> Could you use such a man as myself in your watch and clock repair department? A part-time job would be quite satisfactory to me, and any reasonable pay based on the amount of my work would be suitable.
>
> Yours very truly,
>
> _____
>
> P.S. Records in our front office show that hundreds of our watches have been sold in your territory. Perhaps you could capitalize on that by advertising in your local paper that you were hiring a factory craftsman to service them.

When former co-workers last heard from this man, he was living comfortably in a cluster of Miami palm trees, taking home fifty or sixty dollars a week from a jewelry store and was establishing a reputation as one of the best professional watch men in the city.

Finding an outlet for one's talents takes initiative and sometimes perseverance. Henry Wadsworth Longfellow put it in these picturesque words: "If you only knock long enough and loud enough at the gate, you are sure to wake up somebody."

A few weeks ago I heard a knock on my office door, and a brisk, well-groomed man in a business suit stepped inside. "My name is George Pomeroy," he said. "My son has an office on this floor and when I stop in to see him occasionally I have noticed the lettering on your door: Year Round Publishing Corporation. I couldn't resist the temptation to come in. You see, I've been in publishing all my life. McGraw-Hill in New York."

"Well, this is a real pleasure," I said. "Our little publishing venture is only a tiny speck compared to McGraw-Hill, but I'm happy to know you. Sit down and let's get acquainted. Have you retired?"

"You might call it that," he grinned. "I fought it for two years, but company policy is company policy. At sixty-five—well, here I am."

"How long have you been in Florida?"

"Six months."

"And you still wear a business suit. And long-sleeved shirts?"

"It's my feeble protest," said Mr. Pomeroy with a laugh, "against the whole institution of retirement. Come the day when I put on a sport shirt and pair of shorts, I'll know I'm licked."

George Pomeroy has been stopping in frequently. With each visit I have been impressed with his bubbling energy, his enthusiasm, his zest for continuing, in some capacity, the kind of work to which he had devoted a lifetime. One of these days, I feel, I will have a new partner.

My brother Fredric is an even better example of a race horse turned loose who refuses to nibble the grass. He is romping like a colt and the whole wide world is his pasture. "Fritz," as his friends know him, spent forty years of his life as a Madison Avenue space salesman. His record was spectacular; his contacts numbered in the thousands. But despite his success, I used to wonder what he would do when his selling days were over, especially after I had spent a dismal evening with the late-late show watching the tragic story of an aging salesman who lost his job.

I should have known my brother better. On retirement he bought a modest interest in a new and thriving travel agency and devised a plan that capitalized to the fullest on his extensive contacts. Let Fritz explain it.

"I applied the old principle of advertising sales," he said, "that there's a bigger commission in a schedule of full-page ads than in a single fourteen-liner. So instead of concentrating on selling John Doe and his wife a trip to Baden-Baden, I began organizing group expeditions—hog farmers to the hog-raising countries of Europe, orchid growers to Colombia, archaeologists to the tombs of Egypt, trout fishermen to the lakes of Chile.

"The most exciting trip of all is our 'Gardens Around the World,' now in its fifth year." Exciting, because this world tour of twenty to thirty garden lovers is under the personal guidance of Mr. and Mrs. Fredric Legler. You see, his wife, Elizabeth, is one of America's most celebrated flower arrangers, and now they have found a way to share this great adventure of their later years in a spirit of togetherness.

I could go on reciting case after case of people who have plunged into a new activity in their sixties and have discovered not simply a way to keep busy but a happiness that transcends anything they had known in previous years.

In this complicated world there are thousands of unfilled needs. Did you ever stop to think that organized charity groups usually concentrate only on the pressing needs of the poor—medical care, food, shelter? What about the other hungers—music, art, nature, fun, companionship? The world is crying for donations of talent. Just look around you. No talent is too small. You can play the piano a little and read beginner's music? Aren't there thousands of kids who can't afford music lessons or can afford only the old-fashioned fee of fifty cents or one dollar? Give beginner's lessons! Even if you just rouse their interest and advance them as far as a simple tune and a few scales, you may have opened a whole new world to them.

Your country is waging a war to keep young people in high school. Go to some of your friends and acquaintances and get them to offer one afternoon or evening a week toward helping one young person with his studies. Perhaps a Spanish-speaking neighbor could coach students having a difficult time with their Spanish; a writer or a retired English teacher could help with grammar and composition; and what's the matter with you? Surely you are by now a whiz at arithmetic. Go to your local school and offer your services. Ask them to post a notice on their bulletin board and to advise students having a difficult time that free tutoring is available. Make it a real project. What could put you more into the stream of life than changing the life pattern of some young person?

There are dozens of projects available to those who are willing to open a crack in their imagination. Are your abilities, great or small, no longer needed? Aren't there plenty of people who would love to learn a trade but can't afford to go to a trade school? Can you teach typing or appliance repairing, art, gardening, cooking, or carpentry? Anything you still know and can communicate to others is lost if it stays locked up inside you.

Voltaire, the great French philosopher, once spoke these simple words that should be engraved on the gold watch of every person who retires. "Shun idleness," he said. "It is a rust that attaches itself to the most brilliant metals."

And again, to quote Dale Carnegie, our modern-day philosopher, whose inspiring books have outsold all other volumes in world history, except one, the Holy Bible, "If you want to be happy," wrote Mr. Carnegie, "set yourself a goal that commands your thoughts, liberates your energy and inspires your life. If more of us would practice this basic truth of nature, how much happier we would be."

George Bernard Shaw, in his pungent manner of expressing great truths in reverse, sums it up this way: "The secret of being miserable," he said, "is to have the leisure to bother about whether you are happy or not."

So why brood about your chances of being happy or not in your retirement years? Do something about it. When they turn you loose in the meadow:

1. **Don't be a grass nibbler.**
2. **Romp like a colt.**
3. **Kick up your heels.**
4. **Show the world you've got spirit.**

And like those discarded trotters at Pompano Park, pretty soon you'll be a saddle horse, proudly prancing along the bridle paths, useful, active and happy.

CHAPTER 4

Never Make a U-Turn
on a One-Way Street

*Extolling the past at the expense of the
present is a sign of old age.*
—Samuel Taylor Coleridge

If you were driving along a highway with signs clearly
marked ONE WAY and the car ahead of you suddenly swooped
into a U-turn, you would probably jam on your brakes, blow
your horn and yell in disgust, "You idiot!" Only a very
incompetent driver would be guilty of such a stupid
maneuver.

Yet think of all the people you have known who deliberately make a U-turn on the highway of life and drive against
the traffic that is obviously flowing in one direction—straight
ahead. I am referring to the men—and women, too—many of
them in their fifties and sixties, who are continually living in
the past, turning their thoughts toward yesterday.

I had a business associate several years ago who developed
the irritating habit of launching into lengthy reminiscences
on the pretext that they might suggest a solution to current
problems. Younger members of the firm could not tolerate
his monologues, and when they saw him coming down the
hallway they would scatter in all directions.

It is not always practical or possible to escape from an
insufferable bore by darting around corners. More often you

become trapped in a conversation that starts innocently
enough. If you are alert to the techniques of an inveterate
narrator, you can detect his signal for a U-turn and prepare
yourself accordingly. Be on your guard when he says, "Did I
ever tell you about . . . ?" Sometimes his opening gambit
will be a little less obvious. He may say, "I was in a situation
like that once."

The master raconteur will give you no warning whatever,
no conjunctive phrasing to put you on the alert. He knows
from previous rebuffs that his story must be launched as suddenly as the attack on Pearl Harbor. And your only recourse
is to hear it through, patiently or impatiently, depending on
how polite you want to be.

The tendency to relive the triumphs of yesterday is almost
an occupational disease with retired people. I discovered this
to my sorrow recently when I proposed to the mayor of our
city what I thought was an ingenious plan. I suggested that
retired executives in our area be pooled in a sort of "brain
bank" to be drafted as committee members for the solving of
community problems.

"We tried it," said the mayor, "and it did not work out.
Most of the men who served on our committees were former
officers of big, successful corporations. Instead of concentrating on the problems that needed solution, they spent most of
their time exchanging reminiscences."

There seems to be an almost compulsive need among
retirees to engage in such U-turning conversation. Some
realize themselves that they drive people away by doing this,
and yet they still persist. There is an old anecdote about an
elderly man who visits his doctor and complains, "Doctor, I
have a terrible problem. I talk to myself."

"That's nothing," the doctor responded reassuringly. "Lots of people do."

"But, Doctor," moaned the man, "you don't have any idea what a terrible bore I am!"

There was one retired executive who, during his long and memorable lifetime, never indulged in idle recollections. Right up to the moment of his passing away, at age ninety-four, Bernard Baruch's crisp, incisive opinions were still sought by Presidents. Interviewed by reporters on his last birthday, Bernard Baruch was asked how he managed to keep so alert and informed on current affairs. "I don't dwell on the past," he said. "Today and tomorrow concern me more than yesterday."

There is an old saying that punctuates Mr. Baruch's philosophy: "Little good you'll do watering last year's crops." This doesn't mean, of course, that your experiences are useless and outdated. It's the way you use them that counts. If you are advising a younger person and your experience equips you to feel you know the best road he should take, there is no need to go through your whole life story to prove your point. Why not say, "I found that a good solution is . . ." and let it go at that?

The major ingredient of good conversation is the world of today—not yesterday.

You don't have to be an economics major to keep up with one or two daily papers and some national news magazines. Young people invariably respond eagerly to such remarks as "I'd love to see you do that dance I saw written up in *Life*. What is it—the frug?" instead of "When I was young we really knew how to dance" or "We never would have let our kids do dances like that!"

In other words, move onto the contemporary scene. It's a

busy, exciting world. Young people tend to reject older
people who bore them to death by constantly talking about
the past.

George Washington is one of many statesmen and philosophers who have sounded off on the unwisdom of dwelling on
past glories. "We ought not to look back," said the father of
our country, "unless it is to derive useful lessons from past
errors and for the purpose of profiting from dear-bought
experience."

Another great general, George C. Marshall, put it even
more bluntly: "When a thing is done, it's done. Don't look
back."

Nostalgia has its place in the lives of all of us, but, like
alcohol, it should not be indulged in to excess. Recently I
had occasion to speak long distance to one of the editors of
Modern Maturity, a magazine published in Washington,
D.C., by the American Association of Retired Persons. "Please
forgive me," I said, "if I sound critical. But may I ask why so
many of your articles and pictures are slanted toward the days
of long ago? I should think that people in their sixties and
seventies would not like to be reminded of their age." It was
clear from his reply that our viewpoints on this subject were
miles apart.

The sales manager of one of the most successful retirement
communities in Florida, Lehigh Acres, confessed to me recently that his staff, in selling new homes, no longer stresses
the retirement aspect of the development. They have found
that most elderly citizens prefer to live in a neighborhood
that is sprinkled with younger people. Today the salesmen
wisely drive their prospects past the modern elementary
school as a means of creating a new community image.

Another housing development recently published a full-
page newspaper advertisement with this provocative message:

Where's all the grandpas and grandmas?

Oh, they're here, all right, but it's hard to tell them from the mamas and papas. Imperial Point neighbors refuse to let age be a barrier to active enjoyment of life. You'll find them at gay poolside parties, golfing, fishing or having a spirited game of cards. Buying a home here is the surest way to enjoy ACTIVE retirement.

Many former residents of St. Petersburg have moved to the Fort Lauderdale area because, they say, "There are too many old people in St. Pete. Just because I'm seventy doesn't mean I want to be surrounded by old fogies." What they really mean is "I can't bear to be with people who live in the past."

I suppose that all of us are guilty now and then of making conversational U-turns. The next time you feel an uncontrollable urge to reminisce, ask yourself these questions:

1. Is the experience I am about to relate as entertaining to my listener as it is to me?

2. Is my listener familiar with the personalities involved?

3. Is my story really worth telling?

If your conscience answers "Yes" to all three, you are on safe ground. Proceed at your own risk. If the answer is "No"— bite your tongue and say nothing for three minutes. It is better to be a boor than a bore.

CHAPTER 5

How to Lubricate Your Life for Long and Smooth Driving— Without Friction

All we need to make us really happy is something to be enthusiastic about.
—CHARLES KINGSLEY

When I was a college student majoring in journalism, I got a job one summer vacation on the Chicago City News Bureau. My first assignment was to interview Mr. John G. Shedd, who was then the head of the famous Marshall Field Store. He was to be the principal speaker at a merchandising convention held in the Blackstone Hotel.

As I walked down Michigan Boulevard I wondered how I should begin the conversation. It didn't tell you in the textbooks what to say. "Mr. Shedd, sir, I am a reporter for the City News Bureau." No, that was too stereotyped. Better to approach him this way: "Mr. Shedd, I want to congratulate you on the talk you have just made. And if I may, sir, I would like to ask you a question." Too presumptuous. The more I tried to memorize an opening remark, the more stilted it sounded. And the more confused I became.

I walked around the block. To Wabash Avenue. Back to Michigan Boulevard. Not once but three times. Finally I made my decision. I was keyed up. Excited. Proud to be entrusted with this important assignment. I wouldn't plan the words. I would have faith in my own enthusiasm, faith that I would say the right thing at the right time. I walked up to Mr. Shedd with a broad smile on my face and stretched out my hand. Once the ice was broken, we talked like old friends. The interview was a success. It appeared on page one of the old Chicago *Examiner*. After all these years I have forgotten what I said to Mr. Shedd, but I will always remember what he said to me. At one point in the conversation I smilingly apologized for my exuberance and explained that this was my first interview. "Never apologize for enthusiasm," said Mr. Shedd. "I have told my associates many times that it is far better to be a geyser than a mud puddle."

How colorfully he put it. Yet Mr. Shedd was only echoing the sentiments of other great men before him. It was Charles Schwab who said: *"A man can succeed at almost anything for which he has enthusiasm."*

Frederick Williamson expressed it with even more conviction. "The longer I live," he said, *"the more certain I am that enthusiasm is the most important of all traits or qualifications."*

I can hear you say, "Enthusiasm comes easy for young people, but how can anyone be enthusiastic at sixty-five, especially when they have suddenly been stripped of their job, their importance, and made to feel useless, washed up, non-productive?"

Here's an answer that may bring you hope. Try to think of your life as an automobile that has given faithful service for thousands of miles. It's the only car you will ever own. Now, are you going to let it rust from lack of lubrication? Are you going to let the gears and the pistons get so sticky with carbon and grit that your motor will soon wear out and stop altogether?

The best lubricant a person can have at any age is enthusiasm. If you will look forward to the future with joy and anticipation, if you will seek and find new interests, if you will pour yourself into a new activity with energy and expectation, your life will roll along as smoothly as if it were mounted on steel ball bearings.

I had an experience recently on a jet flight from St. Louis to New York that clearly demonstrated to me the lubricating power of enthusiasm. I had tilted back in a reclining position, disengaged my seat belt and was allowing the muffled hiss of the jet engines to act as a sedative when I became conscious of my fellow passenger in the adjoining seat. He was leaning almost over my lap in a frantic but polite effort to look out the window.

"Would you like to change seats?" I said. "I would just as soon be on the aisle. I'm going to sleep anyway."

"Thank you so much. This is my first ride on a jet. Matter of fact, my first ride on a plane."

Two hours must have passed when an efficient voice on the loud-speaker took me out of my dream world: "This is your captain. We are beginning our descent to New York City. Will you fasten your seat belts, please."

I rubbed my eyes, yawned and glanced at my seat companion. His face was pressed against the window pane.

"Look at all those lights," he said. "Just like a carpet of jewels! That must be Staten Island. There's the Statue of Liberty—and the Battery. What a beautiful sight!"

Then, minutes later, the wheels touched down; the jets braked into a reverse roar and we began the long taxi through paths of blue lights to our gate.

For the first time I was conscious of my companion. He was an elderly man—I would guess in his late seventies—but there was a sparkle of youth in his eyes.

"Well, sir," he said with an enthusiasm that could not be suppressed, "this is the first leg of my journey." His voice betrayed his excitement.

"Going beyond New York?" I asked.

"Goin' around the world," he said, and his face lit up like a little boy's. "Goin' to London, Paris, Rome, Bombay, Hong Kong, Tokyo, Honolulu. You name it."

"And you're making the trip all alone?" I asked. "How come?"

He gave a cackling laugh. "Guess you'd call it sort of a birthday present from myself to me. Turned eighty last week. Told my grandchildren—they're grown up now—by golly, it's time I saw something of this world. Tell you the truth, mister, I've never been out of Kansas till today."

For some, life begins at eighty—a life of carefree adventure. The lucky ones, whose health and financial status permit, can find in foreign travel, if it suits their whims, a wonderful zest for living.

About half of all United States tourists to foreign lands are more than sixty years old. Not all of them are people of means. Most have budgeted their expenses from savings and are choosing this nomadic way of living as the fulfillment of a lifelong dream. And most, if you will observe them closely, have this in common. They are young in heart, enthusiastic, carefree—with a busy life of worries and responsibilities behind them and a future full of adventure before them.

Not everyone can afford the luxury of a flight around the world—but they can lubricate their lives in other ways. I know a man who derives supreme joy in his fascinating collection of salt and pepper shakers—967 of them. Silver, gold, glass, redwood, ebony—even jade. Each new discovery is a triumph that keeps alive his enthusiasm.

Another man, long past his day of retirement, has joined the Peace Corps and is teaching Tunisians how to operate tractors and other earth-moving machines, a skill he had mastered during his active years. No youngster in the Peace Corps can match the enthusiasm of Oscar Haugen, who turned seventy on his last birthday.

At sixty-seven, Miss Ora Ruggles of Laguna Beach, California, is still another example of how a retired person's life can be revitalized by the lubricant of enthusiasm. After more than forty years of hospital work she still gives volunteer aid on occupational therapy. She is active in church and charity endeavors. She belongs to a bridge club. She backs her political convictions with active effort. She lectures on how she pioneered occupational therapy during World War I. She corresponds with hundreds of persons who have benefited through this great modern aid to healing. She paints and sculptures. And during her spare time Miss Ruggles has authored several books.

I can hear you saying, "That's fine for people who are born with that kind of energy. Unfortunately, I haven't got it." That isn't so. You can generate all the energy you need for any task simply by calling on the lubricating power of enthusiasm. William James once said that *"men habitually use only a small part of the powers which they actually possess."*

Medical science is continually proving that the human mind is ageless, that no one grows old by living, only by losing interest in living. Just because you have reached your sixty-fifth birthday is no reason for sitting back in a swivel chair and closing the door on active interests. Your memory may slip occasionally, but your enthusiasm and your creative imagination can actually improve in the years ahead—if you keep yourself mentally and physically alert.

If you loved sports as a youth, you can still get a lot of fun out of golf, croquet or shuffleboard. You can still pitch horseshoes, bowl, ride a bicycle, swim, walk, or sail a boat. You can do almost anything you want to do, if you really want to do it.

There is also such a thing as sedentary enthusiasm. That's the enthusiasm of a bright idea. All the energy you need for that is enough to sit down and let your brain hop around a little. Then, if you come up with a thought about a project that fills you full of enthusiasm, you'll surely have enough energy to make it to the telephone, where many a good idea can bear fruit. Some very ambitious projects have been started in just that way. Someone sat down in a chair, came up with an idea and walked as far as the telephone.

Jennie Lesnick, founder of the Cystic Fibrosis Foundation, must have done just that. In January 1953 she found out that her four-year-old granddaughter was going to die of a little-known disease, cystic fibrosis, that affects at least one out of every 600 children born. When little Patricia died on January 28, Jennie was grief-stricken. But by 1954 Jennie was throwing fund-raising affairs, going on radio and TV, and pushing for a research center to find a cure for the disease.

That means that sometime between January 28 and the next year, Jennie had sat down in a chair to grieve and lament. And at one point or another in that process an idea was born, and Jennie made it to the telephone. She called her granddaughter's pediatrician, Dr. J. W. Geme, and a few other people. In one year the foundation was a reality. Los Angeles Children's Hospital became the research center for Southern California, nine chapters of the Cystic Fibrosis Foundation had been formed, and over $100,000 had been collected!

In a similar fashion, Juliette Gordon Low, in 1912, at the age of fifty-two and going deaf, determined to organize girl-scouting—and did!

You don't have to be a Jennie Lesnick or Juliette Low to get a project off its feet. The rules are: sit down, think about what you once liked to do or once dreamed about doing. Get a bright idea. Let your enthusiasm lubricate that idea with daydreams. Then let that enthusiasm propel you to the telephone. What will it be? A Scrabble-playing group? A literary discussion club with a book a week assigned? Politics? Art? An amateur band or orchestra? Go to the phone and don't be afraid to stick your neck out a little. Not trying is far worse than failure. James Bryant Conant, the famous educator, said it succinctly: "Behold the turtle: He makes progress only when he sticks his neck out."

I believe the most fitting way to close this chapter is to quote the words of Charles Kingsley: *All we need to make us really happy is something to be enthusiastic about.*

CHAPTER 6

How to Pull Out the Plug
and Let Worries Drain Away

Anxiety is the rust of life, destroying its brightness.

—Tryon Edwards

I remember seeing a Broadway play at the Martin Beck Theatre in the days of World War II that taught me a wonderful formula for disposing of worries. It was a comedy by Franz Werfel and S. N. Behrman entitled *Jacobowski and The Colonel.*

The time and the place were just previous to the German invasion of Paris. The cast was magnificent. Louis Calhern was the pompous, swashbuckling French colonel. Oscar Karlweiss, popular Viennese comedian, played the role of Jacobowski, a displaced civilian philosopher.

And here is the dialogue that burned into my mind back in 1943 with such indelible clarity that I can set it down here, word for word, nearly twenty-four years later.

Someone—I think it was the colonel—had just said, "Farewell, Paris!" And Jacobowski, in his charming Viennese dialect, answered, "Have courage! My poor mother, wise woman that she was, always used to say that *no matter what happens in life, there are always two possibilities.* The Germans—either they'll come to Paris or they'll jump to England. If they don't come to Paris, that's good. But if they should come to Paris, *again there are two possibilities*. Either we succeed in escaping, or we don't succeed. If we succeed, that's good, but if we don't, *there are two possibilities*. The Germans, either they'll put us in a good concentration camp or in a bad concentration camp. If in a good concentration camp, that's fine, but if they put us in a bad one, *there are still two possibilities . . ."*

And in the spirit of the comedy, the cynical response, of course, was "Two fine possibilities. Jump in the river—or be shot by the Boche."

The quaint wisdom of Jacobowski's mother applies to most of our worries and fears. I talked to a retired neighbor the other day who confessed to me that he cannot sleep nights because he is so worried that the source of his income may be discontinued. "It's only a small pension," he said. "My company sends me a check every month. They call it sort of a consultant's fee—but there was never any legal contract—just an understanding. Now suppose new people come into control of the company, and they decide to cut me off. What'll I do?"

Remembering Jacobowski's philosophy, I said, " If new people come into control of your company, *there are two possibilities*. Either they decide to keep you on the payroll or they cut you off. If they keep you on, that's fine. If they cut you off, *there are still two possibilities*. You can try to find a job that gives you a comfortable income—or you are unable to find one. If you get steady work, that's good. If not—well, again, *there are two possibilities*. You can collect unemployment insurance from the government or you can increase the mortgage on your home. . . . Say, wait a minute," I said. "Don't you and your wife have social security?"

"Sure we do."

"Well, for heaven's sake, what are you worrying about?"

Most of our worries never happen. They are gremlins of our own creation, but they seem very real at the time. Like the man who imagined himself covered with grasshoppers. "They're crawling all over me," he cried, terror-stricken. "I try to flick 'em off, but they jump right back."

A friend said, "I know how you can get rid of those grasshoppers. Go see my doctor. He's a psychiatrist. He'll help you."

So the poor fellow visited the psychiatrist. "Doc," he said, "what can I do about these horrible green grasshoppers? They're clinging to my coat sleeve and they're all over my face and in my hair!" And he began flicking his imaginary insects, one by one, with his forefinger and thumb. As he kept snapping away he said, "Help me, Doc.!"

The doctor watched him with fascination. Then he stepped back a pace or two and said, in a tone of angry annoyance, "Hey, cut it out! You're flicking those grasshoppers onto me!"

This is a tongue-in-cheek story, but, like an Aesop's fable, it has a moral: *Our worries are like a plague of grasshoppers and most of them exist only in our imagination.*

During my lifetime I suppose I have worried about ten thousand things that have never happened. I used to worry about my children. Riding bicycles to school. Swimming in the town reservoir. Walking home alone after dark. When they were old enough to drive a car I would lie awake nights, waiting anxiously for the sound of wheels in the driveway, the reassuring signal that my loved ones had returned home safe and sound. During my uneasy vigil I would sometimes hear the distant wail of an ambulance siren and it would send shivers of foreboding up and down my spine.

I worried about my health. If I felt a slight pain in my chest, I was sure it was the symptom of a coronary—or possibly lung cancer. And there would be another sleepless night, during which I mentally "put my affairs in order," until somehow the pain vanished, as it always did, leaving me with an ineffable feeling of relief.

Ironically, our worries are the primary cause of the very ills we fear. Dr. George W. Grile, famous American surgeon, once said, "Whatever the cause of fear and worry, the effect can always be noted in the cells, tissues and organs of the body." Specialists in arthritis report that the following factors are nearly always present in arthritic cases: *frustration, chronic anger, tension, apprehension, ill-will* and *habitual worry.*

Worry is also probably the greatest energy eater of all time. You have something to do, a party to attend, tickets to a play you've been longing to see, visitors coming, a project to work on, and, often, a headache accompanies the excitement.

You can say, "Sure I've got a little headache, but that won't stop me. I'll take an aspirin and forget about it." Chances are, with that attitude the headache will take a rapid leave.

Or you can say, "Uh, uh, headache. That's my fourth this month. It seems to me I read somewhere that brain tumors give symptoms like that. I'd better call off that appointment and get to a doctor first thing in the morning. No sense taking aspirin; all that does is mask the symptom. Come to think of it, there's not much sense in seeing a doctor; never heard of an old guy like me coming through a brain operation in one piece." And on and on with what most people frankly call "old-age hypochondria."

If we look hard enough, all of us, young and old, can find

minor symptoms to worry over: an ache here, a ringing in the ears there. Get medical checkups a couple of times a year, but find out too that, surprise of surprises, if you stop worrying, the symptoms often disappear, too.

The same holds true for worrying over defeats. A man or woman who gives up over a headache will usually give up after one defeat as well. Instead of saying, "That dinner party didn't come off too well. Now what went wrong, and how can I make it different next time?" the worrier says instead, "I'll never have another party again as long as I live. Everything went against me and I did the best I knew how. I give up and that's that."

Such a defeatist might well look over Abraham Lincoln's record of resounding defeats. Old Abe lost his job in 1832, was defeated for the Illinois state legislature in that same year, failed in business in 1833. In 1834 it appeared that the tide was turning. Lincoln was elected to the legislature. But sure enough, more trouble was in store. His sweetheart, Ann Rutledge, died in 1835 and a year of grieving brought Abe a nervous breakdown in 1836. It went on like that: defeated for Speaker, 1838; defeated for nomination for Congress, 1843; and then elected to Congress, 1846; once again to be plunged downhill in a lost renomination in 1848; a rejection for his bid to be land officer in 1849; a defeated senatorial attempt in 1854; defeated in his bid for the Vice-Presidential nomination in 1856; and again defeated for the Senate in 1858. He went on, as everybody knows, to the Presidency of the United States in 1860.

As a worrier, Abe would have given up twenty-five years before he became President!

Another big worry which seems to plague women especially is "What will people say?" Worriers on that score seldom have a moment of peace, because no matter what we do there will be some who like it and some who don't.

Why not use the Jacobowski approach to that problem? Decide on what *you* want to do and then say, "If people like it, that will be nice. If some don't, there's nothing I can do about it anyway. And if some do and some don't, that's to be expected, and I'll let the ones who do worry over the ones who don't."

"We should have much peace if we would not busy ourselves with the sayings and doings of others," said Thomas à Kempis, and peace of mind is, of course, the most important kind of peace.

Worry causes its own physical symptoms, which in turn cause more worry. You worry, so you chain-smoke. You chain-smoke, so your breath gets short. Your breath gets short, so you jump into bed. You jump into bed and you don't get any exercise. You don't exercise, so you gain too much weight. You gain too much weight, so you have a heart attack. Then you really have something to worry about!

Cornelia Otis Skinner, daughter of the famous actor and a famous writer on her own steam, describes herself as a most depressed and moody young girl. "Father put up with me for a time," she recollects. "Then one day while we were taking a long walk in the country, he shook me out of my Byronic miasma with an amused but understanding 'Take the pins out of your diaphragm, kid, and start living.'

"Even today the advice holds good for me," she continues. "God knows there are days of tension for everyone. But we are all too prone to fight tension with further tensions. . . . We might do worse than 'take the pins out of our diaphragms and start living.' "

I have often wondered whether the passing years tend to

give us a certain immunity from worries and tensions. Perhaps we merely replace them with another syndrome of anxieties. As our children grow up and have children of their own, they take over the burden.

The other day my daughter confessed to me, "Dad, I used to be furious when you would call for me after those Girl Scout meetings. The other girls were allowed to ride their bikes home after dark. Now that I'm a mother myself, I realize what it means to worry."

Dr. Smiley Blanton, an eminent psychiatrist, says, "Anxiety is the great modern plague." His opinion is confirmed by medical journals which tell us that "thousands of people are suffering from ills caused by pent-up anxiety." What a shameful way to spend our time, especially those of us who are over sixty-five. Here we are, supposedly in the golden period of our lives, and we lose irreplaceable hours brooding over grievances which, in a year's time, will be forgotten by us and by everybody.

I recently met a widow who inherited from her late husband a profitable orange grove near Clermont, Florida. "Aren't you lucky," I said, "to have such an excellent source of income?"

"What do you mean, lucky?" she said with a grimace. "I'm worried sick, half the time, over my groves. If it isn't one thing, it's another. Freezing weather, smudge pots, bugs, hurricanes, thieves, dishonest managers, deflated prices, fruit rotting on the trees because we can't get pickers."

"Have all of those things happened to you?" I asked sympathetically.

"Well, they haven't happened yet—but they could!"

Nine-tenths of our worries can be described the same way. *They haven't happened yet—but they could!*

"But my problems are *real*," you may say. Okay, so they're real. Either you can do something about them or you can't. If there is something to be done, do it. If not, live with the problem and stop worrying over it.

There's the anecdote about the poor man who came to his minister for advice.

"I'm in a terrible fix," he confessed. "Easter is coming and I have no money for an Easter dinner. We can't possibly come to church in the rags we own."

"Let's see now," said the minister. "How much money do you need for a good dinner?"

"Fifteen dollars," the man replied unhappily.

"Clothes for your children?"

"Thirty dollars."

"A decent dress for your wife?"

"Fifteen dollars."

"A new suit for yourself?"

"Forty dollars."

The minister added quickly in his head and said, "You need all together one hundred dollars. Now at least you won't have to worry about Easter dinner, clothes for your children, a dress for your wife and a suit for yourself. You have only one worry. Where to get the hundred dollars."

In the hope of finding a simple cure for the worries and anxieties that plague our lives, I have talked with dozens of doctors and psychiatrists and have studied every book and magazine article I could find on the subject of "neuroses." There seem to be three methods that promise effective relief from this destructive mental habit:

1. The Power of Prayer
2. The Logic of Rationalization
3. The Habit of Positive Thinking

I am omitting tranquilizers, the remedy used by millions, because in my opinion the swallowing of pills to ease tensions is strictly a form of anesthesia, closely related to getting "plotched" at the corner bar.

1. The Power of Prayer

For those who have a strong religious faith, reliance on prayer is an ever-present source of strength and courage. Even psychiatrists recognize that tortured minds can find peace and serenity by turning to a higher power for help instead of trying to fight life's battles alone. One of our leading practitioners, Dr. A. A. Brill, said, "Anyone who is truly religious does not develop a neurosis."

A few years ago Dr. Alexis Carrel, who wrote *Man, the Unknown* and won the Nobel prize for scientific achievement, described the power of prayer in a compelling manner. Dr. Carrel said in a *Reader's Digest* article, "As a physician, I have seen men, after all other therapy had failed, lifted out of disease and melancholy by the serene effort of prayer. . . . In prayer, human beings seek to augment their finite energy by addressing themselves to the Infinite source of all energy. When we pray, we link ourselves with the inexhaustible motive power that spins the universe. We pray that a part of his power be apportioned to our needs. Even in asking, our human deficiencies are filled and we arise strengthened and repaired. . . . Whenever we address God in fervent prayer, we change both soul and body for the better. It could not happen that any man or woman could pray for a single moment without some good result."

In a cynical world, hell-bent on its own destruction, how inspiring are the words of Dr. Carrel—even more because he is not a man of the cloth but a man of science. When doubts and worries are clouding our thoughts, we can find peace and serenity by *"linking ourselves with the inexhaustible motive power that spins the universe."* Prayer gives us the comfort of sharing our burdens, of not being alone. As Henry Ford once said, "With God in charge, I believe that everything will work out for the best in the end. So what is there to worry about?"

2. The Logic of Rationalization

Not everyone possesses a simple faith in the power of prayer to solve his problems. For some, the cold logic of rationalization sometimes serves as a substitute to ease their anxieties. I have found comfort in combining both methods, thus actually doubling my feeling of security. To explain, let me use the example of airplane travel. During my lifetime I have probably flown a total of 300,000 miles on commercial airlines. On most of my trips by air, I experience no fear whatever, but instead a feeling of exhilaration and suppressed excitement. By the law of averages I know that I am safer in a plane than I would be driving a car. I respect the business acumen of insurance companies, and if they are willing to sell me a round-trip policy for five dollars that pays $175,000 in case of death resulting from a plane crash, my chances of survival are better than good. They are 35,000 to one. Of course, I still buy trip insurance. Who could pass up such odds? I hope I never win.

I must confess that there have been moments on my air trips when the law of averages proved to be an ineffectual source of comfort. When the planes were stacked up over an airport in a pea-soup fog. When jagged bolts of lightning fingered the wings. Or blinding blizzards reduced visibility to zero. Or sudden drafts of bumpy air sent dinner trays bouncing along the aisle. These were times when the power of prayer took precedence over the logic of rationalization.

A few months ago my wife and I accompanied a group of friends on a weekend trip to Grand Bahama Island. As we were about to board the plane at Palm Beach, a Mackey Airlines DC-6, one of the women became almost hysterical with fear and refused to go through the gate. "I'm sorry," she said. "I've never been on a plane and I'm scared to death. I just can't do it."

I tried to reassure her. "It's only a twenty-five-minute trip," I said. She shook her head. "No, I can't! I just can't!" I happened to know that she is a devoutly religious woman, so I took her aside and said, in an undertone, which she alone could hear, "I know you have a great faith in prayer. Surely you believe that God is protecting that plane, just as He protects you on the ground." No answer. She stood there, petrified with fear.

Then I tried another approach—the logic of rationalization. "Doris," I said, "did you know that Mackey Airlines, in twenty-five years of service, has never had an accident, nor a single fatality? Think of that—twenty-five years without a fatality. And they fly many, many planes. A total of thousands of miles every day. You will be safer in this plane than you will be driving your car back to Fort Lauderdale."

She still clung to the gate. The stewardess was becoming impatient. Our little group climbed the stairs of the gangway, reluctant but willing to leave our friend behind. Just as the flight attendant was about to shut the door of the plane, we heard the patter of feet on the stairs. "Wait a minute. I'm coming!" Fear had been conquered at last by logic.

A world-famous insurance company, Lloyds of London, has built a fabulously successful business on the tendency of people to worry about things that never happen. Insurance against a drought that might spoil the wheat crops. Insurance against storms that might wreck a ship, or a hurricane that might blow down a building—or an epidemic, or a jewel robbery, or a thousand and one things that we anticipate with dread. James Russell Lowell once said, "The misfortunes hardest to bear are those which never happen."

I realize that the logic of rationalization—call it the law of averages—is not always comforting when the worry concerns the safety of your family or your own health or your financial security. These are the times when most people turn in desperation for help from a divine source. There is a saying that "Man's extremity is God's opportunity."

3. The Habit of Positive Thinking

I believe that the best palliative for the tensions that corrode our peace of mind is the habit of positive thinking. The leading exponent of this dynamic law is Norman Vincent Peale, whose famous book *The Power of Positive Thinking* has not only sold in the millions of copies but has taught millions of people a workable philosophy of living.

"Think positively," said Dr. Peale, "and you set in motion positive forces which bring positive results to pass. Positive thoughts create around yourself an atmosphere propitious to the development of positive outcomes. On the contrary, think negative thoughts and you create around yourself an atmosphere propitious to the development of negative results."

If you will accept this great law of life and practice it every waking moment, you can banish tensions, anxieties, fears and worries and replace them with the products of positive thinking—happiness, security, self-confidence and courage.

"That sounds great," you say. "But how do I begin? Stop worrying? That isn't easy. For example, I've had a bronchial cough for a long time and naturally I'm worried about it. My

doctor says there's nothing really seriously wrong with me—
but I don't know. I don't like the sound of that cough."

So instead of being relieved by your doctor's diagnosis, you
are filling your mind with fear and foreboding. Torturing
yourself with imaginary symptoms of a respiratory disease.
The mental picture you are etching in your mind may
ultimately become a fact if you dwell on it long enough. Do
you recall the Biblical passage, *"The thing which I greatly
feared has come upon me"*?

The first step in acquiring the habit of positive thinking is
to empty your mind of all fears, all worrisome thoughts.
Imagine yourself pulling out the plug from a kitchen sink
and allowing the dirty dish water to go down the drain. That
polluted water is your negative thinking flowing away—your
uneasy fears, your apprehensions, your presentiments, your
premonitions that keep you in a constant dither of anxiety.

Habits are formed by repetition of the same routine. Just
as you would train your pet poodle or your beagle or your
schnauzer to "sit" . . . "stay" . . . "come" by repeating
the same command over and over and over again and insist-
ing on the same obedient action each time, so you must train
yourself in positive thinking by constant reiteration. Say to
yourself ten times, *"I have pulled out the plug and my
worries are draining away. . . . I have pulled out the plug
and my worries are draining away,"* etc.

Picture it clearly. Believe it implicitly. Feel the immense
joy and relief in knowing that your worries, one by one, are
flowing down the drain. The method is not too dissimilar to
Emil Coué's teaching: "Day by day, in every way, I am
getting better and better."

Now start replacing your fears and apprehensions with
positive thoughts. Say to yourself ten times:

"I have faith, courage and peace of mind. God is protecting me and my loved ones from all harm."

"I have faith, courage and peace of mind. God is protecting me and my loved ones from all harm."

"I have faith, courage and peace of mind. God is protecting me and my loved ones from all harm."

There is a reason for this repetition. Go through the routine not once but several times a day—and again at night before you go to sleep. Soon you will be consciously aware of a change in your mental attitude. You will feel a calmness, a sense of security and a "peace of mind that passeth understanding."

Here, then, are the three effective methods for clearing away worries, fears and apprehensions:

1. *The power of prayer. A simple faith in God and a total reliance on His protection and guidance.*

2. *The logic of rationalization. An exercise of judgment, wherein we convince ourselves, intellectually, that the law of averages is working in our favor.*

3. *The habit of positive thinking. A replacement of negative thoughts with thoughts of confidence, courage and inner peace, achieved by mental discipline and constant training.*

CHAPTER 7

How to Be a Nobody
When You've Been a Somebody

*We must adapt ourselves to changing cir-
cumstances.*

—DEAN WILLIAM R. INGE

I have always been such an ardent fan of the New York
Yankees that each year I purchase a single box seat for all of
their pre-season games in the Fort Lauderdale Stadium. This
spring I noticed that the occupant of the seat next to mine
was also alone, and before the first inning of the first game
was over we were discussing the condition of Whitey Ford's
pitching arm, the relative merits of Tom Tresh and Joe
Pepitone, and all the other superficial things that baseball
fans talk about.

When the vendor bellowed, "Get your hot roasted peanuts," I held up two fingers and later my neighbor in the next
seat reciprocated with hot dogs and beer. Before the game was
over we discovered that we lived only two blocks apart, so my
friend said, "If you are coming to the game tomorrow, I'll be
glad to pick you up. No use driving two cars way out here." I
said, "Fine, if you will let me drive you the next day."

Thus began a "baseball friendship" that went on for
eleven pre-season games. Riding to the stadium each day, we
talked about our favorite restaurants, about deep-sea fishing,
harness-track racing, the best kinds of grass for Florida lawns,

and many other topics of purely local interest. I learned that he was from Chicago, that his name was Frank Jenks and that before retirement he had been in some sort of machinery business. And because machinery is so foreign to my interests, I probed no further.

One day I asked a friend if he knew a man named Frank Jenks. "Sure, I know him," said my friend. "Lives over on Cayuga Road. He was president of the biggest farm machinery company in the world—International Harvester."

And that is when I first thought of the title for this chapter, "How to Be a Nobody When You've Been a Somebody." Frank Jenks inspired the idea, but the problem applies to us all. For every one of us is a SOMEBODY in our own little world until the Day of Retirement suddenly makes us a NOBODY. The pilot whose tugboat chuffed and puffed ocean liners into their dockside berths is no longer "Captain," now that he is living on Social Security. The retired shop foreman is no longer "Boss." The retired army sergeant is no longer "Sarge." Retirement is the great leveler. We all become NOBODIES, happy and contented in our new status, or totally miserable, depending upon how well we make the adjustment.

The best advice I can give to a retiree is to sever all sentimental ties that bind you to your old job. I'll go further. Avoid visiting your former place of business. Stay away from restaurants or other familiar haunts where you are apt to run into your former associates. Put all office photographs, newspaper clippings and business mementos on a closet shelf. Make a clean break with the past. Start a new life. And, if possible, move to a new locale.

This may seem like heartless masochism to a person, just retired, who has spent many happy years of his life in the company of friends and co-workers.

Loren Stone learned his lesson the hard way. For many years Loren was the head of the art department of a leading New York advertising agency. He had reached the zenith of prestige in his field and enjoyed the utmost respect among his associates and contemporaries. After a few months of retirement, during which Loren and his wife, Kay, took a leisurely tour through Europe, he stopped in to visit the old company on Madison Avenue.

"I guess that was one of the rudest awakenings I have ever had," said Loren. "My old buddies greeted me warmly enough, but they all seemed terribly busy and preoccupied with jobs that were going through the shop. When I started to tell one of my associates about an incident that happened in Paris, I noticed him glancing at his wrist watch in that cruelly polite way which says all too obviously, "Loren, old boy, I would love to talk with you, but right now I'm working on a rush job."

This attitude is typical of all companies. Once a person is retired he is expected to stay retired and not come back, except perhaps for the briefest greeting: "Glad to see you. How's everything going?" Loren told me ruefully, "That is so true. Now you know why I moved to Florida."

Many years ago I knew a brilliant advertising writer named Gordon Seagrove. He was admired as the genius of the advertising profession, creator of the word "halitosis" and originator of the once-famous Listerine headlines, "Often a Bridesmaid—Never a Bride," and "Once a Prominent Social Leader—Now a Helpless Invalid."

At sixty-five Gordon made the mistake of retiring "part time." He no longer occupied the luxurious corner office but smaller, less imposing quarters down the hall. And because Gordon Seagrove was active only one day a week, he was no longer consulted by clients and rarely by his associates. Feeling the sting of his downgrading, Gordon, who still retained a sense of humor, put up an illustrated sign on his office door that read, "Once a Proud Peacock—Now a Feather Duster!" The next day Gordon decided to retire—full time.

Several years ago a lecturer on biology made a profound statement which I have never forgotten. Because it applies equally to persons who are about to retire, I am quoting it in essence. "All animal life," he said, "is subject to three laws of Nature, and if their species is to survive, they have a choice of the first two. There is no other alternative. These are the laws: 1) ADAPTATION, 2) MIGRATION, and 3) EXTINCTION. He gave as examples 1) the tiger who grew stripes on his body, better to hide in the bamboo forests of the Far East; 2) the migratory birds that fly south to escape the bitter cold winters; and 3) the dinosaurs and pterodactyls who became *extinct* because they did not *adapt* themselves nor *migrate* as a means of survival.

People who face retirement have the same three choices: they ADAPT themselves to their new way of life or they MIGRATE to Florida or California or some other place favorable to retirement, because they are unable or unwilling to adapt themselves to their new environment.

The great majority of men and women approach the leisure years without realizing the shock in store for them. They can understand how a great movie star can suffer a crushing loss of self-esteem when his acting days are over, or how a Senator must feel when he is voted out of office, but they do not seem to realize that retirement can produce the same kind of devasting effect on their own lives. The transition from a SOMEBODY to a NOBODY is one of the cruelest blows the human ego must suffer. The only practical way to ameliorate the problem is to accept the change with finality, make a clean break with the past, and look forward to a new way of life with eagerness and enthusiasm.

Not long ago I discussed this problem with my dentist, Dr. Howard M. Service. Since conversations with a dentist are necessarily one-sided, I will merely quote his answer to the question I managed to ask before my mouth was filled with cotton rolls and saliva tubes.

"Yes," said Dr. Service, "I've devoted a lot of thought to what I am going to do when I give up my practice, which I hope will not be for several years. As you know I make my own gold inlays and bridges, instead of sending the molds to a dental laboratory. Recently I have been experimenting with the molding of tiny solid gold ornaments and flowers and things like that. One of these days I hope to be a source of supply for Tiffany or Cartier." So Dr. Service is well prepared for the day when he will give up being SOMEBODY to become a NOBODY.

Less fortunate is the average businessman who has no special skill to employ as a buffer against boredom in his retirement years. Even the intellectual stimulus of good reading is usually denied these unhappy persons who never took the time, during their middle lives, to cultivate a love of fine books.

"There is nothing quite so gratifying as the vicarious thrill that comes with sharing the experiences and thoughts of great authors," says William H. Dreier of Grinnell, Iowa. Bill retired at age of sixty-three, almost totally deaf. "I have less than five per cent of my hearing," he says, "but I can still enjoy my library. I have a long shelf of volumes written by the great thinkers through history. Reading the words of a Benjamin Franklin, Alexander Hamilton, Voltaire, Thomas Jefferson, Henry Thoreau fills me with a zest for living. They are all anxious to talk with me and their inspiring thoughts make my heart throb with a desire to live a meaningful life, in spite of my handicap. I think the best way to summarize my feeling about great books is to quote the remark made by Bertrand Russell after he had spent several pleasant hours in animated discussion with Aldous Huxley. 'How nice it is,' said Mr. Russell, 'to know something.' "

Sometimes the handicapped are better able to make the adjustment from a SOMEBODY to a NOBODY than the lucky ones who are healthy and normal in every respect. Floyd Padgett of East Palestine, Ohio, was a successful scientific farmer until the loss of a leg ended his active career. Physically unable to carry on with his own farm, he found a way to be useful and happy, despite his handicap. Today Padgett, with his vast fund of knowledge and experience, is channeling helpful information to seventy-four farmers in forty-two foreign lands.

Long ago a retired schoolteacher, a dear old aunt of mine, spent the last twenty-five years of her life (she lived to be ninety) actively corresponding with former pupils whom she had taught through the years. The warmth of their letters brought joy to her life. "Aunt Flo," as they affectionately called her, was still an important SOMEBODY in their memories of the old brick schoolhouse on Bartlett Avenue in Milwaukee.

One of the happiest retired men I know has no hobby, no interest, no activity aside from just being "a wonderful husband." The quotes are supplied by his wife, Martha, who is painfully crippled with arthritis and unable to carry on the simple chores of their household. Don Phillips was a SOMEBODY in his home town of Akron, Ohio. Owner of a manufacturing plant. President of his country club. Member of civic committees. At sixty-five he sold his business and moved to Florida with his ailing wife.

Today Don cooks the meals, does the dishes, buys the food, makes the beds. One day a week a maid comes in for washing and ironing. In the evening, Don watches his color TV along with Martha, when she feels up to it. Sometimes they play Scrabble together, or gin rummy, or take a ride along the beach. When I commiserated with Don for assuming the household duties, he said, "I don't mind. I rather like it. Gives me something to do. And I'm helping Martha. We could get a part-time maid, I suppose, but we like to be alone."

With women the problem can be even more acute— although subtler. So often a woman's life revolves around her children. Often they are gone and on their own long before she hits her sixties. Then, at least, she still has her husband to tend to. Perhaps he is still entertaining business acquaintances at home, and she's the hostess. But when the husband loses his business connections, that's gone too. Preparing meals for two suddenly seems like child's play. The house needs less and less cleaning, and almost all of her activity becomes busy work, made activity.

The more fortunate woman is the one who did not lean entirely on her children for her life activities. Perhaps she was involved in community service, or an amateur theatrical group, or politics; she still can be. Perhaps she had a career too. Then her problems are very similar to her husband's, and she can follow pretty much the same program outlined for him.

Let's look at the worst situation—housewife-mother, suddenly without children and with almost no housework. From a half-nobody to a full nobody. The first trick is reorientation, and that has to take place in your own mind.

Kick out your servant psychology. Say over and over, "My sole useful function is *not* to take care of others. *I am free.* Think of the thousands of slaves emancipated after the Civil War. History books tell us that many could not get used to the idea of being free—especially the older ones. They stayed around the dilapidated plantation of "Ol' Mass," continuing to play the role of old faithful Uncle Tom. That's what you do when you stay in the house desperately wishing that you had a big mess to clean up or a huge dinner to prepare.

Decide that tomorrow morning you are going to accept your freedom. Get out of bed and *rush* through your simple household tasks, eagerly, as if you can't wait to get out the door. Dress up smartly and *leave.* Now head for the local public school, or hospital, or orphan asylum. Walk in and say, "I have plenty of free time. I can help teach reading, or sewing. I can sing to the sick children." You will be surprised at the eager reception you'll get if your attitude is right. Don't walk in with the "I'm bored. I'm resigned to doing-some-busywork-here look." Instead, have the tone of voice and the manner that says, "I'm eager and interested. I know I'll like this."

If you simply can't leave your stove, there are some ways to create a revolution around it. If you've been cooking the same meals for forty years, completely change your style. Pick up a paperback book on French or Chinese or Italian cooking. Start inviting people in to dinner; and if it is too much of a strain on your budget, make an arrangement with another woman in the same boat to switch off the gourmet cooking. You and your husband eat at their house once or twice a week, and vice versa. In other words, change something! Learn new games, new recipes, make new friends, take a class (there's a chapter on that later), even change your looks.

Your part has changed. If you've been "type cast" for forty years and you're no longer the type, do what the actors and actresses do. Change your type. You can start a reading discussion club among the other women, or go in for gardening for the first time. Don't wait for some other bored woman to get you started. You may have been a NOBODY for your whole life. Now try to be a SOMEBODY.

That's exactly what happened to Mrs. Dorothy Lowe of the Bronx, New York. One day she sat down to play with one of her grandchildren. In a moment of inspiration she took some egg shells and began to glue different size pieces onto a cardboard from a laundered shirt. A few years later her eggshell art was on display in homes of friends, and the New York Bank for Savings at 86th Street and Broadway, New York City, had a window display telling the story of her eggshell art.

I am beginning to wonder about the title of this chapter. Perhaps there is no such person as a NOBODY. Admittedly, most of us are SOMEBODIES until we retire. Then, I am beginning to believe, we become SOMEBODY ELSE. And the SOMEBODY ELSE can be a nicer person. A more relaxed person. Less important in a worldly way. But possibly *more important* in a way that counts.

PART 2

How to Keep Busy, Interested and Alert for the Rest of Your Life

CHAPTER 8

There Are 20,000 Things You Can Do— How to Find the One That Suits You Best

The world is filled with interesting things to do.

—DALE CARNEGIE

After reading the first seven chapters of this book, I hope you are convinced that it is better to *do something* in retirement than *do nothing*.

The problem is *what*. *What* can you do? *What* do you really want to do?

The more you think about it, the more confused you are apt to become. Asking advice of friends and relatives does not help; their opinions are usually too subjective. Nor will you find the answer in your public library. There are many volumes on the subject of hobbies, avocations and activities. Someone has estimated the list of Things You Can Do at more than 20,000. Yet no one, to my knowledge, has written a book telling the man or woman of sixty-five how to find the activity that suits their particular needs or talents.

Someday this problem may be solved by computing machines. How simple it would be if you could list your talents and desires, then push a button and let the whirring machine spit out hobbies perfectly suited to your background. If we are to believe what we see on television, even marriages are arranged by a mechanical cupid inside the computer, which pairs up the personalities of certain people who have a natural affinity for each other. Lacking a computer, we must choose the next best method, which seems to be the somewhat more tedious, and perhaps more reliable, process of self-appraisal.

Assuming a sincere desire on your part to search for a congenial or profitable way to spend your time, *how do you decide what is best for you?*

Let's start off by asking a question. *Is income a factor? Is it necessary for you to earn money to bolster your social security, your pension, or any other source of income?*

If so, then your major activity should probably consist of either:

1. A full-time job.
2. A part-time job.
3. A hobby that earns money.
4. A small business of your own.

If your present income is ample for your needs, then, if you wish, you can devote your time to:

1. An interesting hobby.
2. Community service or church work.
3. Travel.
4. Research, study, or reading.
5. Games or sports (fishing, boating, golf, etc.) .

If you need a full-time job

Many people past the age of sixty-five will tell you that it is next to impossible to land a full-time job. It is true that some employers have a policy of hiring only younger people, especially firms that offer pension plans. Other employers, however, have found from experience that older workers are more dependable and are capable of superior judgment. When you apply for a job, avoid large firms which are apt to have pension plans. Companies such as this are usually located in downtown areas and are bombarded with applications. Concentrate on smaller firms in outlying neighborhoods where fewer people apply for jobs.

First decide what kind of work you are best qualified to do. Are there jobs available that would utilize your previous experience? If you cannot decide what you want to do, you may need vocational guidance. An experienced counselor can quickly analyze your talents and tell you the occupations for which you are best fitted. If you cannot locate a vocational-guidance bureau in your area, send one dollar to the Personnel and Guidance Association, 1534 O Street, Washington 5, D.C., and ask for their directory listing all the vocational-guidance agencies in the country.

One of the major stumbling blocks in the path of older persons landing a job is their own attitude. Many men and women over sixty-five believe that they are not physically capable of working even a few hours a week, and yet doctors tell us time and time again that more energy is consumed in boredom, restlessness and general unhappiness than could be consumed on even the most taxing job.

There's a story passed down through the years that a Harvard student was consulting with the late LeBaron Russell Briggs, long the dean of that college. The young man's work had been going rapidly downhill, and the dean asked him why he had failed to complete an important assignment. "I wasn't feeling very well, sir," the student replied. "Young man," said the dean, "I think that you will learn someday that most of the world's work is done by people who aren't feeling very well."

The truth of that reply is obvious all around us. Many of our Presidents, perhaps the busiest people in the whole world, have been far from youngsters. The most famous physicians, missionaries, even explorers have gone on working right to the end. And you must admit that the man or woman who comes home from a job or other useful activity stimulated, interested, with plenty to talk about seems less tired than poor old Mr. Jones, who sits home reflecting on his glorious past and growing more tired and morbid with each passing day.

A pessimistic attitude will reflect in any job interview. Your face, your voice will say, "I know I won't last long on a job." But if your attitude is "A job is just what I need. I'll meet people, maybe learn something new. I'm really excited and eager to work," that will show too. Once you decide what kind of a job you want, prepare a résumé of your employment history and your experience. Start writing letters. Be sure to mention that you are willing to forego participation in pension plans. State your qualifications and assets, such as maturity, judgment, dependability. Avoid asking for sympathy. Don't mention how important it is for you to get employment. And never say you are willing to do "anything."

During my career in advertising I have probably interviewed more than 500 job-seeking copy writers and I was continually amazed at the naïve approach used by many of them. These people were supposed to be experts in the psychology of selling, yet time after time they would use superficial devices which instantly disqualified them, such as, "Mr. Legler, I would consider it a privilege to work under your direction." (Obvious flattery.) Some would say, "What a great opportunity it would be for me to work on this account." (Subjective thinking.)

In selling yourself to a potential employer, it might be well to recall the words of President John F. Kennedy and to paraphrase them for your own guidance: "Think not what the (company) can do for you—but rather what you can do for the (company)."

There are certain types of jobs which are more suitable for men of sixty-five and older, jobs which do not require either physical strain or specialized training. To list a few: retail clerk or floor walker; mail-room clerk; custodian; museum or plant guard; inventory control clerk; collector; taxi dispatcher; manufacturer's representative; receiving clerk; building lobby receptionist; hotel clerk; file clerk; parking-lot attendant; timekeeper; gateman; cigar-counter clerk; stockroom clerk; canvasser; blueprint machine operator; automobile salesman; general office clerk; weigh-master; theater ticket taker.

Women will find that there are many more job openings for them. Those years of child rearing can help you get an assistant's job in a day nursery, a camp mother's spot, a regular baby-sitting job that you can even handle in your own back yard. Perhaps a local knitting shop needs someone to give advice or lessons to its customers. A brief practical baby-care course can give you the piece of paper required to use your knowledge and take care of newborn babies when they first arrive at home. Usually this involves little or no housework. You make the formula and care for the infant at its feeding time and bath time, and you can work full time occasionally. If you can answer telephones or type, there are offices that prefer an older woman to a giggling, boy-crazy teen-ager. There are many busy doctors who love the idea of a grandmotherly person at their reception desk. Of course, a lot of these jobs come under the part-time category as well.

You will find the answer to many employment problems in a free pamphlet published by the New York State Legislative Committee on Problems of the Aging, 270 Broadway, New York, New York. It is entitled *How to Get a Job*. Another called *Suggestions for Workers Over Fifty* is available from the Vocational Guidance Bureau, 1001 Huron Road, Cleveland, Ohio.

If you want a part-time job

Many people over sixty-five desire to supplement their income from Social Security plus private pensions. As you probably know, you are permitted to earn up to $1,500 a year without losing any of your Social Security benefits. Current legislative plans may permit you to earn even more. And you may also receive income from pensions, investments, annuities and rentals from real estate without affecting your Social Security. If you wish, you can work at a full-time job for a few months, perhaps earning a good salary at a seasonal job. Then you can take it easy for the rest of the year and continue to draw checks during each month you are idle. If your total earnings do not exceed $1,500, you do not have to forfeit a single Social Security check. By limiting your monthly earnings to $125 a month you open up a wide range of job opportunities. Younger people require more than $125 a month and are not interested in part-time work. So people over sixty-five have a distinct advantage in selling their services on a part-time basis.

One of the best ways for a retired person to earn money is by selling. You can retain your independence, punch no time clocks, choose your own hours, and control your income by limiting the number of calls to provide you with just the amount of money you need. If you live in northern states you can sell during the summer months and probably make enough to reach your $1,500 income limit. Thus it would not be necessary for you to go from door to door in the winter months. Most of your calls would be in the suburban areas, depending upon the product you sell.

Of course, to sell a product successfully requires patience, tact, persistence, self-confidence and sincerity. You must be able to take rebuffs and to rise above discouragements. Once you begin making sales, you will develop an enthusiasm that will carry over to your customer.

You will find a wide variety of selling opportunities in the pages of the leading salesman's magazines, such as *Salesman's Opportunity,* 850 N. Dearborn Street, Chicago 10, Illinois, and *Specialty Salesman Magazine,* 307 N. Michigan Avenue, Chicago 1, Illinois. There are hundreds of products being sold today successfully by retired people—products such as kitchen tools, brushes, auto accessories, garden tools, books, religious items, greeting cards, and cosmetics. Large sales organizations are aware of the vast changes which are taking place in the shift of populations to the suburban areas and they are rediscovering the profits in door-to-door selling.

Experienced salesmen will tell you never to make a cold call. Always arrange an appointment by telephone, even though you get a certain percentage of turn-downs. One of the most effective methods for getting leads is to offer a small free gift after you make a sale, if your customer will suggest the names of two neighbors who might also be good prospects. You then telephone these people for an appointment. Repeat the process and you will soon find your prospect list growing rapidly. Through this simple plan you can avoid making cold calls.

Of course, some people cannot bring themselves to sell. It

requires, even with appointments lined up, a certain amount of outgoingness. There are dozens of other ways to work part time. Evening work is usually avoided by couples with children or young people who consider the evening their date time. Most shopping areas stay open one or two evenings a week and are amenable to the idea of part-time help on those evenings. The same goes for doctors and dentists who often find it difficult to find part-timers for their late evenings and also for their Saturday office hours. Often such tradespeople or professionals don't bother to advertise for part-time help but limp along with absenteeism and other personnel difficulties. A friendly visit or phone call offering your services for those hard-to-find-help times can pay off with a part-time job.

Examining your old skills can also pay off with a part-time idea. Perhaps you're a former accountant. Why not help out during the rush season? Ex-designers, editors, music arrangers, bakers, cooks, travel-agency bookers, etc., all know just when the rush is on and can earn themselves some extra money by offering their services for those periods. Nobody looks too old to the harried head of an accountant's office a month before tax time or the manager of a travel agency right at the peak of the winter cruise season.

Look around your town or city and think about what others need, and you're sure to come up with some excellent ideas for part-time work.

A hobby that earns money

Sir William Osler says, "No man is really happy without a hobby and it makes precious little difference what the outside interest may be—botany, beetles or butterflies; roses, tulips or irises; fishing, mountaineering or antiques—anything will do as long as he straddles a hobby and rides it hard." Every authority on retirement agrees with Sir William. Life without a hobby can be dull and monotonous.

If you are lucky enough to have a hobby that can become a source of extra income, your happiness will be compounded. It takes imagination and usually a period of trial and error, but if you are determined to make your hobby pay off, the chances are your persistence will be rewarded with success.

Some hobbies lend themselves better than others to earning money. If you are an amateur photographer, for instance, you will find a wide range of available markets that will pay you well for your pictures. But if your leisure-time pursuit is collecting butterflies or autographs, you may have difficulty converting it to cash.

To stimulate your thinking, here are some hobbies which can be capitalized for extra income:

DINNER MUSIC. A competent piano player can supply dinner music at a high grade neighborhood restaurant. Fees range from $15 to $25, plus dinner.

DWARFED TREES. Artificial Japanese Ming trees can be sold for around twenty dollars to florists, gift shops, restaurants, etc. The materials cost less than three dollars, and it takes only three or four hours to finish a tree.

FISH SUPPLIER. An expert pier fisherman can sell his daily catch to local restaurants for three or four dollars. A popular hobby in Florida.

LOBSTER FISHING. Sea-loving boatsmen can easily clear $1,200 in a summer season trapping lobsters off the New England coast.

MAGAZINE CONTRIBUTOR. A good writer with mechanical experience can supply short articles of the "Do-It-Yourself" type to the practical-mechanics magazines. Payments range from ten dollars to thirty-five dollars for each effort accepted.

PICTURE FRAMING. If your hobby is framing pictures with an artistic touch, you may find a ready market with local photographers, gift shops, furniture stores or antique shops. Charge cost of materials plus three dollars an hour for your time.

GROUP PHOTOGRAPHY. If you pride yourself on your photographic skill, arrange with schools and summer camps to take group pictures. Few parents can resist buying an enlargement for one dollar.

CATERING. Any woman who enjoys making delicious canapes or hors d'oeuvres will soon become, with word-of-mouth advertising, the neighborhood "caterer" for cocktail parties. Charge one dollar per guest, which is somewhat lower than a professional caterer's charge.

POODLE BREEDING. If you are a lover of poodle dogs, you can make an extra income of several hundred dollars a year breeding pedigreed pups in a back-yard kennel or spare room. Toys or miniatures a few weeks old fetch $75 to $150— some even higher. This idea applies to any popular breed.

FLOWER GROWING. For green-thumb gardeners, a steady business can be built in certain middle-class neighborhoods, especially in Florida, by growing lavender, tan or yellow chrysanthemums of the smaller variety for supermarkets, which have a steady demand for these popular flowers, especially during the tourist season. Expect to make one dollar per plant or fifty cents per long-stemmed bouquet.

PARAKEET RAISING. If you would like to raise parakeets for money, three or four breeding pairs can produce as many as 200 birds annually. Wholesalers ordinarily pay five dollars apiece for young parakeets; fifteen dollars for a breeding pair.

MUSHROOM GROWING. Raising mushrooms is a year-round hobby that will pay twenty-five dollars per crop grown in a tray measuring five by ten feet.

SHELLCRAFT. If your retirement home is on the west coast of Florida and you have a certain artistic skill, you can make artificial shell flowers and sell them for a handsome profit. You will find details in hobby and craft magazines.

MEDICINAL PLANTS. By collecting herbs, roots and certain medicinal plants, you can supplement your income by several hundred dollars a year. Wholesale drug firms will pay a substantial price for your botanicals. Get full information from Superintendent of Documents, Washington, D.C.

CERAMICS. If metalcraft and ceramics are your forte, you may find a ready market in local gift shops and souvenir stores for distinctive costume jewelry, unusual cuff links and earrings.

MOSAIC TABLES. A popular trend toward ashtrays and coffee tables embellished with mosaic tiles should provide a source of extra income for those with artistic tastes who have successfully developed this hobby.

DOG PORTRAITS. A portrait photographer can charge fifty to seventy-five dollars for a beautiful enlarged color portrait of a pet dog. The promotion of this idea would probably be limited to upper-income communities.

DOLL MAKING. A clever cartoonist, skilled in needlework, can design and sell novel rag dolls to local toy stores.

METALCRAFT. If your hobby is metalcraft, you can design and make original name markers for the front lawns of homes in your neighborhood. If the trend becomes popular, you will be kept busy. Distribution might be made through a local hardware shop or gift shop.

CLAM DIGGING. Once you find a bountiful area, you're set

for season after season. You don't need any equipment except your two hands and a bucket, and you can sell your "catch" to local stands at about twenty-five cents per dozen or get an opener and sell your own for fifty or sixty cents a dozen. Steamed clams go over big too.

HAIR STYLING AND MANICURING. If you have a knack with ladies' hair and fingernails, you can invite customers to your home. Charge less than your local shops and give them a few extras, such as no waiting, privacy, and a cup of coffee and doughnut under the dryer.

SEWING. If your hobby is sewing, try a simple, uniform item like throw cushions. Foam-rubber pads in different shapes and remnant material sell cheaply, and you can offer throw cushions at $1 to $1.50 without zippers, a dollar more for those with zippers. Slipcovers for couches and chairs at a reasonable price can be made fairly easily by a skilled seamstress, and if you don't price them for a huge profit, you'll soon be flooded with requests.

PAINTING. You may never have much luck selling your own originals, but how many artists paint directly on walls? Paint a mural right on your entrance foyer or living-room wall and show it off to your neighbors.

Before long you may have orders for more. Charge three dollars per hour, and if you're a fast worker you'll soon get orders from people who can't afford to commission Dali, Picasso or even a professional mural painter.

WOOD CARVING. Make beautiful book ends, letter holders, etc., especially for Christmas gifts. Handcrafted work is still appreciated and you can sell it for no more than the factory-made item—$1 to $1.50 per end.

BAKING. Nothing can compare with a good home-made cake. Pass the word around that you will make them to order for birthdays and other festivities. Charge a dollar less than your local bakery, and you'll be as busy as you like. Special holiday cookies and cakes for big families also go over well. Word of mouth or simple signs on bulletin boards are good advertisers, and if you bake to order, there will be no stale cakes to throw out.

HOOKING RUGS. Hand-hooked jobs sell for thirty, forty and fifty dollars and more in specialty shops. Charge for the materials plus two or three dollars for every hour you spent making the rug, and guarantee your price will be much lower. Especially popular are hooked rugs with simple pictures for the walls of children's rooms, etc.

Any one of these ideas can develop at such a fast pace that you may have to consider hiring help and going into business with your hobby. At the minimum you can make a little spare cash and enjoy yourself with your favorite hobby. There is, after all, a limit to how much you can use. When your whole house is full of throw cushions, ashtrays, tables, wood carvings or the like, your hobby may seem worn out. But if you have to fill a demand for your talent from others, your hobby never dies.

The list shows only a few of hundreds of ways that hobbies can be made to pay off in extra cash to supplement your income. But don't expect to be successful unless the product you make or service you sell has 1) a recognizable excellence; 2) a market where it can be sold; 3) an appeal to contemporary trends or tastes. Even a modest degree of success in selling a product or service of your own will give you a sense of satisfaction you may never before have experienced.

CHAPTER 9

How to Start
a Business of Your Own

*In every enterprise, consider where you
come out.*

—PUBLIUS SYRUS

The prospect of establishing a small business to supplement
income is appealing to many persons in retirement. There
are many advantages and just as many pitfalls. If the idea
sounds attractive to you, list the pros and cons just to make
sure your decision will be based on sound thinking rather
than emotional desire. You might start off this way:

On the Positive side	On the Negative side
1. I will be my own boss.	1. I am aware that 50 per cent of all small businesses go out of existence within three years.
2. I will be solely responsible for my success or failure.	2. I know that 80 per cent of all small businesses fold up within five years.
3. I need to make only $125 a month net profit, and no more, to supplement my Social Security and pension.	3. I know that the ratio of business failures has increased sharply in the U.S.A. within recent years.

4. I will select a business which I can pre-test—and one that I can start with small capital —from $10 to $100. I will expand on a pay-as-you-go basis, thus I will not risk my savings.

4. I am aware that discount houses sell almost every conceivable item at a price which the small operator cannot meet.

5. I will read and study thoroughly every pamphlet on running a small business supplied by the U.S. Government Printing Office and follow its advice to the letter. I will not act impulsively or without having knowledge of the pitfalls.

5. I know that an inexperienced operator of a small business has two strikes against him from the start.

6. I will make sure there is an adequate demand for my product or my services before I risk any substantial capital.

6. I know that competition from a new shopping center located nearby might put me out of business within a week.

7. I will keep meticulous records.

7. I know that inability to collect money for goods sold on credit has been a pitfall which has wrecked many a small business.

8. I will not build up a high inventory. I will not advance credit. I will not sign leases or pay high rents.

8. I know that manufacturing costs, raw material costs, and shipping costs often nullify projected profits.

You will find many books in your public library on the subject of operating a small business. Other source material is available at a modest price from the U.S. Government Printing Office, Division of Public Documents, Washington 25, D.C. Here are the names of a few pamphlets to start you off:

Developing and Selling New Products (35¢)
Financing a Small Business (15¢)
Record Keeping for Retail Stores (15¢)

Best advice for a person at sixty-five: *Don't risk your capital.* If you limit your investment to a pocket-size business, you cannot lose much if it fails. And remember, all you need to supplement your Social Security income is $125 a month profit. The greatest reward will be the satisfaction of building a business of your own, however small it may be. If you have been working for other people all your life, you will realize at last the joyous experience of making it on your own.

It is not my purpose to provide a Manual of Small Business Opportunities but merely to suggest a few possibilities to illustrate the kinds of profitable enterprise which require a very small investment but an abundance of initiative:

1. Operating a day nursery

Very little investment is needed if you have a basement playroom with a bathroom and a back yard. This can be started gradually, beginning with baby-sitting arrangements for the children of one or two working mothers.

2. Raising flowers

Your equipment is right on hand if you are already an ardent amateur flower-grower. You can sell the cut flowers, or you can sell seeds from special varieties and seedlings for those who don't want to start from scratch. If you live in a city, you can put your green thumb to work on plants.

3. Dealing in antiques

Again, you can start with a few items, and if these succeed you can expand.

4. Operating a refreshment route
among construction projects

A small truck or motorized wagon and a good cook at home and your business is off to a good start. Highway stretches where there are no restaurants, or school areas isolated from town are other good spots for a refreshment route. You can start with hot dogs and sodas and expand to more elaborate sandwiches if all goes well.

5. Repairing bicycles

Very few tools are needed, and your own basement or garage can be your site of operation. Later you might want to expand to fixing up and selling secondhand bikes or renting them by the hour.

6. Operating a rental library

Some people with large book collections have started rental libraries with their own books. Then, when money comes in, they add the latest best sellers to their collections. This is an easy business that can be maintained in a spare room or your own living room.

7. Operating a vending machine

Advertisements abound for vending-machine businesses. But beware of "quick million"-type offers. Start with one or two machines and see how it goes. There is a minimum of servicing and collecting required. Especially interesting are some of the more modern machines that catch the eye (and the dimes) of those who are immune to gum and candy machines. There are now book dispensers, coffee dispensers, fruit-juice dispensers, stocking dispensers, etc. Location is all important, as generally people will prefer to shop for an item in a nearby store if there is one around.

8. A bookkeeping service for retailers

This is strictly for someone with accounting or bookkeeping experience. No amateur should try it.

9. A greeting-card shop

Competition can be keen here, so think about this only if there's a lack of one in your area.

10. Rebuilding furniture

This would include staining and refinishing, modernizing, etc. Don't try this unless you've had luck with your own. A few before-and-after pictures in your storefront window will draw customers, or if you use your basement, you can always run an ad in your local paper.

11. Collecting delinquent bills for small retailers

Not for the timid, this nonetheless can be a profitable business. Your local grocer just doesn't have the time to visit his delinquent customers, and you can work out percentage arrangements.

12. Power-mower rental

Of course, you'll have to invest in at least a few power mowers to start and know how to repair them. If you're successful, you can always add other items for rent—power tools, floor scraping machines, etc.

13. Boat rental

Ideal if you live near water and have a little capital to invest in a few boats. Later you can add skin-diving equipment and hire one of the local kids to teach customers the art of scuba diving, water skiing, etc.

14. Used-car surveyor

No capital required at all here. All you need is that know-how about cars. A small ad in the local paper and word of mouth about your unfailing honesty as an advisor and you'll be on the road to a neat little business with no overhead.

15. Rural electrician

Your knowledge, your hands, and no capital needed.

16. Rug-cleaning service

You can start with one man, one machine, and wind up with six men and machines!

17. Catering service for diabetics

This can expand to other menus too—salt-free diets, low-calorie diets, etc. There have even been catering services specializing in gourmet dishes for bachelors and working girls.

18. Floor-polishing service

As with rug cleaning, you can keep it small or expand it.

19. Delivery service for stores

This can be as simple as two boys and two bikes or you and a small secondhand pickup truck.

20. Compiling mail-order lists

This is a tedious clerical procedure, but all that it requires is a typewriter and clear thinking.

21. Home service "fix-it" man

This could include everything from the family iron to a 1960 radio or TV. The advantage is that the customer doesn't have to lug the goods to your shop and wait days to pick it up. Your advantage is that you don't even need a shop.

The government pamphlet "Meeting the Needs of Older People at the Community Level" tells about the "party aides" in one community. "This came, as do most such projects," it states, "from the idea of one person, who reasoned, 'All of us like to give parties, but few have domestic help. Yet there are retired women who would make wonderful helpers at parties. Why not have a system whereby these older persons could help out as party aides?'

"A program was soon developed. Party aides were easily recruited from senior activity centers. The women took a 15-hour course of instruction in which they learned how to make hors d'oeuvres, mix drinks, serve, and a great many other things of this nature. An ad was placed in the newspaper, 'Party Aides Available, $1.25 Per Hour,' and a telephone number was listed. The person who handled the telephone service was a homebound, bedridden lady with a telephone by her side. She took calls and then, going down her list, called one of the party aides.

"These people are now very busy; the demand for party helpers has far exceeded the supply. I asked one party aide, 'How do you like it?' She said, 'I love it—I go to a party now every week!' For her it is a social activity; and she is making money too."

It would require a volume the size of the Manhattan telephone book to describe all of the possible opportunities for starting a small business. For the same reason I am confining this chapter to those activities which can provide a source of supplementary income.

A description of "do something" activities, in which you can participate for the sheer joy of doing something, will be covered in subsequent chapters.

CHAPTER 10

If You Haven't the Foggiest Idea
of What You Want to Do—
Start a Button Bowl

To find happiness we must seek for it in a
focus outside ourselves.

—W. Beram Wolfe

When I was a little boy my mother used to let me play with a wooden bowl in which she kept buttons. Mother-of-pearl buttons, brass buttons, bone buttons, wooden buttons. A vast assortment which she had snipped off old pants and shirts and overcoats through the years. We called it the "button bowl."

This childhood memory made such an indelible impression that I have used the words "button bowl" ever since as a synonym for a research file where I could deposit snippings from magazines, letters, pamphlets and miscellaneous papers that I wanted to keep for later reference. It has occurred to me that a "button bowl" containing slips of paper listing various Things I Might Want to do After I Retire should be an excellent idea.

I have a friend who started such a "button bowl" at my suggestion a few weeks before retirement and his experience proved so interesting that I am relating it here as a possible source of encouragement for others who may be eager for something to do when they reach sixty-five.

Jim Brockton dreaded the day when they would remove the little bronze plaque from his desk embossed with the words MR. BROCKTON, ASSISTANT CASHIER. He hoped the bank would let him take it home with him along with his other scanty belongings—a solid-gold pen and pencil set, a couple of Prentice-Hall books on taxation and investments, and a thin manila file of personal papers.

"I've been sitting at this desk for thirty-five years," he told me almost tearfully. "It's like the end of the world."

"Or the start of a new world," I said, sounding even to myself like a Pollyanna.

"Horse feathers! Don't give me that old wheeze about 'life begins at sixty-five.' "

"Haven't you got a hobby—or *something?*"

"Not even *something*. You know I don't play golf. I hate bridge. Fishing I loathe. I get seasick on boats. I'm not civic-minded. And don't expect me to go in for finger-painting. I tell you, when I retire, I'm finished. I've had it."

"Why don't you start a button bowl?" I suggested.

"A what?"

"A button bowl."

"Don't be funny."

Finally I got through to Jim. He seemed to understand what I was talking about. I didn't see him again for three months. One day my telephone rang and it was Jim.

"Just thought you would like to know what's in my button bowl," said Jim, and his voice sounded a little more cheerful. "I've been doing a lot of thinking—about things I might like to do. When I was a kid I used to go mushroom hunting in the woods. I was quite an expert at identifying different varieties. So I sent to the Department of Agriculture for a book on mushroom growing."

"Good for you, Jim," I said with real excitement.

"Are you kidding," said Jim. "I read that book and if you think I'm going to have a basement full of horse manure, you're crazy. Compost, they call it. But it set me thinking. I thought I might like to grow orchids. So I sent for another book called *How to Grow Orchids.*"

"Wonderful," I said.

"Let me finish," said Jim. "I'm not going to raise orchids. They're too delicate. Too expensive. And it just doesn't appeal to me. But I found another book on *Hydroponic Farming* and it gave me an idea. You know, growing vegetables in water with chemicals. I built a little greenhouse in my back yard. And I want you to come over and see it. They're beginning to sprout. Beans and tomatoes and beets."

So Jim Brockton found his answer in a "button bowl." If you think the analogy is a little farfetched, try it yourself. Just remember, the "button bowl" is only a symbol.

Unless you are one of those fortunate persons who cannot wait for the day of retirement to jump headlong into a full-time hobby, the future may look bleak and empty. That is the time to start thinking. Be your own psychiatrist, or "head-shrinker," as the younger set might say. Analyze your faults and foibles as well as your talents and aptitudes.

Here is a simple check-chart which may prove helpful in suggesting an activity compatible with your particular temperament. I make no claim for its infallibility and frankly admit that this oversimplified method will probably be regarded with scorn by the professional personality analysts whose techniques for fitting square pegs into square holes are far more complicated (and expensive). All this test requires is simple honesty. No Rorschach ink blots. No drawing of nude pictures to determine psychotic tendencies. No completion of sentences nor filling in of missing words to ferret out prejudices.

Are you inclined to be careless . . . or meticulous . . . ?
Are you clever . . . or clumsy . . . with your hands . . . ?
Are you creative, artistic . . . or somewhat unimaginative . . . ?
Are you patient . . . or restless . . . ?
Are you gregarious, the friend-making type . . . or inclined to be shy, retiring . . . ?
Are you consistent . . . or capricious . . . ?
Are you the intellectual, studious type . . . or a rugged individual, a man's man . . . ?
Are you musical . . . or tone-deaf . . . ?
Are you uninhibited, outspoken . . . or cautious and reserved in your opinions . . . ?
Are you excitable . . . or phlegmatic . . . ?
Are you energetic . . . or do you like to take things easy . . . ?
Are you athletic . . . or sedentary . . . ?
Are you an introvert . . . or an extrovert . . . ?
Are you idealistic . . . or perhaps a trifle cynical . . . ?

An honest self-appraisal may help you to eliminate certain activities for which you are patently disqualified. Or vice versa. It may suggest an avocation perfectly suited to your personality, your talents and aptitudes.

Let us say that you are *excitable*. The *restless* type. Somewhat *capricious*. An *extrovert*. If you know these things about yourself you are more apt to fill your "button bowl" with Things to Do that make sense. What about politics? A civic responsibility? There are innumerable opportunities in public service for men who have these qualifications. The mayor of our village, a retiree who had spent a lifetime as a liaison man for a large public utility company, checks high on all of these personality traits. Ed Ingram, "Mr. Mayor" as we call him, has another quality that astounds his friends and neighbors—a boundless energy. Our mayor is in his "City Hall" at seven o'clock in the morning, and all day long he is dashing hither and yon, devoting his energies to the affairs of the community, its zoning problems, traffic tie-ups, police-department regulations, lawsuits and litigations.

No fancy salary keeps Ed Ingram's interest in high gear. The office of mayor in our village is strictly an honorary position—a labor of love. Yet somehow I feel that Ed's reward is the supreme satisfaction of getting things done with dispatch and diplomacy—plus the knowledge that his neighbors and friends are continually awed by his dynamic leadership.

Going back to the check-chart, let us say that you are *patient, meticulous, clever with your hands, artistic* and *creative.* You can fill your "button bowl" to overflowing with suggestions for consideration, such as these:

Get information on CERAMICS
Get information on METALCRAFT
Get information on INSIGNIA PAINTING
Get information on COPPER ETCHING
Get information on WATER COLORS—OILS
Get information on GLASS BLOWING
Get information on WEAVING TAPESTRIES.

A letter addressed to the American Craftsmen's Cooperative Council, 29 West 53rd Street, New York 19, New York, will bring you details that will help you make up your mind as to which of these, or other allied arts, are suited to your tastes and talents.

If you are *intellectual, studious, idealistic* and *introverted,* here are a few ideas to cram into your "button bowl."

Investigate research for public library on historical documents or on local civic history

Investigate reading and recording books for the blind

Investigate newspaper and magazine clipping service

Investigate genealogical research for your own family or for prominent families who may pay well for such a study

Investigate preparation of documented histories of large industrial corporations for contract fee

Investigate collection of first editions; air-mail stamps from foreign countries; old Bibles; crucifixes; antique jewelry; Early Americana

There are, of course, many people who could once check off certain items and no longer can. This can be a special problem for the man or woman who was once *active* and *athletic* and now must check *sedentary* because of doctor's orders or the law of the protesting legs. No longer can they race toward the goal posts for a touchdown, cycle cross country, bat in a home run or do a swan dive. Mentally these people are still athletic. They wouldn't dream of embarking on a research project or taking up ceramics. Their hearts are still out there with the ball, even though their legs are confined to the chaise longue.

If only they realized that they can still check *athletic* and readjust their first love to a new role! Recently, President Johnson announced that as part of the government anti-poverty program older citizens would be put to work as "foster-grandparents" to underprivileged youngsters. But it's no secret that the wheels of government programs turn slowly, and there is no law against stealing the idea for yourself, even improving on it.

All you have to do is think in terms of all of those youngsters around your area who may never know the joy of a sudden turn of a bike wheel onto a road with a spectacular bit of scenery, or pulling the trigger and shooting off a dead-center bull's-eye. There could be over-sixty-fivers all over the country running rifle-shooting classes, planning bicycle trips, coaching baseball, basketball and swimming teams. Often all those kids need is someone who wants to start it—not for money (which they don't have) but for love.

Guaranteed your yard would be filled with happy youngsters if you passed the word around that you were going to give free skeet-shooting lessons, or golf tips, or were organizing a basketball team. Almost every characteristic listed on the check-chart suggests some activity that uses your capabilities.

For instance, you say you are clever with your hands? Have a once-a-week basement or back-yard class in your favorite handicraft, be it furniture making, ceramics, carving or sewing. If you are artistic and creative, nothing makes painting more exciting than supervising a half-dozen youngsters who never had the chance to try oil paints before.

You're gregarious, the friend-making type? Be a group leader for a young people's discussion club. Nothing could do you more good if you are perhaps a trifle cynical. Are you musical? That's an obvious one. Give free or reasonable music lessons, organize a band or trio or small orchestra. And if you are that man's-man type, take on some of the "tough guys" on the block and try your hand at "big brothering" them. There is no more rewarding experience for the intellectual type than bringing to light a budding young author or poet. Start a writing workshop where everybody reads and listens to one another's productions and discusses the work.

So when you start filling your button bowl, fill part of it with the younger generation in mind. The possibilities for filling it are endless.

Instead of a barren existence from sixty-five onward, you can glorify each day you live with joyous anticipation and the tingling excitement that comes only to those who keep active. Just remember to

DO SOMETHING! AND DO IT AS THOUGH YOUR LIFE DEPENDED UPON IT—BECAUSE IT DOES!

CHAPTER 11

Read This—If You Are Tempted
to Buy a Motel When You Retire

*He is truly wise who gains wisdom from
another's mishap.*

—Publius Syrus

Ten hours of solo driving with a stop for a hamburger and a cup of coffee makes for a long, tiring day. What I wanted most in life at this moment was a hot shower, a good dinner and a comfortable bed.

And I wouldn't have long to wait, for a billboard told me the next town was only six miles up the road—Steep Valley. What an odd name. Steep Valley. Somehow it sounded familiar. And then I remembered. George and Ethel Cartright. Of course! For two years George and Ethel had talked about little else but Steep Valley and the quaint little inn they had discovered hidden away on a hillside "just flaming, my dear, with azaleas, dogwood and magnolia blossoms."

"Of course, we'll have to wait until George retires," Ethel used to say.

And George would interrupt her with a description of the cabins he was going to build. "Each one air-conditioned, with showers and comfortable beds and TV in every room. You know, there's a lot of money to be made in the motel business."

Soon the glowing neons of Steep Valley flashed the names

of a dozen roadside motels, one after another. I stopped at an impressive place and zigzagged my way among a score of parked automobiles into the office.

"Sorry, mister, we're filled up. I snapped on the 'no vacancy' sign an hour ago."

I smiled and thought, Good old George. He was so right. There's money in this business.

"I wonder if you could tell me," I said, "if a Mr. and Mrs. George Cartright own a motel in Steep Valley. They're old friends of mine. Came down here a couple of years ago. I've forgotten the name of their place."

"The Cartrights? Sure, I knew them. They were nice people."

"What do you mean—*were* nice people?"

"George and Ethel moved upstate about six months ago. Sold their place. Couldn't make a go of it. If you ask me, they never should have put a motel way up there on the ridge."

There's an old saying, "Make a better mousetrap than your neighbor and the world will beat a path to your door"— but it doesn't apply to the motel business.

The cardinal rule for a successful motel operation is *traffic*. A main highway means putting up with roaring trucks and blaring horns and a steady stream of headlights—but it can also mean "no vacancy" signs.

I guess as long as there are Georges and Ethels who build their dream of retirement around picturesque motels off the beaten track there will be disillusionments and, worse still, the tragic loss of lifetime savings.

Generally speaking, a small motel is not very profitable. The owner usually has also to be the manager—and often it's a twenty-four-hour-a-day job. For the average individual of retirement age, it's exhausting work.

During February and March, motel operators in Southern areas—Florida, for example—often put out "no vacancy" signs and turn customers away. This condition, though, lasts only a few weeks at most. June, July and August usually are also good tourist months. During the rest of the year, however, there are plenty of accommodations available.

In a good tourist location almost anywhere in Florida you could expect about 90 per cent occupancy in the winter months. For a typical tourist operation, occupancy probably would run from 50 to 60 per cent during the summer and in December, and around 30 to 40 per cent the rest of the year. In less competitive areas the percentages might be a little higher.

One thing which inexperienced operators sometimes find it hard to learn is that the winter income must be hoarded for use during the lean months. An experienced motel owner on the Gold Coast of Florida reports: "Four months of the year you make money, four months you break even, four months you lose money."

Of course the number of tourists visiting Florida is increasing every year. According to one recent prediction the number of annual visitors will be eighteen million by 1970—an increase of three million over the present rate. Keep in mind, however, that the supply of motel rooms remains well ahead of the demand. Scores of new motels are built every year.

According to one estimate, only about half of all Florida motels are profitable. It has been calculated that more than 40 per cent of them change hands every year.

A good motel should return not less than 10 per cent on a buyer's investment. Make certain the return includes some salary to you as the operator; if the salary is included, the return on your money may not be as great as it seems. You can figure on paying out about 40 per cent for operating expenses.

In estimating the cost of a motel, there is a rule of thumb which says the price should be about equal to three to five times the gross annual income. Don't depend too heavily on this, however; there are too many variables.

The down payment required is usually about 30 to 50 per cent, though often you can get it with much less—as little as 10 per cent. Experienced operators contend that in order to have a financially healthy situation, you should put down at least one-third.

While financing is usually available for the purchase of a motel, it is often the financing that gets the buyer into difficulty. If you are determined to own a motel, make a reasonable down payment; otherwise the interest charges will eat heavily into your revenues.

Keep in mind that the broker, if he has the motel among his listings of property for sale, represents the seller and is duty bound to get the seller's price if he can. On the other hand, if you don't like the seller's price, you can make a counter offer and the broker is duty bound to carry the offer to the owner.

The best sites for a motel are on traveled highways or near the beaches. Surveys show that motorists, when choosing their motels, look for restaurants, air conditioning and swimming pools, in that order. The motel without a good pool has a hard time competing with those which have them.

If you are thinking of a small motel, bear in mind that with anything less than twenty units, the owner is pretty well chained to the place; the revenue won't permit him to hire much help. With a motel of more than twenty units, the owner's lot is a little better.

Tempting as the idea of motel ownership may be, best advice is to go slow. Double-check every aspect of price, financing and operating expenses—as well as the soundness of the location. And face up to the unpleasant truth that many retirees have had unhappy experiences with motels.

CHAPTER 12

How to Use
Your Most Valuable Asset—*Experience*

*No personal consideration should stand in
the way of performing a public duty.*
—ULYSSES S. GRANT

Some people claim to set their clocks each morning by the drone of a passing plane or train.

A few years ago, my unfailing time signal, usually heard as I gulped my toast and coffee, was the familiar "whooosh, whooosh, whooosh" of my next-door neighbor's car starter. But this Monday morning the driveway between our homes was strangely silent.

Big Joe Gilbraith was probably sleeping late. Or, more likely, he was wide awake, from force of habit, and was just lying in his bed languidly enjoying his new freedom—the delicious realization of a long-anticipated retirement.

Over the weekend Big Joe had told me about the dinner his company had given in his honor. How they had risen to their feet to applaud his farewell remarks.

"And look what the fellows gave me," Joe said proudly as he peeled the watch off his wrist and read aloud the inscription:

TO THE
WORLD'S GREATEST SALESMAN
JOSEPH CHARLES GILBRAITH

"How about that!" I said. "You know, Joe, I envy you. I've got five years to go before I can retire. What are you going to do with yourself?"

"Just sit on my good old rockin' chair. Nothing to worry about! No sales quotas. No customers to pamper. Boy, I've got it made!"

During the next few months, my business took me out of town much of the time and I saw Big Joe only occasionally—in his driveway washing his car or pushing a cart at the supermarket. One evening Joe came over to our house and said, "Henry, I've got to talk to you. This retirement is for the birds. I'm going absolutely nuts sitting around day after day doing nothing."

"Haven't you any hobbies?"

"None! All I ever knew was selling. It was my whole life."

"Want a suggestion?"

"That's why I'm letting my hair down. Shoot!"

"Do you know Reverend Lindsay?"

"Our minister? Sure!" Big Joe laughed. "What do you want him to do—pray for me?"

"Quit the kidding. I'm serious. Go and see him. He's got a job for you. The biggest job in town."

I wasn't sure that Joe would follow up my suggestion. And a lot of time went by before I knew. Six months, at least.

It came in the mail. An announcement from Reverend Lindsay to each member of the congregation. The building fund for the new church had gone over the top. One hundred and fifty thousand dollars! And in the last paragraph there was a glowing tribute to "the man whose tireless energy had made the drive a success, Joseph Charles Gilbraith," as Reverend Lindsay put it, "the World's Greatest Salesman!"

One of the most tragic aspects of retirement is the mistaken belief that the surrendering of a lifelong job means the end of usefulness to society. Nothing could be further from the truth. Nearly every community has a group of advisory boards staffed by citizens with time to contribute. These boards help develop such things as libraries, parks, museums, beautification programs, airports, community colleges and hospitals. There are never enough workers to go around.

The retiree who opens his mind and his heart to some form of church or community service can find satisfactions that are far more enduring than the triumphs of a business career.

In countless communities of this country, wherever retired people have gathered in noticeable numbers, the cry is repeatedly heard, "Why don't we use the minds and the experience of our senior citizens to help us solve our problem?"

In one such community a perceptive young woman newspaper editor published an inspiring article on the outstanding individuals who had retired there. A scientist. An educator. An inventor of electronic devices. An author. An architect. She called it "our county's Brain Bank!" In another community the largest bank set out to catalogue the broad experience that lay at the beck and call of the city's political and civic leaders among the retired people.

The bank's officers felt strongly that this priceless experience should not be permitted to go to waste—that it should be made available to the local government agencies and civic committees which face so many difficult problems in the fields of taxation, education, welfare, law enforcement, recreation and politics.

In a resort city which depends heavily on tourists to support its economy, a civic leader declared publicly, "We have among our retired people some of the shrewdest advertising and public relations executives in the country. Let's ask them how we can attract more tourists."

The pattern is being repeated over and over all across the

country. Political and business leaders, in city after city, are coming to the realization that retirees are an enormous asset—that they have both the know-how and the time to make great contributions to the general welfare.

No talent, no skill, no experience achieved over a period of a working lifetime need ever go to waste. If you grimly picture your retirement years as a dead end of loneliness, you will have only yourself to blame.

The truth is, this country has more need for the experience of retirees than it has ever had. Every city, every town, every village and hamlet faces problems of great scope. The nation is in the midst of a population explosion. In the midst of a crime explosion. In the midst of a culture explosion. And a taxation explosion.

There are countless younger political and civic leaders who don't know which way to turn. Some will even admit it. They are in sore need of the best advice they can get. And communities which cater to retirees are discovering that the best counsel available comes from men and women experienced in these problem fields. From retired people, who now have time to put that experience to work on behalf of their neighbors.

Retirement gives an individual a precious gift that is often denied to younger leaders who are trying to build careers and families in today's complex and competitive world.

That gift is time to think.

Today's retiree who is concerned with a community problem can think about it while fishing from a skiff in the middle of a placid stream, or while in the garage refinishing a piece of furniture.

There in the quiet, while the young people cope with buying and selling and jangling telephones downtown, the

THE BEST OF YOUR LIFE

man who has served his time in the working world can
mentally assemble all he has seen and heard and read and
been taught and put it to bear on the matter at hand.

One of America's most successful commercial airlines uses
as its advertising slogan, "The priceless extra of experience."
This "priceless extra" can be the retiree's continuing gift to
the world. He has only to make certain that he applies it in
the proper manner—allowing his ideas to be leavened and
shaped by new advances and current conditions.

Experience loses much of its value if it is glued too tightly
to old ways and old conditions. Reshaping experience to new
situations will help to keep the retiree young, keep his mind
racing ahead. So far ahead, in fact, that younger fellows will
sometimes lag behind. Remember, there are "young fogies"
in the world just as there are "old fogies."

Some men's minds get set in concrete in their thirties.
Some business executives, some holders of political office,
even though age-wise presumably in their prime, are unable
or unwilling to see beyond the next fiscal year.

Unfortunately you cannot expect every community to send
out a call for retirees to ponder its problems. Some areas have
yet to realize what this "brain bank" of experience is capable
of contributing.

Where can you go to offer your services after you retire?
To civic clubs? Rotary, Kiwanis, Lions? These are open
doors. To neighborhood improvement associations? A direct
route. Taxpayers' leagues? Hospitals? Theater guilds? All of
these.

In many communities the city councils have volunteer
advisory boards at work in several fields. Planning, recreation, transportation.

Possibly you can initiate a "brain bank" movement in the

town where you elect to settle. Visit the editor or publisher of
the local newspaper. Point out the immense amount of time
and mental capacity available to any community through its
retired citizens.

You and others like you constitute a veritable treasure
house of hard-won wisdom. It would be a shame indeed if all
you have learned and experienced were allowed to go to
waste.

CHAPTER 13

Three Words That Can Open a Golden New World for You

Build a better mousetrap and the world will beat a path to your door.
—RALPH WALDO EMERSON

In the early days of television there was a popular program entitled "The Millionaire." The stories were farfetched and quite improbable, yet the program had a high rating because people enjoyed the vicarious thrill of suddenly receiving a check for "one million dollars, tax free, from an unknown benefactor."

By the time we reach sixty-five, most of us are willing to swap our dreams of becoming a millionaire for a modest pension, or even for a Social Security check. But in the hearts of many there still burns an unquenchable hope for THE BIG IDEA that will someday make them rich.

These are the people whose personality traits check high on *imagination, curiosity, ingenuity, inventiveness,* and, perhaps most of all, *persistence.* Age is no barrier to an exploring mind. Age, in fact, can be an asset, for the man of sixty-five has time to think and time to dream. And while the pot of gold at the end of the rainbow is usually never found, except by a lucky few, there is always a consolation prize—the joy of the search itself.

The formula for success of a new idea is so simple, it can be expressed in three words:

DO SOMETHING BETTER.

These words have made fortunes not just for manufacturers and business concerns, not just for engineers and inventors, but for thousands of unskilled men and women, young and old, who found a way to *do something better.*

The opportunities for thinking up new ideas are all around us—in the home, in the kitchen, in the bathroom, in the back yard. You have probably used a product in your toilet bowl called a Jonny Mop—but did you know that this useful accessory was dreamed up by the wife of a famous composer? She presented the idea to Personal Products, Incorporated, makers of Modess Sanitary Pads, and today she receives a royalty on every Jonny Mop sold.

What could be more trivial than a wooden golf tee, but because golf is a popular sport, the millions of people who play it willingly paid a fortune to its inventor.

The snap-open beer can is another recently invented device that proves how quickly American business will accept an idea if it promises to DO SOMETHING BETTER. An adaptation of the same device is now threatening to revolutionize the canned-food industry by dispensing with the need for can openers.

Someone dreamed up a kitchen roll of cellophane bags for storing leftover foods in a fresh condition, and Baggies, a popular new product, was born.

A new adhesive bandage that can be pulled gently off minor cuts and burns and bruises was described as "Ouchless" and achieved instant success. Plastic ice buckets, frozen foods of every kind and description, easy-feed razor-blade containers, disposable single-use carbon paper, charcoal filter cigarettes, prepared cake mixes are but a few of the thousands of new products that have come into national usage because they DO SOMETHING BETTER.

In the past decade a vast new industry of aerosol spray products has developed a new crop of millionaires. When George Spitzer invented Rise Shave Cream a few years ago the Chicago *Tribune* devoted an editorial to his achievement. "The inventor of the new kind of shaving soap that comes in cans and is squirted out like whipped cream," said the *Tribune,* "deserves the Nobel Peace Prize."

Most of the great ideas that have brought fame and fortune to their inventors are simple devices that were created to fill a need. For generations women performed messy kitchen tasks with soiled cloths and rags until someone said, "Why don't they make a paper towel for the kitchen?" That was thirty-five years ago and I was the someone who made the query. The result: a $250,000,000 paper towel industry. Unhappily, my reward was only the self-satisfaction of knowing that I had spawned the suggestion.

Your golden idea may come to you like a bolt of lightning while you are standing under the shower or mowing your lawn or even sitting in a sickbed nursing a cold. Let us assume that you have just taken your temperature with a thermometer. You hold it under the light, twist it and turn it, squint your eyes and say, "Why don't they make these darn things so you can read the figures?"

Why don't they? Here is an opportunity to DO SOMETHING BETTER. How about a magnifying glass? You slide the thermometer back into its case. Why not make the case a rounded magnifying glass? Then that little red line of mercury would be easy to see and the temperature figures would be greatly enlarged and easily visible. Perhaps you have found a way to DO SOMETHING BETTER.

Why stop there? What else can you do to improve the thermometer? How about a self-contained tiny flashlight that illuminates the figures? Could it be built into the case? And speaking of the case, the inside of that little black cylinder must be crawling with germs. Not everyone is cautious or considerate enough to wash off the thermometer and wipe it clean. How about a germicidal case? Come to think of it, thermometers are personal things, like a toothbrush. Why not sell them in pairs—"His" and "Hers" thermometers?

Apply the same kind of thinking to any product in general use. Study it. Be critical. What is wrong with it? How would you improve it—make it better, safer, more convenient, more useful, more attractive, more economical, more comfortable, more disposable?

This is the kind of creative thinking that advertising men call "brainstorming." A few years ago Marvin Small wrote a fascinating book entitled *How to Attain Financial Security* in which he presented a "Brainstorming Chart." It was intended to stimulate inventive thinking with questions and answers such as these, to be applied to almost any product, process or service:

Is there an EASIER way to do it?
Is there a QUICKER way to do it?
Is there a PLEASANTER way to do it?
Is there a LESS PERISHABLE way to do it?
Is there a SAFER way to do it?
Is there a MORE HEALTHFUL way to do it?
Is there a MORE COMFORTABLE way to do it?
Is there a CLEANER or NEATER way to do it?

Is there a SURER way to do it?
Is there a CHEAPER way to do it?
Is there a way to increase its USEFULNESS?
Can it be made MORE ATTRACTIVE, SMARTER?
Can it be adapted to SOME OTHER USE?
Can something be added to ENHANCE ITS VALUE?
Can a COMBINATION WITH OTHER DEVICES be evolved?
Can it be made DISPOSABLE or PORTABLE?
Can the DISTRIBUTION METHODS be improved?
What other way can it be IMPROVED?

If you will expend the same mental energy applying Marvin Small's "Brainstorming Chart" to products around the house as you would to solving a crossword puzzle, I will guarantee you more fun, more stimulation—and much more satisfaction should you be lucky enough to come up with THE BIG IDEA.

Make a game of it. Start with the kitchen. Take one item at a time. Go through the questions step by step. Apply them to your flour sifter. Your measuring cups. Your electric toaster. Your can opener. Ice cube trays. Egg beater. Turkey baster. Garbage container. Condiment dispensers. Pot holders. Knife sharpener. Brooms. Brushes. Mops. Dusters. Soaps. Detergents. Bleaches. If a certain question does not stimulate tangible ideas for improvement, skip to the next question. For example, someone recently came up with an idea for plastic, watertight garbage bags to be fastened to the inside door of the cabinet under the kitchen sink. This new product, now advertised on television, might have been suggested by the question, "Can you make it more disposable?"

You might spend an entire day, or several days, in the kitchen alone. Then proceed to the pantry, to the hundreds of different kinds of foods. Canned foods. Packaged foods. Bulk foods. Frozen foods. For inspiration go to your supermarket and make notes of the hundreds of items which might be MADE BETTER, PACKAGED BETTER, OR DISPENSED BETTER. You will be amazed at the number of new products that are constantly being displayed in your local food store. Some of these could have been yours, with a little concentrated effort and a lot of imagination.

Here is a retirement activity more exciting than solitaire, more stimulating than a game of gin rummy. When you have covered the kitchen and pantry, start on the garage. Examine each item in your tool chest. Your wrenches. Your hammers. Screw drivers. Drills. Scroll saw. Nut-and-bolt containers. Measuring sticks. Then your garden tools. Rakes. Spades. Hoes. Pruners. Clippers. And your paint supplies. Brushes. Paint pails. Turpentine containers. Think of all the improved products being offered constantly by your local hardware store. Wouldn't you be proud and happy to be the inventor of a useful product, a product better in its field than anything previously conceived by man?

You are ready now for the living room. The lamps. Bookcases. Lounging chairs. Tables. Cigarette boxes. Magazine racks. Look around you. Check off each item, step by step, with the "Brainstorming Chart"—not in a perfunctory way, but thoughtfully and inventively, searching always for betterment, in one area or another.

The bathroom is a treasure house of unfinished ideas—a potential gold mine for the creative mind. Start with the disorderly medicine cabinet—and most of them are. There must be a better way to segregate and store cosmetics, prescription medicines, shaving implements and all of the drugstore items that find their way into that inadequate storage chest behind the mirror. And what about the bathtub, the shower spray, the soap containers, the faucet handles, the laundry basket, the towel racks? Has each and every item reached the point of perfection? Or is there still room for improvement?

As you pass sixty-five and merge into your seventies, you will be more conscious of the need for certain home conveniences especially designed for the advancing years. Alert housing developers are already showing initiative in this area. Some of the latest model homes advertise special comforts for the elderly—such things as waist-high wall sockets for electric cords; non-slip kitchen floors; shelves and cabinets all at arms' length—none that requires stooping or bending; wider doors that permit the entrance and egress of wheelchairs; and a score of other conveniences. The surface has just been scratched. Here is a comparatively new field for exploration that offers a promising challenge to inventive thinkers.

Just for fun and to pass the time, I played the Brainstorming Game recently on a two-hour jet flight to New York City. With nothing but a pencil and a paper tablet for making notes, I managed to come up with seventeen different ideas for new and improved products. This method is what I call "Random Brainstorming" rather than by categories. Either way can be productive; and either way can be fun. Here are my notes, scribbled on the plane ride:

1. FIDDLE STIX. Plastic drinking stirring sticks, coated on lower end with a soft-drink flavor—strawberry, raspberry, lemon, lime, etc. Kids stir them in ice water, flavor melts, makes a soft drink.

2. MINUTE CAR-WASH PADS. Circular, non-scratching cellulose pads impregnated with soap (like Brillo). Big as a

saucer. Half inch thick. Dunk in a pail of water and wash your car. Packed one dozen in a circular cardboard container.

3. JELLY WHIP. Conventional fluffy-soft whipped butter, but fruit-flavored. Strawberry, raspberry, grape, etc. Spread it on bread. Eliminates need for jelly.

4. AQUA SADDLE. For swimming-pool sitters. Shaped like a motorcycle saddle. Made of smooth plastic. Air-sealed in for buoyancy. Sit astride. Holds you up so only your head and shoulders are above water.

5. GIANT ROLLERS. Rubber-tired roller skates. Each wheel six inches in diameter. For fast silent skating on smooth pavements. Sold attached to shoes, like ice skates.

6. PARKING FLAGS. Brightly colored silk flags with snap-on fastener. To be affixed to radio aerials of cars, so car can be located more easily in crowded parking lots. Alternative: colored disks with initial letter.

7. ROMAN FOUNTAIN. Circular hose sprinkler for lawn, with red or green spotlight in middle of circle. Becomes beautifully illuminated lawn fountain at night. A decorative touch for outdoor parties.

8. TURP 'N TEENA. Paint brush with transparent plastic handle containing turpentine. Push button to release a few drops of turpentine through hairs of brush to thin out the paint. Handle of brush can be refilled from bottle of turpentine.

9. TINTERS. Prescription eye glasses with top half of each lens tinted for sun shade, similar to the tinted top section of windshields on automobiles.

10. GAY BLADE. Kitchen carving knife in scabbard. The scabbard contains self-sharpening device. Knife blade is automatically sharpened as it is inserted or pulled from scabbard.

11. MAGIC PITCHER. Plastic pitcher similar in texture to

plastic drinking cups that are thrown away. Inside of pitcher coated with a soft-drink flavor which dissolves when pitcher is filled with ice water. Makes twelve soft drinks. Sold in cellophane seal to keep it clean and sanitary in supermarket.

12. WALLET CLAMP. Attention motorcar manufacturers. Dashboard glove compartment soon becomes filled with road maps, Kleenex, Windex, rags, tobacco pouches, etc. Some of us like to keep wallets containing our credit cards in this compartment. Please put a wallet clamp on the inside of the glove-compartment door. It would be a real convenience.

13. VITA-SHAKER. A vitamin shaker, like a salt and pepper shaker. Mixed vitamins in crystal form, similar to salt. Shaker kept permanently on dinner table alongside salt and pepper shakers. Family encouraged to sprinkle their vitamins on food, all you need for each day's vitamin quota. Vitamin supply replenished from container like Morton's Salt container.

14. KREDIT KARD. A fascinating modern game similar in some respects to Monopoly. Players issued Kredit Kards for gasoline, restaurant meals, motels, florists, air travel, long-distance phone calls, etc. Also imitation paper money. Players incur debts, must settle periodically for expenditures.

15. FLYING SAUCERS. Colorful plastic plates which children can spin on the end of a three-foot long flexible stick, like Japanese jugglers. Could become a popular schoolyard pastime, like yo-yo.

16. HIDE-ROGEN BOMB. An aerosol insect killer with a thin, three-foot-long spout, enabling you to reach spiders and insects that hide in ceiling crevices on screened porch, in closets and attics.

17. BEST BETS. Small device for top of TV cabinet. Schedules your favorite program channels for afternoon or eve-

ning. You study program listings in newspaper, set the device, and follow it for uninterrupted listening. Example: 6:30—Ch. 7; 7:00—Ch. 4; 8:00—Ch. 10, etc.

Perhaps these random ideas will suggest other products or devices which might have commercial value. Let your thoughts explore the things that interest you most. A new kind of golf tee that doesn't disappear when you whack the ball. A car jack that won't sink into the soft earth when you have to pull off the road to change a tire. A tiny electric buffer for polishing silverware.

If you happen to be a deep-sea fisherman you might spend a pleasant and profitable hour, between strikes, in a critical examination of your rod and reel. What an awkward device! With a hundred-pound sailfish on the end of your line, your hand must wind that little spool until your thumb and fingers are numb with exhaustion. Why don't they make a retrieving device which would be just as sportsmanlike but less tiring?

Retain the reel for winding the line, or for letting your catch run it out. But imagine a lever about two feet long, parallel to the rod, with a grip at the top end, and a hinge and ratchet at the lower end. Instead of that infernal winding, you would pull on the lever and release it slowly to play your fish, pull again and release, and again and again, until your catch was alongside, ready to be gaffed.

Securing patents and having models made of your new or improved idea can be an expensive step in the creative process. Reputable engineers have built successful businesses making models for wealthy retirees who earnestly believe they have found THE BIG IDEA. Some retirees, not wealthy, pour their life savings into hand-built models which cost from $500 to $10,000. And many have nothing to show for their efforts but an impractical gadget on the closet shelf.

Best advice is to BEWARE and BE SURE when your dream product reaches the stage requiring investment.

It is not my purpose to supply the rules and regulations for submission of ideas and inventions, nor to suggest how they should be presented, financed and marketed. Here are some sources of information, however, which go into considerable detail on all of these important steps:

How to Attain Financial Security and Self-Confidence, by Marvin Small; publisher, Simon and Schuster, Inc., New York. One of the most inspiring books ever written on the subject of creative thinking.

The Inventor's Patent Handbook, by Stacy V. Jones, the patent columnist for the *New York Times.* Publisher, The Dial Press, New York. A practical book of information for the amateur and the professional. An indispensable guide.

Answers to Questions Frequently Asked About Patents. single copies free from U.S. Patent Office, Washington, D.C. 20231

Patents and Inventions: An Information Aid for Inventors. 15 cents. Write the Superintendent of Documents, Washington, D.C. 20402

How to Obtain Information From U.S. Patents. 20 cents. Write Superintendent of Documents, Washington, D.C. 20402

In a recent issue, *Advertising Age* predicted that 70 per cent of the products which will be displayed on supermarket shelves twenty-five years from now are not in existence today.

What a challenge to people with inventive minds! What an opportunity for those of us who have retired from the rigors of business, to think, to dream, to let our imaginations soar into the wild blue yonder of million dollar ideas!

And if we fail to hit the jackpot, who cares? It was fun trying.

PART 3

How You Can Feel Thirty-Nine the Rest of Your Life

CHAPTER 14

The Secret of Staying Youthful

Winter is on my head but spring is in my heart.
— VICTOR HUGO

There is a feature in our daily newspaper entitled, "To These, Farewell"—a sadly sentimental variant of the black-bordered obituary column. Every day I read it with morbid fascination, and every day I am disturbed by the same recurring phrases:

"He was 68 and had been ill for some time."
"He was 71. Death was due to natural causes."
"He was 65 and had recently retired."

I often find myself wondering how many of these untimely deaths are self-inflicted—not with pills or bullets or carbon monoxide but with an instrument of self-destruction far more subtle and just as lethal: the poison of depression.

A few years ago I had the rare privilege of spending a full day in conversation with Dr. Hans Selye of the University of Montreal, the world's leading authority on stress. It is Dr. Selye's contention that stress is the cause of most diseases. His theory, now accepted by the medical profession, is that prolonged or excessive tension creates an imbalance in the body's metabolism—and that nature has provided a corrective in the secretions of the adrenal and pituitary glands. When stress is continued in violent outbursts or in a simmering state over a long period of time, the glandular corrective is insufficient to counteract the imbalance and the body becomes susceptible to attack in its weakest areas.

If this sounds like medical jargon, it simply means that prolonged tension—such as resentment, anger, bitterness, discouragement, vindictiveness and self-pity—are attitudes which eventually produce ill health.

One of the most brilliant creative advertising men I have ever known brought about his own destruction through a long-continued pent-up rage against the president of his company. Frustrated by the unimaginative attitude of his superior, he resigned his $50,000-a-year position in a burst of temper and, instead of seeking a more congenial berth in a competitive company, he nursed his anger in the solitude of his penthouse apartment until it became an obsession. Former friends could not tolerate his diatribes and shunned him. Within six months he collapsed of a heart attack, unquestionably brought on by his bitterness and animosity.

Dr. Miner Cooper, a San Francisco physician, in an article entitled "Heart to Heart Advice About Heart Trouble," says, "When I tell you that I have known a patient's blood pressure to jump sixty points almost instantaneously in response to an outburst of anger, you can understand what strain such reactions throw upon the heart."

The inability to adapt oneself to retirement can produce an emotional stress, which, though not so violent as anger, may be equally destructive if allowed to continue unchecked. Some men use their new leisure to nurse their feelings of disillusionment and thus become easy prey for neuroses, hypochondria and bodily decline.

Women especially suffer from fears of growing old. Many

of the excess wrinkles and lines they worry about are caused precisely by that worry. Youth, of course, has become a big commercial byword, and everywhere women look they see that finger shaking at them from billboards: "Stay young," "Banish gray forever," "Can you tell this mother and daughter apart?"

As one who spent a lifetime creating such slogans, I must confess that, if women would stop worrying so much about the outer woman and concentrate on inner happiness, the outer shell would respond with more success than the most expensive hormone creams or hair-dyeing jobs.

Garson Kanin, the famous playwright-director, said once, "A woman stays young as long as she's capable of changing her opinion."

I think that's a good formulation, because it covers a wide area. A woman who has been telling herself "I'm old and useless. Once you lose your looks there's nothing left" will change her whole life if she says instead "Hollywood has brainwashed me into thinking that every wrinkle is a tragedy. When I was a smooth-faced, empty-headed teenager, I didn't have half of what I have to offer now—experience, maturity, a sense of perspective. In my younger days, if I had a pimple on my chin I could barely speak to people until it went away. Look at me now! Wrinkles here and there and I'm still good company."

While most of us at sixty-five are certainly not happy in the realization that we have passed our physical peak, it is a misconception to believe that our lives, from here onward, must follow a downhill path to senescence or, even worse, to senility. We cannot hide our age like an ostrich hides its head, but we can cultivate a youthful spirit that will manifest itself in continuing happiness and health.

If we are willing to make a clean break with the past and to accept retirement as a stimulating challenge, we may find this fresh approach in itself a rejuvenating experience.

My years after sixty-five have brought me the deepest satisfactions of my entire life. I am happily bewildered at the incredible array of opportunities that have opened up in every direction. There are seldom enough hours in a day to accomplish all the activities which I type on my office agenda at eight o'clock each morning. Sometimes this list numbers thirty-five or forty "Things to Do Today." On such occasions my office telephone will ring at 6:30 in the evening and my wife will say plaintively, "When are you coming home for dinner?" A sharp contrast from my Park Avenue days when I used to watch the clock in midafternoon to make sure I would not miss the 5:23 at Grand Central Station.

Post-retirement activities can be a joyous experience if we choose to make them so. If we lack the courage and imagination to seek new interests, we may find ourselves drifting into a drab routine of intellectual and physical stagnation, slowly sinking into the bog of discontent.

By searching, each of us can find, within the limits of our own talents and capacities, an outlet for self-expression. And though our new achievements may be humble, they reward us with a sense of stimulation. For eventually we learn that all things in life are relative, and the truest satisfactions are those that come from within. External triumphs are too often laced with vanity—and when the applause dies down, we are left with nothing but silence—and the chill feeling of belonging to yesterday.

In striving to stay youthful for the rest of our lives we must face up to the fact, with honesty and humility, that happiness is a figment of our imagination and exists only within the confines of our own thoughts. This does not make it any less real. I suppose that we at sixty-five are not unlike a woman who emerges from a hair-dressing establishment with chin held high and a self-confident mien as she surveys her little world. Who would deny that her hairdo was worth the price?

The cynics will say that this carefully cultivated aura of youth is a sham world, destined to explode the moment we look in the mirror. They fail to understand that the youth we seek to preserve is indestructible—the youth of the spirit. Sometimes friends and neighbors, watching me cavort like a forty-year-old, will say to my wife, "When is he going to slow up?" And with deep understanding, God bless her, she answers, "Never, I hope!"

I wonder if the secret of staying young at sixty-five is not, perhaps, the realization that for the first time in our lives complete freedom of choice is restored to the individual. We can work or play as we choose. We can abandon forever the pretense of keeping up with the Joneses. We can say what we think at all times, without shaping our words for political expediency. Satisfaction and self-respect become the goals in life rather than promotions and pay increases.

The mood of the moment determines each activity. We can get up at dawn for a brisk walk on the beach. Or sleep until noon if it suits our fancy. We can waste a whole day shopping for a gadget. Or turn out a prodigious work-load on some self-imposed project. We do what we do simply because we want to do it—and not for any other reason.

Once we cut the strings, we are forever free from the routines, the restraints and the obligations that enslaved us. With a delicious feeling of superiority, we remember how our business associates used to say to each other at the end of each week, "T.G.I.F." (Thank goodness, it's Friday) . Life for us has become one everlasting weekend. Staying youthful under such favorable conditions can be and should be a stimulating experience.

Despite our new freedom, it isn't easy to abandon habits of our preretirement days. For example, as a former advertising man, I cannot resist the temptation to summarize this chapter with a device as old as advertising itself:

Do This—And You Will Stay Youthful

Seek new friendships.
Think positive thoughts.
Avoid emotional stress.
Yield to the demands of retirement.

Yearn for spiritual understanding.
Open your mind to new ideas.
Utilize your natural talents.
Take frequent walks.
Have regular medical check-ups.
Find a new interest.
Understand your limitations.
Lubricate your life with enthusiasm.

CHAPTER 15

How to Wash Out
Tired Thoughts Instantly

*Most people who are tired need not be
tired at all.*
—MARIE BEYNON RAY

I was sorry to read a newspaper report the other day about
the Food and Drug Administration cracking down on advertising claims of the multi-vitamins and mineral-supplements
manufacturers. Under the new regulations these drug products will have to carry a special label explaining that "Vitamins and minerals are supplied in abundant amounts by the
food we eat. . . . There is no specific basis for recommending routine use of dietary supplements."

Perhaps such legislation is warranted, perhaps not, yet I
have no doubt that millions of people who faithfully dose
themselves with vitamin pills every day feel stronger and
healthier because of this self-imposed regimen. After all, psychiatrists now agree that 90 per cent of chronic fatigue in this
world stems from psychological causes—neurosis, anxiety and
just plain boredom.

So whether you dose yourself with pills or not, let me
advance a prescription that doesn't come in pill form and
doesn't get filled at the pharmacy. Here is new hope for you
who have aching bones and muscles. Unless you have an
organic illness, I will tell you why you are tired and how you

may get over it—quickly, easily and permanently. I will give you the secret of releasing, within yourself, an abundance of energy and a storehouse of strength that will astound you.

The most penetrating lessons of the Bible were taught by parables. So let's start with the story of Bart Goodlow, a city editor some years ago with the old New York *Telegram*.

Bart was a tall, angular man with drooping shoulders and a sallow complexion. Yet he had never had a day's illness in his life. Like most devoted newspapermen, Bart had practically no interest outside of his work. Leisure, hobbies, golf were, in his opinion, a waste of time. He thrived in a world of confusion. The tension of deadlines, the pounding of tele-types and the whirr of giant presses were a tonic that kept his energy at top level. He was never tired, except on vacations.

When Bart Goodlow turned sixty, his family talked him into retiring. "Bart, dear," his wife would say, "you can't keep up this pace. You'll have a nervous breakdown!"

She was right. Bart did have a nervous breakdown, but not until six months after he had left the newspaper. At their little home in Forest Hills, he was a fish out of water. Restless. Chronically tired. His muscles weary with aching. His mind rusty and stultified from disuse.

Some time later Bart and his wife left New York and headed South. That was the last news I had of Bart Goodlow until six months ago. I was driving through a small town in Virginia and had stopped at a drugstore for a sandwich and a Coke. On the stool next to mine was a tall, stooped man with white hair. It was Bart. He greeted me like a long-lost friend.

"Are you going to be in town long?"

"Maybe ten minutes," I said.

"Make it fifteen and come around the corner. I want to show you my shop."

It was a typical small-town newspaper office. A roll-top desk. An old-fashioned letter press in the back room. A couple of battered typewriters. A bank of files.

"I bought it five years ago," said Bart. "It's just a weekly newspaper. Sort of a one-man show, but I'm having the time of my life. And say, you should read my editorials. 'Battling Bart,' they call me! Would you believe it? The local boys want to run me for Congress."

"You look great, Bart," I said.

"Never felt better in my life!"

For every Bart Goodlow who finds his niche there are tens of thousands of retired persons who never find it. Most of them are too tired to look. Mistakenly they regard their aching bodies as the inevitable toll of age.

If you were to tell them that their fatigue stems from boredom, they wouldn't believe it. Yet psychologists have proved, time after time, that boredom seeps through the body like a poison, causing muscles to ache and energy to drain away.

A ten-year study by Harvard University on the subject of fatigue among factory workers concluded that, "the phenomenon formerly called fatigue is better described as boredom. It is boredom that causes a reduced rate of working."

Marie Beynon Ray, whose famous book *How Never to Be Tired* has helped thousands conquer the disease of fatigue, says, "Recent investigations into industrial fatigue stress more and more the part played by boredom. With work constantly more mechanized, less and less physical effort is demanded of the worker. And yet fatigue increases. It must be because the task is more monotonous, more boring. At the end of the day, the worker has not a lessened *capacity* to work, but a lessened *desire* to work."

This same condition applies a hundredfold to the retired person who has no hobby, no work, no special interest. With nothing important to do, day after day, life naturally becomes *more monotonous, more boring,* with the result that there is a lessened *desire* to seek a new interest. No wonder so many of our senior citizens need Medicare.

We rarely get tired when we are doing something interesting and exciting. To illustrate, let's take the case of Jennie Talbot, a widow who lives on our street. She was always complaining that she was tired. She had a headache. She had a backache. She went to bed every night right after dinner— too exhausted to watch television, too drowsy to read a book.

One day the telephone rang. "Mrs. Talbot? Are you Mrs. Jennie Talbot? . . . Well, congratulations! You have just won our 'Lucky Sweepstakes.' "

Jennie was about to hang up when the excited voice said, "Your prize is a trip to New York—a suite at the Waldorf, tickets to the top shows, all expenses for two, you and your husband."

"I have no husband. I'm a widow."

"Well, then, invite your best friend. . . . A messenger will stop at your house tomorrow with the airline tickets, the theater tickets and a check for five hundred dollars."

Jennie leaped out of bed, threw on a bathrobe and skipped across the lawn to the house next door. She jabbed the bell with her finger and rapped her knuckles on the door. "Martha! . . . Martha! Are you home?"

Martha opened the door. "For heaven's sake, Jennie, what's the trouble?"

And Jennie, flushed with excitement, poured out the news of her sudden good fortune. For one blissful week Jennie

Talbot, brimming with energy, accompanied by her close friend, Martha, whirled through Fifth Avenue stores, dined at sumptuous restaurants, applauded curtain calls, traipsed through art museums and glassware exhibits—even sat with rapt attention at a concert in Lewisohn Stadium.

Gone and forgotten, for the moment at least, were the headaches and backaches. Gone was the desire to fall into bed, exhausted and weary, the moment dinner was over.

Was Jennie really tired during all those months and years of self-confinement? Of course she was. She was exhausted because she was bored with life. But a miracle happened when Jennie's telephone number was fatefully picked from a revolving drum.

Tiredness from boredom is not only the province of the old. The younger generation, perhaps less patient, shows the same symptoms. I remember a mismatched pair in a restaurant one night. They both worked for a computer firm, he as a programmer and she as a secretary. They were out on a dinner date after work, and since I was dining alone their loud voices almost dropped on my plate.

He leaned forward eagerly, excited about his day's work. "Remember the program I was telling you about? The one that will cut the billing work in half?" His eyes were wide awake and sparkling. If I hadn't heard the words I would have thought he was in the midst of a romantic speech.

She, on the other hand, stifled a tired yawn. Her eyes were glazed and they wandered from his eager face over the sea of diners. "No, I don't remember," she replied.

"Oh, sure you do," he said, encouraging her. "I told you about it the other night. They had Jim on it first and then they turned it over to me because they liked the job I did on the order department." Pride rang out in his voice and he barely seemed to notice her faltering posture, her weary expression.

Oh, Lord, I thought, it's like the dormouse in *Alice in Wonderland*. Any minute her head's going to be down on that plate and she'll even snore!

And so it went for a tortured half hour, until I, the unwilling listener, could bear no more and went my way.

Do you remember the homespun philosophy of Captain Andy, skipper of the *Cotton Blossom*, in Jerome Kern's delightful old musical *Show Boat*? It went something like this: *"The lucky folks are the ones that get to do the things they enjoy doing."* Such people are seldom bored and seldom tired.

But how do you get to do the things you like? One way, of course, is to like the things you do. Simple little tasks like pruning a boxwood hedge or cooking a brace of quail can be as glamorous and absorbing as you choose to make them.

One of the great charms of the British novelist and poet D. H. Lawrence, according to Aldous Huxley, was his passionate interest in practically everything. "He could cook, he could sew, he could darn a stocking and milk a cow, he was an efficient woodcutter and a good hand at embroidery; fires always burned when he laid them, and a floor, after Lawrence had scrubbed it, was thoroughly clean."

How could such a man be bored or complain of being tired?

It's your own fault if you find life deadly dull. All around you are things waiting to be done. Fish waiting to be caught. Books waiting to be read. Articles waiting to be written. Pictures waiting to be painted. You can participate if you can qualify. All it takes is *desire*—an insatiable curiosity and a refusal to resign yourself to boredom.

And what about talent? Forget it. You and I are not concerned with fame, with posterity. All we really want is a modicum of happiness—and a middling chance to shed that tired feeling.

"But," you say, "I used to be a bookkeeper before I retired. I never want to see another row of figures as long as I live! What's for me?"

All the more reason to start out fresh, to switch to a new and exciting interest in a wholly different field. Did you know that O. Henry was once a bank teller, Earl Stanley Gardner a lawyer, Lloyd Douglas a minister and Somerset Maugham a doctor? Perhaps they never wanted to see another bank statement, preach another sermon or prescribe another pill.

It may seem difficult at first to find your slot in life, but eventually you will fall into the right groove as smoothly as the nickels and dimes and quarters that are tossed into a highway toll box.

In many ways the task of finding your groove has been made much easier. Not long ago the only advice given to elderly people was the frantic necessity of somehow avoiding old age. Today the attitude has changed radically. Older people are no longer obsessed with hiding their ages. Now they enjoy their particular stage of life—minimizing its difficulties and utilizing its virtues.

In this new, enlightened era, here is your blueprint for action—nine rules to follow for a happier, richer life—a life without tiredness, without boredom:

1. Stop feeling sorry for yourself. Repeat out loud, ten times a day, "I'm glad I'm alive—and well!"

2. Be curious about everything. Be enthusiastic. Be ex-

cited—and that sodden feeling of boredom will dissolve like a morning mist.

3. Never, but never again, say, *"I'm tired!"*

4. Repeat to yourself fifty times a day, "I have *unlimited energy*. I'm calling on it *right now!*"

5. Find a new interest. Not tomorrow—but *today!* Go to an art store. Visit the library. Register at night school. Stop at a bowling alley. Do something! Do *anything!* But don't put it off. Act now.

6. Make new friends. Join a club. Say "Hi there!" to a stranger at least once a day.

7. Smile when you don't feel like smiling.

8. Take a deep breath. Fill your lungs with good, clean air. Exhale slowly. Then do it again.

9. Walk. Don't ride—unless you have a long way to go. Walking is exhilarating. Walking does not dissipate energy. It creates energy.

CHAPTER 16

A New Kind of Exercise That Makes You Feel Young and Vigorous

Every man is the builder of a temple called his body.

—HENRY DAVID THOREAU

What would you give to turn back the calendar ten years? I don't mean on events—that's impossible, of course—but on your physical fitness. How would you like to feel as good as you felt ten years ago?

If you are sixty-five, wouldn't you like to feel as strong, as alert and as energetic as you were at fifty-five? Or if you are fifty-five, wouldn't you like to have the hale and hearty vigor you enjoyed at forty-five?

You can do it—if you are in reasonably good health and are not suffering from some organic disorder. All it takes is moderation in your diet and a new kind of exercise known as isometric contraction, or the pitting of a muscle against strong resistance for a few seconds every day.

Too many of the exercises in vogue today are physically exhausting. Push-ups, deep knee bends and other strenuous forms of calisthenics may be muscle-conditioners for youngsters in their teens, but they invite disaster for people in their fifties, sixties and seventies.

I have invented a name for the exercises based on isometric

contraction, which I hope will give this system a popular vogue. I call them: FLEXERCISES because the technique involves the flexing or tensing of your muscles against each other for a single brief effort of a few seconds. No body motion is involved. No jogging. No rope-skipping. No Indian clubs. No weight lifting.

The isometric system is used with great effectiveness by United States and Russian athletes training for the Olympic Games and other sports events. You can adapt this same series of Flexercises as a daily "work-out" to give you better posture, good muscle tone and a feeling of well-being.

Here are seven Flexercises which, if practiced with persistence, will give you a healthier, more enjoyable outlook on life. Between each Flexercise be sure to take a breathing spell.

Flexercise No. 1. Head, Neck, Wrists. Lock your fingers and place your palms against your forehead. For five seconds, push your head forward as you try to push it back with your hands.

Flexercise No. 2. Arms, Shoulders, Neck. Put your right palm against the right side of your head and push. For five seconds, resist this pressure with your neck muscles. Then try the same Flexercise with your left hand against the left side of your head.

Flexercise No. 3. Stomach, Forearms, Legs. Place your hands just above your knees and assume a semi-squatting position. For five seconds, try to rise up as you resist rising by pushing your hands downward.

Flexercise No. 4. Chest, Arms. Clasp your hands in front of your chest and for five seconds let your hands have a "tug-of-war," each pulling in the opposite direction.

Flexercise No. 5. Stomach, Thighs, Arms. Sit in a chair. Raise right leg, flex knee until it is chin high. Clasp hands around knee and pull for five seconds as you try to lower your leg to sitting posture against the tug of your hands. Now try same Flexercise with left leg raised.

Flexercise No. 6. Hands, Arms. Sit beside table. Clasp hands with elbows on table. For five seconds have a table "wrestling match" between your two hands.

Flexercise No. 7. Arms, Wrists, Neck. Bend over and clasp your hands behind your head. Interlock fingers. For five seconds, try to straighten up into a standing posture as you resist the action with your clasped hands.

You will find these Flexercises less exhausting than a game of handball, tennis or golf. If you apply yourself too strenuously to the above routine, cut down the time of muscle resistance from five seconds to three seconds.

Remember, the preservation of your health is vital to your happiness. Neglect of your physical condition, or abuse of it, can be disastrous to all the plans you might have made for your wonderful new leisure.

Without overpampering yourself or damaging your mental state with overconcern about your health, you can and should follow a few rudimentary rules:

1. **Periodic physical examinations.** Each of these check-ups should include an electrocardiogram, a chest X ray, rectal examination, blood count, urinalysis, inspection of the cervix (for women) and of the prostate (for men).

2. **Sensible attention to your daily diet.** Make certain that your food intake is properly balanced for vitamins, minerals, proteins, water and fiber—and fats and carbohydrates in lim-

ited amounts. Visit your doctor for the specific purpose of discussing with him your personal diet requirements.

3. A moderate amount of exercise. The Flexercises described above should be ample physical activity if augmented by daily walks of a mile or even a half mile.

4. Sufficient rest during the day. Take a light nap in the afternoon. Avoid the temptation to spend half the day in bed. Avoid the habit of falling asleep in front of the television set.

5. Consultation with your doctor at the first sign of an unusual complaint or physical condition. Neglect increases hazards.

6. Avoidance of accident situations—around the house or out in public places. Avoid such things as slippery floors, high ladders, badly lighted areas, dangerous traffic.

7. A cheerful outlook. This is most important and cannot be stressed too emphatically. The daily state of your mind should be of primary concern to you. Give it the same attention you give the state of your body.

Always remember that your health is more important to you than to anyone else. If you don't guard it, who will? Successful retirement embraces a certain degree of selfishness. Don't allow yourself to be imposed upon in ways that might endanger your physical health or your peace of mind.

If you play golf, know your limit and never play to the point of exhaustion. Don't "go 18 holes" if it tires you out. Resist the temptation to demonstrate how hale and hearty you are in spite of being a retiree.

Watch the heat and the sun. For you, the noonday hours in summer, or in a subtropical climate, are the best time to be indoors. Take your outings in the cool of the mornings or in midafternoon.

Just as overeating is ill-advised, so can undereating have its dangers. It is true that older people require fewer calories, because their expenditure of energy is lower. But you can easily develop a tendency to eat too little. It is essential that your daily food intake be sizable enough to sustain you and sufficient to give you the bulk you need.

Each day's diet should include some form of protein—meat, fish or fowl; a green vegetable, a yellow vegetable, an egg and something leafy. Keep a rein on your intake of fats and sweets. Don't let your friends or writers on dietary subjects prescribe for you. Know your own particular requirements, based on your weight, your exercise habits, your physical condition and your weaknesses.

After retirement age, your doctor should occupy a definite place in your life circle. Make a friend and confidant of him. Put your trust in him. He can prolong your life and help you accomplish the fullest enjoyment of the lengthened span of your years.

Consult him at once whenever you note any worrisome little change in your physical condition. Unusual shortness of breath. Unaccustomed fatigue. Pains where there had been none before. Sleeplessness. Spitting up blood. Changes in the nature of your stool or urine.

Avoid situations that can bring about a sudden and tragic change in your health. A fall, a jolt, a sudden wrench, a sprain or strain can cause a heart-breaking halt to all your plans for a rich and carefree future.

Finally, to perpetuate that "ten years younger feeling," make up your mind to:

1. Have a regular series of medical check-ups every six months, if you are not already following such a program.

2. Know exactly what your health situation is, where you are sound and where you might be verging on trouble.

3. Gear your activities to habits that offer you the best chance of enjoying many vigorous years.

CHAPTER 17

Read This—and
You Will Never Again
Worry about Insomnia

*Worrying about insomnia will hurt you
far more than insomnia.*
—DALE CARNEGIE

The first significant advertising campaign I ever wrote, nearly forty years ago, was on "The Importance of Sleep." It was for the Simmons Beautyrest Mattress, and as the copywriter on the account it was my job to interview famous personalities, such as Henry Ford, Harvey Firestone, Admiral Richard E. Byrd and other top people whose opinions would be regarded as authoritative. Without exception, these leaders of their day stressed the need for getting eight or nine consecutive hours of sound sleep every night.

How outmoded are the dogmas of yesterday. For modern medical science has proved conclusively that every individual runs on a different sleep budget. Toscanini rarely slept more than five hours a night, whereas Calvin Coolidge needed more than twice that much sleep. Coolidge slept eleven hours out of every twenty-four.

During his entire lifetime Samuel Untermyer, the famous international lawyer, never had a sound night's sleep. At the peak of his career he would work until midnight and get up at five o'clock in the morning to start the next day's routine. He lived to be eighty-one.

About twenty years ago Bob and Vera Savage, close friends and neighbors, spent the night at our home in Larchmont, New York. We played cards until eleven o'clock and then turned off the lights and went to bed. At about three o'clock in the morning I thought I heard a slight noise in the living room and tiptoed downstairs to investigate. It was Vera, reading a magazine.

"Can't sleep?" I asked sympathetically.

"Oh, I never sleep more than four hours," said Vera.

"Never?"

"Never! It doesn't bother me. I just get up and read."

"Don't you ever feel tired the next day?"

"No, I don't. Four hours of sleep is all I seem to need."

A few months ago, after a lapse of years, Bob and Vera Savage again became our neighbors. I said, "Vera, tell me. Do you still sleep only four hours a night?"

"Same old routine! I go to bed at midnight and I'm up at four o'clock."

"What do you do? Read?"

"Here, let me show you!" Vera opened a closet door, and there, stacked in the corner, were twenty or thirty cardboard boxes—jigsaw puzzles. "These are the complicated kind," said Vera. "Five hundred pieces—some of them even fifteen hundred! Takes me a whole week to complete one—but it's fun."

"How do you keep so healthy and vigorous?"

"I just don't worry!"

That's the answer. In fact, it's the answer for anyone who may be troubled with insomnia. *Just don't worry!* As long as you are getting all the sleep you require, whether it is four hours or ten, you will not suffer any loss of vitality or undue fatigue. If you feel tired and nervous because you cannot sleep, just remember, it's the worry that does the damage, not the insomnia itself.

Dr. Nathaniel Kleitman, whose forty years of research on sleep at the University of Chicago earned world-wide acclaim, says, "People who worry about insomnia usually sleep far more than they realize." This was true in my own case. I cannot recall when I have slept soundly through the night. No matter what time I go to bed, I wake up, on the average, ten times before morning.

This wakefulness used to bother me and I would toss and turn, trying desperately to go back to sleep. Minutes seemed like hours. In the morning I would tell my wife, "I didn't sleep a wink last night." I was frequently exhausted from fatigue and worry. I was convinced that my health would eventually break under the strain—until one day I read an article by Dr. Kleitman in which he said, "The average amount of sleep required is no more applicable to a particular individual than an average size hat or shoe would be." And he mentioned several prominent people who find four or five hours of sleep sufficient.

Another physician, Dr. William Von Stein, told me that the act of falling asleep is relaxing in itself. "We do not necessarily require sleep for a long duration," said Dr. Von Stein. "Even a cat nap of five minutes during the day can bring refreshment to a tired brain."

I still wake up ten times a night, but I have stopped worrying about it, and as a result I go to sleep again in moments. I have even convinced myself that sleep in small doses is more refreshing than "sleeping like a log" for eight or nine hours at a stretch. Recently the *Reader's Digest* confirmed my belief with a statement to the effect that "students have found two three-hour sleep periods more refreshing than a single eight-hour span."

More and more doctors are advising frequent daytime naps, especially for older people. Dr. Alton Ochsner of New Orleans' Ochsner Clinic says, "The siesta habit is a good one. It is difficult for many to store up a day's energy needs with a single stretch of night sleep."

Dr. Hans Selye of the University of Montreal, in his famous book *The Stress of Life,* says, "A day of hard work can make you sleep like a log or it can keep you awake all night. This sounds contradictory, but if you care to analyze the work that helps you sleep and the work that keeps you awake, there is a difference.

"A stressful activity which has come to a definite stop prepares you for rest and sleep: but one which sets up self-maintaining tensions keeps you awake." This is just another way of saying, *Never take your problems to bed with you.* If you are keyed up with excitement over an unfinished project or problem and your mind keeps churning after you turn in for the night, don't expect to induce sleep by enforced relaxation. You won't be helped by sheep-counting, warm milk, hot baths and so forth unless you have implicit faith in these conventional remedies. Under such conditions the sleeping pill is the only sure way, but not always the wise way, to induce quick sleep.

Dr. Selye warns against the habit of overworking the body or mind before going to bed. "Be especially careful," he says, "to avoid the senseless repetition of the same task when you are already exhausted." The simple act of attempting to solve a crossword puzzle in the evening can set up tensions that will keep your mind boiling in a fitful and kaleidoscopic pattern for hours as you try to sleep.

Psychologists and neurosurgeons explain it this way: People call it nervous tension but it's really muscular tension. The nervous system brings it on, but the actual tension is in the muscles. The tense muscles keep sending messages back to the brain, keeping the brain wide awake and active. This process is called kinesthesis. The result is often a night of frantic insomnia. It calls for relaxation of those tense muscles that keep nagging the brain to stay awake; and from that stem the cure-alls for muscle relaxing—walks, warm baths, a glass of wine, etc. In extreme cases doctors sometimes teach insomniacs consciously to relax their muscles one by one.

Let me repeat, though: You are not suffering from genuine insomnia if you require less sleep than your neighbor. You'll know it if you're missing sleep that you need. At the U.S. Army Glen Research Station outside of Washington, D.C., extensive sleep studies were recently conducted. The Army wanted to find out just how much sleep a man could do without, and what the results were at each stage.

The men were tested in tasks that required vigilance such as monitoring a radarscope. After a day without sleep, performance was much poorer with obvious complete lapses in the job. Yet the men claimed that they were not a bit sleepy. Later on creative thinking slipped; the men had trouble making choices. At a day and a half or two days, most of the men started "seeing things." Their eyes burned and their vision was double or badly blurred. At the fifty- or sixty-hour mark, although the men knew that what they were seeing wasn't really there, many of them thought that the room was smoke-filled or the floor uneven.

At one hundred hours the visions became reality. A New York disk jockey, after 200 hours without sleep, thought that the doctor was wearing a suit of worms and the nurse was covered with saliva. Most of the men, in fact, at the 100-hour mark had full-blown mental derangements and finally went into delirium tremens.

All this is not to frighten you but to let you know that you are probably getting more sleep than you think. If your own individual sleep-need were eight hours per night and you were getting only three or four, you would have symptoms that would tell you sleep was needed. But if you feel chipper and see clearly (with your spectacles, if you wear them, of course) , chances are you are not suffering from insomnia but you're applying your neighbor's rule to yourself. After all, you eat more or less than he does, talk more or less, sing more or less on key than he, laugh more or less.

If you are troubled with insomnia, this list of don'ts may help to minimize your problem:

1. Don't worry about it. Remember, worry causes more damage than sleeplessness.
2. Don't eat a heavy meal before retiring.
3. Don't repeat the same task to the point of exhaustion.
4. Don't get the sleeping-pill habit.
5. Don't get unduly excited before retiring.
6. Don't take your problems to bed with you.
7. And don't think you require the conventional eight hours of sleep every night.

Maybe you need only four hours or six hours. Or perhaps you need ten hours. How do you know what your sleep budget should be? Here is a common-sense rule to follow:

If you wake up spontaneously in the morning, refreshed and ready for a day of work or a day of play, you are getting all the sleep you need. But if you feel tired, run down and physically exhausted, especially in the afternoon—then you may not be getting your quota. So go to bed at ten instead of eleven, even if it means missing the late-late movie.

But mainly, *don't worry*. And don't spend money foolishly on solutions for sleeplessness. Just keeping from worry may provide your cure. I would like to end this chapter with a famous story about a sleepless old man—Jason Hardwick was his name.

Old man Hardwick had severe insomnia. He had spent fortunes on relaxant pills and specialists, but the insomnia continued night after night. Finally a famous doctor was recommended, guaranteed to cure Hardwick's troubles.

When the doctor arrived, the whole family was eagerly awaiting him. "Let me see your father alone," the doctor told the assembled clan. Once alone with the ailing man, the doctor said, "Now do whatever I do." He raised his hands up and did three quick knee bends; the old man falteringly followed suit. Then the doctor walked to the window and panted five times, then breathed deeply twice. The old man followed suit. There were five or six more such operations, all of which Hardwick followed faithfully.

Then the doctor wheeled around and stared piercingly at Hardwick. "Now go to bed," he said in a slow monotone, *"and sleep!* I command it." He pointed a rigid finger at the bed, staring relentlessly at Hardwick.

The old man settled down on the bed and closed his eyes.

Then the doctor left the room and marched triumphantly into the living room. "You may all go in to your father now," he told the waiting assemblage. "You will find him sound asleep."

They all entered the bedroom, and the youngest son tip-toed over to Hardwick's bed. He whispered gently into his father's ear, "Papa, it's me. Are you sleeping?"

Very carefully old man Hardwick opened one eye and asked, "That maniac . . . is he still here?"

CHAPTER 18

How to Avoid a Heart Attack— and What to Do If You Have One

Nothing in life is to be feared. It is only to be understood.

—MARIE CURIE

A man shuffled into my office the other day with a haunted expression in his eyes. He wanted a copy of my book *Retiring in Florida.* I usually talk with such people to probe their viewpoints on retirement, and my $64 question is always "What are you doing to keep yourself busy?"

This fellow, about sixty-six, said, "Not a darn thing!"

"Aren't you afraid you'll get bored doing nothing?"

"Well, you see—" and his tone was apologetic—"I had a coronary a couple of years ago and my doctor advised me to sell my business and take life easy."

His comment was typical of dozens of men I have met who, mistakenly or deliberately, use a former heart ailment as an excuse for total inactivity.

These people are traveling on the downhill road to invalidism. They do not realize that when a man is sixty-five or seventy he needs to *do something* just to keep alive. Discouragement can be fatal. At this age it is only one short step from futility to senility.

Pampering oneself after a heart attack is a precaution which doctors advise, but only up to a point. After a period of rest and recovery, there are many examples of men resuming a normal life without ill effects. Everyone knows that General Dwight Eisenhower, during his first term as President of the United States, suffered a severe coronary attack and recovered sufficiently to serve another full term in the White House. General Eisenhower, now in his seventies, still leads an active life, alternating between his Gettysburg farm and the lush golf courses of Palm Desert. President Lyndon B. Johnson is another notable example of an active man who has survived heart disease, yet today occupies the most important position in the world, with untold responsibilities.

But despite these and other well-publicized examples of men in public life and in business who have resumed normal living after a heart attack, there are many who are crushed psychologically by the experience and never seem to recover. A subconscious fear hangs over them, for the rest of their lives, like the sword of Damocles. These are people who need a psychological rebirth. It is not easy to abandon the fears that are planted in the subconscious mind during the long period of rest following a heart attack. Yet fear itself is a form of tension—and tension is something to be avoided by heart patients, just like other strong emotions—anger, hatred, sorrow.

It isn't hard to understand why anxiety is bad for one's heart, whether there has been a heart attack or not. Ask yourself what your physical symptoms are when you hear a sudden piece of bad news, or when you're unhappy or very worried about something. Almost everyone will answer that his chest seems "tight," that his breathing is difficult, or he'll say there's a "knife in my chest." He'll say that if he's nine or ninety.

Of course, some anxieties are bound to occur in life or you're just not living. But one of the things a heart patient should remember is that the heart doesn't know whether you're anxious over *its* state of health or over something else.

Another good thing to remember is that your heart is the strongest part of your body. Often, when life itself is failing, when other organs are damaged beyond repair, the heart beats faithfully on for an amazing period of time. Blessed with great recuperative powers, it literally repairs itself. In many cases a "dead" man has been brought back to life by heart massage—often to live on for many years. But the heart needs the cooperation of you, its host. Many people who suffer a heart attack submit to depression. They feel they have little to live for anyway. Sometimes, for the first time, they have something to think about, something to talk about —and because they never had an interest, a hobby, a love, their heart attack becomes their interest.

I paid a visit to a sick young friend in the hospital several years back. She was a child of fourteen, and all she could talk about was getting out of that hospital. "When can I leave?" she kept pleading. "Ask the doctor for me, please. I can't wait to get out. I have so many things I want to do."

She pointed to an empty bed across the room. "The lady who stayed there," she said, "do you know what she did this morning? she *gave herself a heart attack!*"

I must have looked a bit dubious.

"Oh, it's true. I mean it. She came here after a heart attack about two months ago. The doctor came in this morning and told her she was in good shape. Her heart was almost normal again—there was almost no damage done. He told her she could go home. But the minute he left the room she began to fuss. 'He doesn't know what he's talking about,' she said. 'My daughter must have put him up to it so she could save money. I can tell I'm still plenty sick. Why, right now I can feel that awful pain and my heart is thumping and jumping right out of my chest! If they throw me out of here I'll fall on the street dead. I won't leave. That's all there is to it!'

"Sure enough, within two hours she was back in emergency, back in an oxygen tent with a fresh heart attack—a much worse one this time."

My wise young friend went on with her story. "I think I know what happened. All she ever talked about since I came here was her heart attack. I tried to change the subject a few times—talk about school and friends and cheerful things—but it was always as though she never had anything else happen in her life. When her daughter came to visit her, she always mentioned later that she saw her daughter only once a year before the attack. She used to say that people think of you only when you're dying. I believe she wanted to have another attack rather than give up her sickness. Her heart is her hobby now, her whole interest in life—everything."

Cases like this are not rare, although sometimes they are less dramatic. Thousands of people make sickness their favorite pastime.

Take the story about the elderly woman who accidentally pays a visit to the office of a noted scholar. She thought his title of "Doctor" meant that he was a member of the medical profession.

"Doctor," she complained, "I suffer terribly from my kidneys. Would you please . . ."

"Madam," he interrupted gently, "there's a ladies' room just down the hall on your left."

Even those who have no desire to make a lifetime pursuit out of their heart attack find it difficult to abandon their fears. But one cannot go through life avoiding every form of emotional excitement and physical exercise without becoming a total invalid. The only intelligent solution for a person who has suffered a heart attack is to acquire an attitude of moderation in all things. Medical men generally agree that the heart patient who pampers himself by staying in bed most of the time has less chance of living than the man who resumes normal, but moderated, activities.

What are the most irksome restrictions that usually follow a heart attack? Well, your doctor may tell you to cut down on your smoking or quit altogether. Reports indicate that nicotine constricts the blood vessels and forces the heart to pump harder. As a result, your blood pressure goes up.

You will probably have to give up strenuous forms of exercise such as tennis, rowing, deep-sea fishing, shoveling snow or sawing wood. But you can still have the pleasure of walks, of short swims in warm water, and you can play golf if you use an electric cart. Your doctor will prescribe in some detail the amount of exercise you can or should take, and he will give you a few sensible rules to follow. The American Heart Association has prepared booklets to help people with heart disease simplify their routine of living. Ask your doctor or your local heart association for this literature. Your physician is the person best qualified to answer all your questions. Discuss your fears and worries openly with him. Be careful not to get overtired, overchilled or overexcited—and you can look forward to many useful years of active life.

Aside from those who have actually experienced heart trouble, there are millions who live in fear of it. Studies show that almost 50 per cent of all people who seek medical help today are suffering from ailments caused or aggravated by such emotional disturbances as prolonged worry, anxiety or fear. Neurotic people especially tend to ascribe their illnesses to the heart more than to any other part of the body.

A close friend, whose name I shall not mention, told me that he had been suffering almost constantly from heart palpitation. He was convinced that he had a serious heart condition, although careful examinations showed no organic involvement. He was having increasing difficulty in breathing. He said his chest felt heavy. Eventually, with his doctor's help, he realized that his physical problem was caused by an emotional disturbance. He was in business with his father and the relationship had never been harmonious. The load on his chest consisted of resentment, irritation and guilt. When the conflict was resolved, his heart symptoms quickly disappeared and there were no further recurrences.

Kenneth C. Hutchin, M.D., in his excellent book *Heart Disease and High Blood Pressure,* says, "Nine out of ten with a pain in the chest imagine that they have heart disease. Nine out of ten with a pain in the chest have *not* got heart disease."

Pains in the area of the heart, or palpitations, are often caused by gas in the stomach. Sometimes excessive stomach acidity causes a pain in the chest known as heartburn. Pressure on intercostal nerves, disturbance in the gall bladder, rheumatism—all these may cause pain which many people mistakenly believe to be heart trouble. Regardless of these reassuring facts, if you are stricken with a severe pain in the chest out of a clear blue sky, it is best to send for a doctor without delay. There is always the chance that it may be a coronary attack, and speed is important.

Another condition which sometimes causes exaggerated

fears is high blood pressure—otherwise known as hypertension, a condition which affects about five million Americans. There is a popular belief that high blood pressure is caused by the aging process. This is not true. If you are getting along in years, there is no medical reason for you to believe that you are developing high blood pressure.

There are many factors which can cause a variation in your blood pressure—such things as temperature of the atmosphere, time of day, your emotional state, even the technique of the doctor who makes the reading. Doctors know that some patients become nervous during a medical examination, and this apprehension in itself can cause a difference of twenty or thirty points in blood pressure.

Even discounting nervous tension or emotional upsets, your blood pressure can vary from hour to hour. It can register higher while you are standing on your feet than when you are sitting down, or higher when you are rushing around than when you have been resting.

Some people who are chronic worriers suffer from a condition known as essential hypertension, and even though their blood pressure is higher than average, there is little tendency for the condition to worsen. This is the commonest type of high blood pressure, comprising about 80 per cent of all cases.

One thing you can count on for a certainty: High blood pressure cannot be cured by worry—but it can be caused by worry. If stressful thinking can raise your blood pressure thirty or forty points, just imagine the harm you are doing yourself by constantly worrying about your condition.

Some doctors say that the anxiety of the patient does more harm than the high blood pressure itself, and their treatment is aimed at reducing tension. This is not easy, because many people tend to exaggerate their doctor's advice and read into it more than was intended. Thus their anxiety is actually increased and they tend to withdraw from normal activities, becoming chronic invalids instead of merely slowing the tempo of their lives. At the other extreme are the patients who take their doctors' advice too lightly and ignore the simple measures that might have helped them.

Much has been written about the dangers of overweight and the strain it places on the heart. One doctor estimates that for every ten pounds you are overweight, the extra load on your heart is the equivalent of pumping blood through an additional six miles of blood vessels. Think about that the next time you weigh yourself.

In their award-winning book *Your Heart Has Nine Lives*, Alton Blakeslee of the Associated Press and Jeremiah Stamler, M.D., Chairman of the Council on Arteriosclerosis of the American Heart Association, sound this warning: "At middle age, the overweight man—depending on the amount of his blubber—is two or three times more susceptible to coronary heart disease than his neighbor of normal weight. If he has gained 20 per cent or more over his youthful desirable weight, for example, he is at least twice as prone to a coronary as the man who stayed lean."

I know a young man and his wife in their early forties who are both overweight by twenty or thirty pounds. Both began to experience worrisome heart palpitations and both were advised by their doctor that they had a serious condition of high blood pressure. The remedy raised a big problem in their lives. It was simply "Eat less! Drink less!"

Habits acquired over a period of years are not easy to break. It was their custom to mix a tall shaker of Martinis before the evening meal. Then, each night, during a gourmet dinner of rich, highly spiced foods, sauces, gravies and desserts, they would replenish their crystal glasses, time after time, from a full gallon of wine which they kept on the table. The result was inevitable. Today they are paying the penalty for overindulgence.

"We are an overnourished nation," says Paul Dudley White, M.D., a founder of the American Heart Association, "and we should wake up and regard excessive food intake as a serious health hazard—an intoxication with a slow and insidiously harmful effect, not so acute or dramatic as intoxication by alcohol or drugs, but almost as damaging."

Again, doctor's orders may be a bigger bonus than you realize. With strong motivation and your doctor's insistence, you may become a slimmer, more attractive person. Another side gain may be that, without the compensation of bored nibbling, you may find much more promising ways of spending your time. Doctor's orders may cause you to make a "raid on life" instead of a raid on the refrigerator.

Along with people who withdraw from life after a heart attack there are certainly just as many who do the opposite. Their close proximity to death shakes them up a bit. With the concept of fleeing time pressed home to them, they decide to change their lives, do something with their time. Instead of detaching themselves from human activities, they simply slow up their tempo a little. The doctor will tell you to try to cultivate equanimity, calmness, composure and peace of mind under circumstances which, at one time, may have caused you to blow your top. Composure and its companion virtues are most easily maintained in happy surroundings. People who are bored and bitter tend to blow their tops often. Your heart attack may be the jumping-off point to a decision to improve your marriage, your friendships, your activities. It may mean the obliteration of all the things that originally led to your heart attack in the first place.

What can be done to prevent heart trouble? How can you protect your heart and your health? A simple formula for living habits designed to safeguard your heart has been prepared by the Metropolitan Life Insurance Company. It is reproduced here, with their permission:

1. Watch your weight, and keep it under control. As a precaution, it is a good idea to know what your best weight should be, and then eat and exercise to keep yourself at that weight. Weight control is essential to health in general.

2. Eat nutritious meals, and take stock of your eating habits from time to time. Make sure that each day your menus include foods from the four basic food groups: meat, poultry and fish; milk and milk products; vegetables and fruits; breads and cereals. Restrict yourself on very rich, high-calorie foods.

3. Get some regular exercise, even if it is just taking a walk every day. Moderate exercise appears to help protect against hypertension and coronary heart disease. Besides, everyone needs a certain amount of physical activity just to stay in good condition. After middle age, however, it is best to avoid sudden strenuous exercise which you are not accustomed to.

4. Avoid excessive smoking, because there seems to be a statistical relationship between heavy cigarette smoking and cardiovascular disorders. To be on the safe side, remember that word: moderation.

5. Learn to relax, and take tension in stride. Intense and persistent emotional tension can and does play a part in physical ailments. A person under constant emotional strain runs a greater risk of acquiring heart and blood vessel ailments.

6. Have periodic checkups. A thorough medical examination is the only way to detect heart and circulatory disorders. Beginning at about age 40, an electrocardiogram is usually taken at periodic health examinations. Regular checkups protect your heart, and your health.

CHAPTER 19

The Cheapest Medicine on Earth—
and the Best

The best medicine is to stop thinking about yourself, and start thinking about other people.

—FREDERIC LOOMIS

If Ellie Baldwin had lived fifty years ago, her neighbors would have called her—behind her back, of course—a "chronic complainer." Today they use the more sophisticated but equally unflattering term "hypochondriac." For no matter what the occasion, a bridge party or a Sunday supper, Ellie always leaves early—or can't come at all—because of "a frightful headache, my dear," or "swollen glands," or a "terrible case of diverticulitis—that's what my doctor calls it"—or "just a miserable cold."

Ellie doesn't enjoy being sick. And her ills are by no means imaginary. She'll have a runny nose or a deep chest cough or an itchy rash, and all these symptoms are quite real and quite painful.

I discussed Ellie's case with a doctor several months ago, without revealing her name.

"Of course, you understand," he said, "it is impossible to make an accurate diagnosis without a complete physical check-up. However, from the way you describe this person, I would guess that her problem is psychosomatic. . . . Is she married?"

"No, she's a widow. Her husband died about five years ago. She lives by herself in a small apartment. So far as I know, she has no activities or interests of any kind."

"That may be her trouble. Is she attractive? Intelligent?"

"Very much so. Why do you ask?"

"I need a receptionist for my office. Someone with a nice appearance and personality to make appointments with my patients—and greet them when they come in. General office duties, filing, invoices—that sort of thing."

"No medical experience?"

"It really isn't necessary. I have a nurse who acts as my assistant."

I talked to Ellie. At first she resisted the whole idea—positively refused to consider it. Later she phoned me.

"I've been thinking about your suggestion, and I've changed my mind. I'd like to try it."

That was two months ago. The other day I happened to meet my doctor friend in the elevator of my office building. As we rode up together I said, "How is your new receptionist?"

"Great! Simply great! I've been meaning to call you and thank you for recommending her."

"Any problem with absenteeism?"

"She hasn't missed a single day. And—you'll never believe this—Mrs. Baldwin has never once complained about a headache or any of those other chronic ailments you told me she used to have."

The elevator stopped at my floor, so I did not have an opportunity to ask the doctor the key question, "So you think her problem was entirely psychological?" But Ellie had answered it for me.

For many of the symptomatic illnesses that plague our lives, the cheapest medicine on earth—and the best—is

SOMETHING TO DO! Few persons realize how much their happiness and health are dependent on their work—whatever it may be. As Charles Kingsley once said, "Thank God every morning when you get up that you have something to do which must be done, whether you like it or not. Being forced to work, and forced to do your best, will breed in you temperance, self-control, strength of will, contentment and a hundred other virtues which the idle never know."

W. Beran Wolfe, a noted psychiatrist who, during his lifetime, helped thousands of malcontents to find a happier life, used to tell his patients, "If you live only for yourself, you are always in immediate danger of being bored to death with the repetition of your own views and interests. No one," he said, "has learned the meaning of living until he has surrendered his ego to the service of his fellow men."

Years ago I met a man in Palm Springs, California, who was crippled with arthritis. His body was stooped; his arms and legs were twisted and contorted with pain. When he told me that he was the pianist at Chi-Chi, a popular restaurant in the area, I found it hard to believe. "Won't you and your wife come down for dinner tonight?" he said. "I start playing about seven o'clock."

We sat at a table near the piano, and, sure enough, at a few minutes before seven the man came hobbling in with two canes, plumped himself down on the piano stool and started to play.

We were fascinated. Those fingers that seemed so cruelly bent now danced over the keys with infinite precision. His repertoire included not only the popular melodies of the day, but the familiar refrains of Chopin, Strauss, Bach and Beethoven.

I had read stories about actors who went on stage to play

their parts when their bodies were racked with pain. "The play must go on" is the expression immortalized by their courage. But this was the first time I had experienced at close range the dogged determination of a man who refused to let his infirmities beat him down.

The psychologist Lynde C. Steckle, in his excellent book *Problems of Human Adjustment,* points out one of the gravest dangers of focusing on bodily ailments.

First of all, one alienates one's friends. Nobody—no, no-body—even another chronic complainer, enjoys hearing the details of our physiological problems. People will stop offering a simple greeting like "How are you" and may even stop saying "Hello" altogether if they are assaulted with a barrage of clinical descriptions everytime they greet you. Not only will you be left alone with your aches and pains, but you'll be left alone in general.

Secondly, Dr. Steckle puts forth another interesting theory. He conjectures that people who think constantly about their ailments cannot help but live in the past. As they moan over their rheumatism they cannot help but add a sorrowful comment such as "I remember when these legs of mine could run a five-minute mile" or "I can't hit a ping-pong ball the way I used to hit a tennis ball." Such comparisons can only drive people further and further into the past—and particularly into sorrowful mourning for days gone by. Dr. Steckle quotes two lines from Tennyson to illustrate what happens to those who "seek reunion with a former self:"

> *But how carve way i' the life that lies before,*
> *If bent on groaning for the past?*

Making sickness a hobby is embittering and boring to others and is even likely to make you sicker!

Most of us learn to live with our aches and pains. Yet those who have never made the effort, in retirement, to seek and find a substitute for their former busy lives are more apt to be plagued with nagging ailments. Feeling useless, tired and old is the quickest and surest road to the cemetery.

Again, let me call on W. Beran Wolfe to sound a trumpet of hope for those who will listen:

"The best insurance," wrote Mr. Wolfe, "against melancholia, depression and a sense of futility in old age is the development of wide horizons and the cultivation of mental elasticity and interest in the world. Unlike the flesh, the spirit does not decay with the years.

"Many of the happiest (and healthiest) individuals in the world are men and women in their sixties, seventies and eighties, who have contributed richly to the world's work during their maturity, and at the same time, have cultivated sufficient awareness and interest in the undying cultural activities to make their leisure a delight.

"The older men grow, the more they realize that it is only by putting the focus of their activities in some movement greater than their own individual ego, that they can attain peace and security in old age."

PART 4

How to Find Inner Peace and Contentment in the Years Ahead

CHAPTER 20

A New Way to Pray
That Works Miracles
Even for Non-Churchgoers

*God is not a cosmic bellboy for whom we
can press a button to get things done.*
—HARRY EMERSON FOSDICK

What you read in the next ten pages will either: 1) shock you; 2) anger you; 3) impress you; or 4) change your entire life.

I am not a religious person. Nor a sacrilegious person. Nor an atheist. Nor an agnostic. Nor a pagan. But I am going to turn the spotlight of common sense on certain religious practices and beliefs, and if you don't like what you see, you had better skip this chapter.

Let me start off by saying that religion has failed millions of people. Or perhaps you would prefer to have me say that millions of people have failed religion. Both statements are correct.

During our active years, most of us are so preoccupied with making a living or conducting a business or managing a household that we have little time for religious study or for the cultivation of spiritual values. Later, when we abdicate our responsibilities and when the years seem to be passing much too quickly, we feel the need of effecting some sort of reconciliation with God.

So we turn to the church of our choice, but too often we find that the spiritual values we are seeking have been decorated and camouflaged and embroidered with creeds and formulas and doctrines and apologies. And because most of us are unable to comprehend this theological dogma, we shrug it off as the architecture of religion.

We bow our heads. Kneel in prayer. Look at the stained-glass windows. Join in the singing of hymns. Listen to the organ music. And later tell our neighbors, "What a nice sermon." Church for us has become an aesthetic experience that fills an emotional need but leaves us vaguely remote from God.

Perhaps it is just as well that way. For as we grow older we find that we have become calloused by life's stern realities and are unable to accept the anthropomorphic concept of the Great Creator that was pictured so vividly in the family Bible of our childhood days. Vaguely we recall the illustration: a bearded man in flowing robes on a throne in the sky with a bolt of lightning emerging from the staff in his hand and, all around Him, beams of sunlight splitting angry black clouds.

Much more comforting is the present-day concept of a kindly Father watching over his children, doling out little favors to all who petition Him with fervor and humility.

The institution of prayer, beseeching the Supreme Power of the Universe to help us out of our difficulties, is probably the greatest build-up of the human ego that mankind has ever devised. If we were to try to contact the president of General Motors or U.S. Steel by telephone, we would have to go through several undersecretaries or department heads and would finally be told, "Sorry, he cannot talk with you now. I'll connect you with one of our vice-presidents."

And yet, no matter how humble our station in life, we

have the audacity, the presumptuous arrogance to believe that we can get through to God at any instant of our own choosing and that somehow He will take time off to listen to our troubles. In one simple act we have promoted ourselves from an infinitesimal speck on this earth—which is, after all, only a speck in the solar system, which is again just a tiny fragment in the universe of solar systems—to a top-level confidential relationship with the boss of the whole shebang, the Divine Creator.

There is a little anecdote about a pious man—let's call him Rudy—who prayed loudly ten times a day and followed each and every tiniest detail of ritual of his religion. Nonetheless he ran into continual bad luck. His wife died; his daughter ran off with the town drunk; his business failed; he was in debt up to his neck; etc., etc. And each time bad luck hit him anew, and every day in between catastrophes, he would stand in front of his house, look up at the heavens and say something like this: "O God, how can you do this to me? I'm a religious man. Don't I pray to you constantly? Don't I follow your laws to the letter? And what do you do to me? You bring me misfortune! Grief! Misery! And my neighbor who never prays, who hasn't walked into a church in twenty years, what do you do to him? You bring him luck! A beautiful healthy wife, six happy children, success in business! O God, why do you treat me this way?"

Each and every day Rudy would say something like that, directing his supplications toward heaven and waiting, waiting, for an answer. Then one day his humble house burned down. Rudy now had nothing—no wife, no children, no job, no home.

Again he turned his eyes toward heaven and made a longer and whinier speech than ever. And then, lo and behold, the clouds parted. And through the early-morning mist Rudy heard a mighty voice from above.

"At last you are answering me," shrieked Rudy in near hysteria. "Tell me, O God, why have you treated me this way?"

A great voice boomed from the sky, almost knocking Rudy off his feet.

"Rudy, my friend, if only you didn't *nag* me so much!"

I do not speak disrespectfully of prayer. Nor do I deny its efficacy. There are too many millions of documented proofs that prayers have been answered from Biblical days to modern times. My only purpose is to seek a *raison d'être*, an explanation for this phenomenon, which will lift the act of praying out of the supernatural and mystic unknown and into the realm of understanding.

I agree with Santayana, who says that religion has unhappily ceased to be wisdom and has become "superstition overlaid with reasoning." Perhaps this explains why religion is divided into narrow sects, each believing itself to be the propounder of the only truth.

Lin Yutang, in his gayly serious and profoundly naïve masterpiece *The Importance of Living*, says that such religion "nourishes a man's selfishness not only by making it impossible for him to be broad-minded toward other sects, but also by turning the practice of religion into a private bargain between God and himself, in which the party of the first part is glorified by the party of the second part, singing hymns and calling upon His name on every conceivable occasion, and in return the party of the first part is to bless the party of the second part, bless particularly himself more than any other person and his own family more than any other family."

Is it any wonder that so many sincere people look upon prayer as a futile gesture which cannot produce results because its motivation is so frequently and so obviously selfish?

With great humility I would like to offer a concept of prayer which I fervently hope may satisfy the doubts and disbeliefs of millions whose prayers have not been answered. It is a strangely simple philosophy, with a longer record of demonstrable results than that of any creed or sect or religion in world history. The key to this great spiritual Power is a single letter of the alphabet—*the letter "O."*

If the people of all nations would practice the philosophy outlined in the next few paragraphs, there would be no danger of a nuclear holocaust. Aggressions would subside. Crime would vanish. Murder would be unknown. Brotherly love and civil rights would be a fact of life and not a political football. Retired people in their sixties, seventies and eighties would discover a new world of happiness, peace and contentment instead of a lonely world of bitterness and despair. The millennium would be here in all its glory. A utopia for all humanity to enjoy.

That sounds like a big order. But read on, and you will see that the promise can be fulfilled, at least for those individuals who are willing to pay the price.

This new way to pray starts with the word *God.* Insert an extra letter "o" and God spells *Good.* Throughout the history of mankind there is incontrovertible proof that God is synonymous with Good. The striving toward Good and the condemnation of evil is the essence of all religions, stripped of their mysticism, their orthodox tenets, their legends and their allegories. All religions proclaim the omnipotence of God. Then, if God is synonymous with Good, Good is omnipotent.

The definition of omnipotence is "the infinite, unlimited source of all power."

Thus Good is the "Infinite, Unlimited Source of All Power."

It follows naturally that if we have faith in Good, if we reflect Good in our lives, if we think Good thoughts, and exclude the opposite of Good from our consciousness, we have within us an *Infinite, Unlimited Source of Power.*

Just what is Good, and what is the opposite of Good? Here is a partial list of basic characteristics which may serve as a guide:

Good	The Opposite of Good
Kindness	Selfishness
Consideration	Anger
Courage	Fear
Honesty	Dishonesty
Humility	Conceit
Wisdom	Ignorance
Love	Hatred
Confidence	Self-Pity
Faith	Anxiety
Peace of Mind	Discontent
Gratitude	Distrust
Diligence	Laziness
Generosity	Greed
Truthfulness	Falsity
Loyalty	Disloyalty
Trust	Jealousy
Friendliness	Cruelty

Can you imagine what would happen in our world, which is dominated today by fear and misery and hatred and selfishness and political ambition, if human beings would abandon the traits and characteristics listed as "The Opposite of Good" and if they would, conversely, fill their minds with nothing but Good thoughts—kindness, consideration, brotherly love, truthfulness, honesty, humility, gratitude?

Even the Rudy of our earlier anecdote could probably have profited from this method. With much time spent in praying and dogma, there is more than a small chance that Rudy had neglected his family, worked very little and trusted wholeheartedly instead in his daily supplications to God. His neighbor, on the other hand, may have been in reality the truly religious one of the two. If he put the "O in God" and went about his business taking care of his family and friends, loving his children and not blaming the Lord every time trouble hit, it follows logically that he would have better luck than Rudy. Those who feel sorry for themselves usually wind up with something to feel sorry about. I never saw a long face yet that drew smiles from others.

The story is told of the overzealous churchman visiting a dying woman in the hospital. Since she was a young girl, the woman had unselfishly served others—never marrying in order to take care of her parents first, and then her younger sisters and brothers. Uncomplainingly she had scrubbed, cooked, mended and tended throughout her joyless life.

The churchman leaned over the bed and asked, "Have you ever been confirmed?"

"No" came the sad reply.

"What will you say to the Lord when he asks you that?" he continued relentlessly.

"I . . . I'll show him my hands," she said shyly.

I have called upon the *Infinite, Unlimited Source of All Power* in a moment of dire need, when I was stricken with smallpox and my doctor said, "There is nothing we can do." Faced with a death sentence, or at best a body scarred and pock-marked, I emptied the poison pockets of my mind of all despair, fear, anxiety, foreboding and self-pity and filled the void with thoughts of courage, harmony, health, perfection and faith. I called on the Infinite Law of Good, the Infinite Law of God, if you will. I denounced smallpox as an imposter, an aberrated mental condition posing as a law, a false belief—as untrue as a mistake in arithmetic, as unreal as a mirage in the desert.

And suddenly my mind seemed flooded with a great light. It was almost like coming out of a dark tunnel into the bright sunlight. My fears had evaporated like a morning mist and I felt a great sense of joy and triumph and relief. In less than a week I was feeling healthy, normal and strong. The pustules on my body, arms, face, hands and legs began to recede, to wither away, and in two or three weeks disappeared altogether, without a trace, without a scar.

The doctors were amazed. "You are very lucky," they said. "A most unusual case."

This experience taught me that all things are possible through prayer. Not the prayer of supplication. Not the distorted, fear-inspired lip service that many people believe to be prayer. Fear and faith are deadly enemies, and one must always destroy the other. The prayer that heals the sick is the prayer of calm and quiet faith—*total faith*—the prayer of understanding, wherein we tune our thoughts to the wave length of the *Infinite Power of the Universe, the Power of Good.*

More and more, modern medicine is proving mental attitudes as a causative factor in illness. Psychology, psychiatry and psychosomatic treatment are employed by many hospitals in diagnosis and therapy. Doctors are discovering that many physical and mental ills are deeply rooted in emotions of hatred, desire for revenge, chronic irritation and deep-seated fears. And they are more than willing to concede the healing power of prayer, especially when prayer is coupled with a fervent desire for self-purification. Physicians know that when the cause of illness is removed, the body will heal itself.

Sometimes our prayers go unanswered, and we wonder why. The following incident may suggest the reason. Recently I walked into a department store where color television sets were being sold. I was fascinated by the long rows of TV screens that were tuned to the same program. The pictures on some of the sets were brilliant with natural color, as flawless, sharp and true as a Technicolor movie. On others, the pictures were distorted, the colors scrambled in a mélange of unreality. Women with green cheeks and purple lips. Men with pink foreheads and lavender ears.

Just at that moment two store customers walked along the aisle. One of them said, "Look at those ghastly pictures! I wouldn't have a color television set in my house!" And they went on their way.

I asked the salesman, "What's the matter with these TV pictures?" and he replied, "They're not properly tuned." And with a twist or two of the dial, he put the pictures back in focus.

I thought to myself, What a perfect analogy to prayers that go unanswered! They are simply out of focus with the Infinite Power of the Universe. We can control the image that appears on the "television tube" of our personal lives by twisting the dials of our conscious mind. If our thoughts are filled with fear, intolerance, anger or self-pity, our picture will be distorted and ugly. We can adjust the image simply by changing our thoughts.

Those of us who have passed our sixty-fifth birthday are perhaps more conscious of the need for a power outside of ourselves than younger people who are immersed in the affairs of business or the responsibilities of parenthood. We have time to think, time to ponder the true meaning of life. We hunger for a method of praying that has greater portent than the mumbo-jumbo of threadbare words. We want a God that permeates every cell of our bodies and brains, every particle of space in the universe—a God with more power and energy than atomic force. And if it takes a revolution of our thinking processes to release this great energy on our behalf, we say, "Let's go! Show us how!"

Here, then, in three steps, is the way to pray that works miracles—even for non-churchgoers:

Step One: *Expunge from your conscious mind all negative thoughts—fear, intolerance, envy, anger, self-pity, vanity, shame, selfishness, impatience. Banish forever these impostors that are masquerading as real.*

Step Two: *Flood your consciousness with an abundance of Good thoughts—forgiveness, consideration, kindness, confidence, faith, courage, humility, love, peace of mind, patience. Not just for a few minutes. Not for just an hour. But day after day, until this way of thinking becomes your way of life.*

Step Three: *Surrender yourself to the Infinite, Unlimited Law of Good. Have total faith that Good is Omnipotent.*

If you will open your heart sincerely to this great law of the universe, you will be able to conquer every problem that confronts you. You will gradually be surrounded by new friends, true friends. Your health will improve. Your sense of security will be firm and unshakable. Your life will move in an orderly sequence of harmony, fulfillment and happiness.

Is this any less than the Infinite Power that Christ used to heal the sick? Jesus' teachings were expressed in the metaphorical language of Biblical days. He said, "If ye have faith as a grain of mustard seed, ye shall say unto this mountain, remove hence to yonder place, and it shall remove; and nothing shall be impossible unto you" (Matthew 17:20). Jesus called this Infinite Power of the Universe "Our Father which art in Heaven." In all reverence, and with deep humility, we have been describing the identical law of the universe as the "Infinite Power of Good."

When we understand that God and Good are One and the Same, we will, perhaps, be reinspired to attend our church or temple or synagogue with a new and richer appreciation of its spiritual values. And we will become more closely identified with the Divine Creator when we have learned to practice and to preach this four-word prayer with all our heart and all our soul:

"In Good we trust."

CHAPTER 21

How to Banish the Boredom
That Leads to Ills, Pills—and Wills

I must lose myself in action lest I wither in despair.

—ALFRED, LORD TENNYSON

I was having lunch in a restaurant alone not long ago, a bad habit I have acquired recently, when I felt a hand on my shoulder.

A voice said, "Could you, by any chance, be Sergeant Legler?" I looked up into the wrinkled face of a white-haired elderly man. There was something vaguely familiar about his features.

"Did you say 'Sergeant'? Are you kidding? That was World War One. Forty-nine years ago!"

"Don't you remember Private Patterson?"

"Of course, but he was a young guy, twenty years old! Don't tell me you are Harry Patterson!"

"I sure am."

For a moment I was speechless. "I can't believe it. Nearly fifty years. How did you recognize me, Harry? I'm an old duffer, just like you."

Patterson grinned. "I'll be honest with you. I heard you were living in town—and you remotely resembled the guy that used to make me peel potatoes, Sergeant, sir!"

"Stop the kidding. What are you doing here?"

"Retired, I suppose like you! And bored to death doing *absolutely nothing.*"

"Join me for lunch."

For the next half hour Harry and I enjoyed the unique experience of dusting off memories half a century old. Then we closed the gap on yesterday and talked about today.

Harry said, "I'm going stark, raving mad with nothing to do. How do *you* kill time?"

"I'm busy as a bird dog." And I told him about my activities. "I've got an idea for you, Harry. Hear me out." And I described with honest enthusiasm the fantastic scope of adult courses which are available to retired men and women in our local schools and colleges. Daytime courses. Nighttime courses. Foreign languages. Political science. Literature. Commercial art. Oil painting. Retailing. Importing. Travel-agency operation. Fiction writing. "Harry, I've made a study of this thing called Adult Education—and it's simply terrific. Not like school and college in the old days that used to be such a chore. It's fun! And you meet people. Loads of people. People of our own age."

Harry appeared to be vaguely interested. "Might be something to it," he said.

A few weeks went by. My phone rang. "How about letting me take you to lunch?" said my old-time friend. For the next hour I visited with a different Harry Patterson. He was cheerful, excited, and eager to tell me about his enrollment in our local adult school system. "Three nights a week," he said. "It's really very interesting. I was intrigued by what you said about travel-agency operation. I'm fascinated with it. Something I always wanted to do. I'm going to get a job with a travel agency, and when I know the ropes I'm going to open my own."

"No longer bored?"

"How could I be? I'm having a ball—and I've met a lot of nice people."

Adult education, in my opinion, is one of the most exciting concepts of the twentieth century—and it holds out so many benefits to the retired person that it might have been created for him alone.

What does it mean to enroll in an adult-education class? It means spending from one to three nights a week, or mornings or afternoons, in a classroom or workshop or laboratory, just as a college student does. The classes may be held in the local high-school building or at a community college or a university, or even somewhere in your neighborhood—in a library or social hall. Adult-education leaders throughout the country are imbued with the necessity for taking these programs to the people and offering the kinds and varieties of courses that people of the community seek or demand.

A young woman I know gave the following description of a guitar class for beginners she enrolled in at an adult-education program in Levittown, Long Island:

"It was fun from the very first night. First of all, anybody could take the class. There was no entrance examination and you didn't have to prove that you were as musically endowed as Yehudi Menuhin or Jascha Heifetz. We had about fifteen people in the class—two teen-agers and the rest of us ranged from our early twenties up to a man who told us he was eighty-seven. The instructor was a man of about forty who really taught us but in a relaxed, friendly way. By the end of the first evening everybody in the room could play two chords; but the big treat came when the instructor told us that those two chords could carry us through a couple of dozen songs. The whole class played 'Jingle Bells' six times, and by the sixth time it almost sounded like 'Jingle Bells' and we were all laughing with pleasure and congratulating ourselves.

"After the class was over we went to the corner diner for coffee. We were all happy and wide awake, and we talked until midnight, becoming good friends. That's the way it went all term long, and some really lasting friendships came out of that class. Several of the people went on to the more advanced class, while others decided to take this or that class together. Mr. Standler, the eighty-seven-year-old, went on with me to a TV scriptwriting class. He turned out some very funny scripts and was a terrific critic of other people's stuff. I've been 'adult-educationing' it ever since. This year I'm going to take an auto-mechanics class for beginners. You see, I'm tired of getting stuck on the road and begging for help. I want at least to know my rear axle from the windshield wiper."

The extent of the curriculum available depends, of course, on how well adult education has been developed in the locality which you select for your retirement. For example, just scan this broad range of courses offered in a Florida community which is outstanding in this field:

Vocational Courses: bookkeeping, shorthand, typing, real-estate selling, travel-agency operation, use of business machines, commercial art, hotel front-desk work, window dressing, importing and exporting, cost accounting, construction estimating, advertising, retailing, electronic data processing, automotive mechanics.

Academic Subjects: history, philosophy, social sciences, languages (Spanish, French, Russian, etc.), mathematics, literature, short-story writing.

The Arts: oil painting, choral singing, playing the organ, music appreciation.

Home Skills: basic cooking, advanced preparation of gour-

met meals, basic and advanced sewing, dressmaking, uphol-
stering, choosing a wardrobe, interior decorating.

A well-developed program also will have an evening high
school for adults who never completed public-school education. It will offer U.S. government tests under which anyone
who never obtained a high-school diploma can demonstrate
that his general knowledge qualifies him to hold one.

In communities where adult education is being given the
attention that it deserves, retired persons, and other students
as well, remain year after year, pursuing subjects that have
always interested them, adding to their store of academic
knowledge and acquiring new skills and making new friends.

If this kind of study were valuable for no other reason, it
would be valuable for the opportunities it offers to the
retired person for widening his circle of acquaintances. A
friendship struck up in a school classroom virtually guaran-
tees, moreover, that certain mutual interests exist—and suggests that the newfound acquaintance is a person of intelligence and initiative.

How much does it cost to enroll in an adult-education
class? It varies, of course, from locality to locality, but as a
general rule the fees are nominal—$1.50 a semester, for
example, for a standard course. Another kind of course might
require an investment of ten to twenty dollars for special
books or supplies. If you should elect to take a course for
college credit under a university extension program, you
would pay a tuition fee commensurate with the tuition costs
charged by the institution on its campus—perhaps from fifty
dollars up. Basically, however, the philosophy of adult education these days calls for nothing more than token registration
fees. The programs are supported by local taxes similar to the
public-school taxes.

Great advances are being made in the field of junior colleges. These gains have opened promising new opportunities to the retired person who enjoys expanding knowledge and keeping his mind sharp. Junior colleges consist of the first and second year of college. They are public institutions, tax-supported, as opposed to the private junior colleges, which also fulfill an important function. The high-school graduate in a community may move directly into his local junior college and get the first two years of his higher education there at a fraction of the cost of going away to a distant city as a boarding student. In thus expanding public-school education for two years beyond high school, educators have created wonderful new opportunities for adults with time on their hands and the inclination to study.

Generally speaking, the junior-college curriculum is available to all, though the retired person who undertakes to enroll may find the young high-school graduates getting first preference, and rightly so, in courses and hours. He may be required to take evening classes. Nevertheless, the typical community-college program offers both academic and vocational courses in the depth and variety that the specific locality demands and is willing to pay for, through taxation.

If adult education interests you, don't expect to find it at its best in a community which skimps on its education dollar in order to keep taxes down. You will have to anticipate that property taxes for school purposes will be higher where the educational establishment is adequate and up to date.

What is your chance of becoming a teacher in an adult-education program? It may be excellent, depending upon the education and experience you can offer, though not necessarily teaching experience. In countless adult-education programs across the nation, retired industrial, business and professional people are putting their skills to work. A machinist, a drill-press operator, an accountant, an office manager or anyone on the executive, professional or technical level may find such an opportunity in the area which he selects for his retirement.

If there is a demand for a class in business office procedures, someone experienced in this field will be sought to supply the instruction. If the young men in the community want courses in welding, the teacher must be a welder, or must have been one in the past.

If you have any knack for communicating to others the knowledge and experience that you have accumulated in your field over the years, you may very well find a place as a teacher in some adult-education establishment. This applies to women, of course, as well as to men. Young women who aspire to be secretaries, for example, must be taught by a woman who has been a secretary.

Donald P. Kent, Director of the Office of Aging of the Welfare Administration, U.S. Department of Health, Education and Welfare, in a speech before the Annual Conference of the Indiana State Commission on the Aging and Aged, discussed similar programs around the country.

"In Winnetka, Illinois, for example, retired persons aid the schools by working with those students we call 'underachievers.' In every school system there are such students whom we know should be doing much better than they are. The question becomes 'How do you stimulate them?' Usually, the answer lies in a person-to-person relationship. So in Winnetka they are using the retired person to work with these under-achievers. The initial results of this project are very encouraging. Virtually all of the under-achievers have shown marked improvement by having an adult work closely with them. As important as the individual contact is, I suspect that the qualities of age—wisdom, patience, tolerance, and objectivity—help significantly in this progress.

"This program with under-achievers has been so successful that it has been extended to the 'gifted' and average students. Here the emphasis is on enrichment—on stimulating and assisting the younger people to broaden their horizons by digging deeper into the sciences, humanities and other fields.

"I recall a city where retired people are conducting nature walks. They are giving instruction to children, and adults, too. In another city one may take a guided tour of the museum with a retired art critic.

"In New York City older persons are giving still another educational service. They come into the classroom in what is called the 'Eye-Witness to History' program. In our older people we have an amazing resource. We have people in our society who saw the first automobile, who witnessed the first flight of the airplane. They can describe to the students what happened the first day an automobile was driven down the street. Or they can describe what happened in World War I."

All of these ideas could be put to work in your community. Sometimes it means that *you* have to suggest them. One way is to attend the local parents-association meeting at your neighborhood school and raise such suggestions, or go to the director of the adult-education program and present your ideas to him. If there's nothing started now, *you* can help make that start and be part of it.

You need never lack for companionship. You need never feel that your mind is growing dull or your abilities are going to waste. Many individuals have enjoyed their most reward-ing accomplishments after reaching retirement. And just in case you think I may be overexpansive in my enthusiasm, let me quote verbatim the comments of individual students, all over sixty-five, who are finding the answer to their boredom in the classroom.

George C. Henderson, sixty-seven: "Mrs. Henderson and I are planning to spend several months next year in Barcelona. We are both taking a refresher course in Spanish and are enjoying the experience immensely. We help each other with our lessons and are able to converse in Spanish at home."

Mabel Germaine, sixty-five: "Since I started to take an advanced course in sewing at our local high school, I have made some very pretty dresses and shifts for my grandchildren. It is keeping me busy where I used to be bored with nothing to occupy my time."

Harold Jensen, sixty-six: "I own a small motel and I thought it might help me to put the place on a paying basis if I spent a couple of nights each week studying hotel management in our junior college adult-education classes. I've learned a lot and I am going to enroll in other courses that I think would be helpful."

Emma Stanton, sixty-seven: "When I learned they were giving a course in playing the organ, I enrolled as a student. I have always played the piano fairly well, but I must say that learning to play the organ has opened up a new world of pleasure for me. I bought myself a small secondhand Hammond and our house is flooded with music most of the time."

Frank Ellsworth, sixty-nine: "Just to keep myself busy, I have been taking courses in real-estate selling. I have become so interested I am going to apply for a salesman's license. I am sure I can pass the test. It's never too late to learn."

Thomas Evans, sixty-five: "I'll be quite frank with you. I enrolled in the oil-painting classes because I was bored doing nothing. I am not very talented, but I have made a number of new friends and find the course quite interesting."

Dale Carnegie once said: "Are you bored with life? Then throw yourself into some work you believe in with all your heart, and you will find a happiness that you had thought could never be yours."

CHAPTER 22

How to Jump
Out of the Dumps

*I had the blues because I had no shoes—
until upon the street, I met a man who
had no feet.*

—HAROLD ABBOTT

Did you ever hear of Mr. Lugubrious Blue and Mr. Smiley Glad? Probably not—unless you are well over fifty and spent your boyhood in the Middle West. Back in the 1920s, these two oddly contrasting characters, created by the famous cartoonist John T. McCutcheon, were a front-page feature of the Chicago *Tribune*.

Their conversation, printed in type under the picture, was a typical cracker-barrel discussion about topics of the day. And as their names implied, Mr. Lugubrious Blue was the long-faced pessimist and Mr. Smiley Glad the unquenchable optimist. No matter what topic was discussed—woman suffrage, the Teapot Dome scandal, Prohibition or the stock-market crash—Mr. Lugubrious Blue's comments were invariably cynical, while the imperturbable Mr. Glad always emphasized the brighter side of life.

The cartoon taught an important lesson. It showed how our viewpoints can create a mood of utter despair or joy, whichever thoughts we choose to entertain. I have often wished that, if John T. McCutcheon were alive today, he could be induced to re-create his two famous characters as retirees, sitting on a park bench, discussing the pros and cons of their new life of leisure. Their conversation might go something like this:

SMILEY GLAD: Congratulations, Mr. Blue. I hear you have retired.

LUGUBRIOUS BLUE: You mean *condolences!* I didn't retire. They booted me out!

SMILEY GLAD: Why, for heaven's sake? I thought you were one of the top men on the totem pole.

LUGUBRIOUS BLUE: Company policy. When you turn sixty-five, out you go, no matter what kind of a job you're doing.

SMILEY GLAD: Surely you got a pension.

LUGUBRIOUS BLUE: Bah! A few lousy bucks. How am I going to live on it, when I've been getting a nice, fat salary?

SMILEY GLAD: It takes a little readjustment, L.B. Mira and I get along fine on our pension plus our Social Security. Frankly, I'm the happiest guy in the world. No more alarm clocks. No more commuting. No more office politics.

LUGUBRIOUS BLUE: Well, I'm bored to death. Nothin' to do! My old business pals give me the brush-off. Why? Because I'm no longer useful to them?

SMILEY GLAD: You'll have time to live, L.B. Get acquainted with your children.

LUGUBRIOUS BLUE: Nonsense! We've become baby-sitters for my married daughter.

SMILEY GLAD: Do something, man! Get yourself a part-time job. Get a hobby. Go into community service.

LUGUBRIOUS BLUE: Are you kidding? Why should I do something I don't want to do? I've got news for you. I haven't been feeling too well lately. I don't know how much longer I'll be around the campus.

SMILEY GLAD: You're really in a bad way, L.B. Let me give you some advice. You'd better get yourself a new outlook. Why don't you cut the string? Move to Florida. Get some fun out of life.

LUGUBRIOUS BLUE: On my pension? Couldn't afford it!

SMILEY GLAD: We've got a little house down there. Twelve thousand bucks. Fifty-two dollars a month mortgage. Got our own pool. Our house is on a lake. Not far from the beach. Wonderful fishing.

LUGUBRIOUS BLUE: Baloney, S.G.! You always were the eternal optimist. You know me. I'd die of loneliness. I don't know a soul down there.

SMILEY GLAD: You'll make friends. We did—best friends we ever had. Join a neighborhood club. Finest thing that ever happened to us.

LUGUBRIOUS BLUE: Forget it! That's not for me. My company says I'm finished. So I'm finished—washed up. I'm going to sit on my backside and do nothing. Absolutely nothing!

This little dialogue is not an exaggeration. If you are in your forties or fifties, let this serve as a warning.

I have a neighbor who reminded me of Mr. Lugubrious Blue. Frank Dahm was a butter-and-egg man from Cleveland —successful, well liked, popular among his business associates until that dismal day when he retired. Then he was lost, confused, depressed. He bought a home in Florida, but instead of doing something he did "absolutely nothing." Frank wouldn't even prune his hibiscus bushes, but sat day after day staring at the blue sky, waiting—waiting for what?

One day he confessed to me his boredom. I commiserated and, like Mr. Smiley Glad, urged him to get a part-time job. A month later Frank solved his problem. He dug into his retirement savings, bought a desirable building lot in a residential section, and with the help of a local contractor began the construction of a nicely designed speculative house. From that moment on, Frank Dahm was a different person—energetic, excited, enthusiastic.

Women tend at least as much toward the Lugubrious Blue side as their husbands. If they had careers, the effect of retirement is not far different. Then, with such an emphasis on glamor and looks in our society, the prospect of physical aging looms even more horrendous to the fair sex. Often one of two dreadful solutions comes into play. The older woman becomes the frantic teen-ager, dressing herself in miniskirts and tight sweaters, placing coy little bows in brightly dyed hair, and acting coy. Or, equally tragic, she wears old black dresses, tight-bun hairdos, cameo brooches and thick stockings.

The older woman who had been a housewife all her life may go into deep, idle melancholia or, in contrast, she may while away her time on compulsive cleaning binges, chasing after dirt that no longer accumulates rapidly, washing invisible spots off ceilings, dragging out the vacuum cleaner every time one speck of ash approaches the carpet.

If you were asked what disease is the most prevalent among retired persons, you might say "heart disease." You would be wrong. The most virulent disease is Depression, with a capital "D."

Felix Von Mendelsohn, M.D., in the *Encyclopedia of Mental Health,* defines depression as "a state of mind, a mental disorder, characterized by a lowering of the individual's vitality, his mood, desires, hopes, aspirations and his self-esteem. It may range from no more than a mild feeling of tiredness and sadness to the most profound state of apathy with complete psychotic disregard for reality."

The depressed person usually has no appetite, loses weight,

sleeps poorly. Ordinary tasks become burdensome and difficult. His general attitude is one of all-pervading pessimism.
Unless depression is conquered, it can interfere with normal
bodily functions and bring on more serious disorders.

As Dr. Joseph F. Montague once said, "You do not get
ulcers from what you eat. You get ulcers from what is eating
you." Physicians are fully aware that extreme depression and
self-pity, if continued over a period of time, can result in
gastric disturbances, thyroid deficiencies, kidney ailments and
many other illnesses. Perhaps this explains why the mortality
rate is so high among retired persons who cannot adjust
themselves to their new environment.

The treatment of depression varies with its type and mag-
nitude. Dr. Von Mendelsohn says, "Neurotic depressions must
be handled in one way, psychotic depressions in another, and
agitated depressions need a still different approach." If you
are concerned over an increasing tendency toward melancholia, you will be wise to consult a physician to diagnose the
cause and prescribe the cure.

Here are some of the therapeutic measures in general use,
determined, of course, by the degree and kind of depression:

1. Change Your Environment. Sometimes it is advisable to
remove a patient from a locale or a situation where a family
conflict or other circumstances have been a contributing
factor to the depression.

2. Do Something—Keep Busy. Psychiatrists call it "occupational therapy" and it works wonders—depending upon the
willingness of the individual to participate. Avoid tasks too
difficult or unpleasant, as these may accentuate the depression. Best activity is one that produces a sense of accomplishment, even though it may be of minor importance.

3. Acquire a Philosophy. The practice of showing good will, tolerance, friendliness toward others can be a deterrent to depression. Dr. Alfred Adler, the famous psychiatrist, said that he often told his patients how they could cure melancholy in fourteen days with this simple formula: *"Try to think every day how you can please someone!"* This remedy may be difficult for those who are so immersed in self-pity that they cannot project their thoughts to others.

4. Read the Bible. For many people who are distraught, the Bible is a constant source of help. There are hundreds of passages which provide hope and inspiration. It promises protection from a Power greater than ourselves and produces a peace of mind and a reliance on a supreme being that overcomes depression.

5. Talk Hopefully. "An effective cure for depression," says Norman Vincent Peale, "is the practice of hope. The more hope you build up within your mind, the more quickly your depressed feelings will lift. . . . When you awaken in the morning, tell yourself, 'This is going to be a great day. . . . I am going to do something constructive today.' Then keep on talking hopefully all day long. By saying the words, you start the process which leads to the actual fact."

6. See a Psychiatrist. Effectiveness of psychotherapy is disputed. It has proven valuable as a treatment for neurotic depression, which usually has its cause in psychological conflict. Whether or not psychotherapy is needed must be evaluated individually for each patient.

7. Take Antidepressant Drugs. Such remedies should be prescribed only by a physician, because some drugs may produce undesirable side effects. Most are rarely ever effective immediately. Neurotic depression responds to anti-depressant drugs better than psychotic depression.

8. Submit to Shock Therapy. Seldom used today except in extreme cases of psychotic depression, where urgency is necessary to avert suicide. Patients sometimes respond after two or three treatments. Rarely used in mild forms of reactive depression.

9. Replace Negative Thoughts. An effective method for conquering depression. Every time you think a negative thought, replace it instantly with all the will power you can muster. When you lapse into a mood of discouragement and gloom, sweep those offending thoughts out of your mind. Replace them with confidence and joy. Erase *all* negative thoughts instantly just as you would erase chalk marks from a blackboard. Make your own thought pattern. *You can do it— if you try.*

Depression is as contagious as the measles. A perfectly cheerful person living with a glum one cannot maintain his cheer for long. There is nothing more disheartening than a long face, red eyes and pessimistic comments.

Not only is the virus of depression contagious but it is chronic, and it nourishes itself, worsening hour by hour. If you wake up in the morning and say, "Ugh, another day. What's the good of it all?" there is no doubt that it will be a terrible and useless day. No one will smile or stop to chat with you—not for long, anyway. Your dour looks, your sour thoughts will come through in your posture and in your voice. If your friends don't catch your depression, they are surely going to walk away fast to escape contagion.

The "virus of depression" is no respecter of persons. It attacks not only the idle pessimist, like Mr. Lugubrious Blue, but often, without warning, strikes a devastating blow at the Smiley Glads. I know. For, despite my usually bubbling disposition, I have just recovered from a severe attack of melancholy—so devastating, so overwhelming it almost (to use a British colloquialism) "did me in."

For six weeks I wallowed in self-pity, unable to write, unable to think clearly. And for no apparent cause. I made eight, nine, ten false starts on Chapter 22, only to tear each sheet from the typewriter, crumble it into an angry wad and hurl it toward the wastebasket.

I sought solace in the words I had written in previous chapters, but they mocked me as monstrous platitudes. I said to myself: "How can I pretend to inspire others when my own enthusiasms are proving so volatile, so tenuous? I decided to chuck the whole project. I felt tired, listless, despondent, ready for the human junkyard. My legs ached. My mind was sodden. I felt pains in places where there had been no pains before.

In a morbid mood, I wrote to my good friend, publisher and adviser, Leon Shimkin, confessing my "woeful discouragement," admitting my inadequacy and suggesting that I consign my unfinished manuscript to the nearest bonfire. I expected a mild rebuke, which I hoped would thrash me out of my depression.

Instead, God bless him, Leon wrote, "I offer you not merely sympathy, but empathy, for your 'woeful discouragement.' Here is my constructive suggestion. Don't stop being discouraged. Hold onto those feelings and make an asset out of them. Put down a careful description of just how discouraged a person can be in a fashion which everybody will understand because they think you understand. Then figure out how to deal with the problem. Then write a chapter on 'How to Jump Out of the Dumps.' Try this prescription and see what happens."

Reading Leon's letter, I smiled for the first time in weeks. His kindly words of encouragement were, to me, like a Biblical voice booming from the mountaintop and I determined to follow his advice. Strangely enough I was cured in twenty-four hours—not by acquiring a philosophy, not by reading the Bible, not by antidepressant drugs nor by any of the methods outlined on previous pages. I experienced a new kind of shock therapy, new at least for me, that snapped me out of my depression *instantaneously!*

On my calendar-for-the-day was a visit to the printing plant where I was to check the galley proofs on one of my Florida publications. The linotype operator was still clicking the keys, so I wandered over to his machine and watched his nimble fingers as he finished setting the last few lines of the text. The roar of the presses created a bedlam of confusion.

I shouted over his shoulder, "All finished?" He paid no attention. I thought perhaps the noise had drowned out my voice, so I yelled still louder: *"Job all finished?"* He ignored my question, gathered up the lead slugs and handed them to the man who operated the proofing press. I said to the proofer, "Not very friendly, is he?" The proofman said, "He didn't hear you. Joe's a deaf mute."

"No kidding? And he operates that complicated linotype machine?"

"Joe's the best man we've got."

Later I complimented the manager of the plant on the galley proofs. Not a single mistake. Not a misspelled word, which was rare indeed. I asked him about the linotype operator.

"Joe's a good man," he said. "A perfectionist! Noise doesn't bother him. In fact, he doesn't even hear it."

"Where did you get him?" I asked.

"From the Handicapped Adult Headquarters. We have several employees from the same place. Did you notice the heavy-set fellow in the offset department—George Janowski? Does meticulous work. He's a double amputee. Two wooden legs. Railroad accident when he was a kid. There's another young fellow out in the bindery. Hard-working. Conscientious. Jimmy Pablo. He's a dwarf!"

Driving home from the plant, I couldn't keep my thoughts off these handicapped people. What courage! What determination! And there must be, I thought, thousands like them—the lame, the halt and the blind. Fighting for a livelihood against terrible odds. Refusing to accept charity. Developing skills to compete and even to surpass normal, healthy human beings. Giving a day's work for a day's pay.

Then I began to realize what a weak, spoiled, ungrateful person I had become in recent weeks, racked with self-pity. And for what reason? None!

That night, before I went to bed, I said a prayer—not a prayer of supplication but a prayer of gratitude. With an overwhelming surge of relief and thanksgiving, I said these words:

I am grateful that I have my eyesight.

I am grateful that I have my hearing, my speech.

I am grateful that I have my legs, my arms, my healthy body and good digestion.

I am grateful that I have a loving family—that no tragedy, no serious sickness, no accident has blighted my home and loved ones.

I am grateful that my needs are filled, that I can live in comfort with no haunting fear of poverty hanging over my household.

I am grateful for my friends.

I am grateful for whatever talents I may have acquired, and for the opportunity to express them constructively.

I am grateful, grateful, grateful.

In ten minutes I went to sleep and woke up refreshed. The depression that had clouded my mind for days and weeks was gone—dissolved—like a dense fog burned out by the sunlight.

I had learned, in my own way,

"How to Jump Out of the Dumps."

CHAPTER 23

Do This—and You Will Become a New Person in Seven Days

I never go into a hotel or a barber shop or a store without saying something agreeable to everyone I meet.

        —WILLIAM LYON PHELPS

The desire to be "somebody else" is deep-rooted in most human beings. If you ever read Grimm's fairy tales as a child, you will remember how often a wicked witch or a fairy godmother waved a magic wand and changed the poor little shepherd boy into a handsome prince or the kitchen scullery maid into a beautiful princess.

We never tire of the same romantic theme, whether it be a Danny Kaye in *The Secret Life of Walter Mitty* or a middle-aged baseball fan who, suddenly and mysteriously, became the home-run hitter Shoeless Joe from Hannibal, Mo. in the motion-picture musical *Damn Yankees.*

The same Freudian wish to escape from ourselves explains why men grow mustaches. Why brunettes become blondes. Why plastic surgeons reshape noses and take tucks in paunchy chins. Strangely enough, the desire to be something other than what we are is usually limited to externals. We are willing to suffer agonies having our complexions sandpapered, but we balk at the thought of sandpapering our prejudices.

The reshaping of our personalities requires a major operation which most people are unwilling to experience. It is painful surgery to cut away selfishness. To remove the gangrenous growth of resentments. But it must be done if we are to become the person we would like to be.

In the next dozen pages I am going to describe a method by which *you can become a new person in seven days.* The technique is not original. It was employed by Pythagoras, the Greek philosopher, in 500 B.C. and centuries later by Benjamin Franklin, who described his method in considerable detail.

"I wished to live without committing any fault at any time," said Franklin in his autobiography, "and as I knew, or thought I knew, what was right and what was wrong, I did not see why I might not always do the one and avoid the other."

The only difference between Benjamin Franklin's method and mine is the length of time allotted to the self-purification process. Franklin devoted a full week to the mastery of a single virtue and elimination of its opposite. He expected to become a New Person in thirteen weeks. In this swifter moving world of today, I have shortened the course to seven days, a sort of "cram session," with each day devoted to the mastery of a single virtue and the elimination of its opposite. And I have taken a few liberties with Franklin's list of virtues, replacing his Frugality with Forgiveness and Justice with Generosity.

Here is the seven-day list of constructive habits, with their destructive antitheses:

Sunday—devoted to KINDNESS and the elimination of INTOLERANCE.

Monday—devoted to FORGIVENESS and the elimination of RESENTMENT.

Tuesday—devoted to HUMILITY and the elimination of CONCEIT.

Wednesday—devoted to SELF-CONFIDENCE and the elimination of SELF-PITY.

Thursday—devoted to FAITH and the elimination of ANXIETY.

Friday—devoted to GENEROSITY and the elimination of SELFISHNESS.

Saturday—devoted to MODERATION and the elimination of SELF-INDULGENCE.

There have been many inspiring books offering prayers to guide us through each day. I remember one in particular which reflected great warmth and wisdom and humanity, *The Prayers of Peter Marshall,* a collection of the daily messages Dr. Marshall delivered before the Senate of the United States while he was chaplain from 1947 to 1949.

The seven-day method I am proposing is far more arduous and demanding than the fleeting moment of spiritual uplift provided by a daily prayer. Taken seriously, it is comparable to the training of an astronaut. It requires alertness and awareness every instant of every day from breakfast to bedtime. You may decide after a single day that the routine is far too strenuous, and polish it off with some such remark as "Who wants to be perfect?"

Benjamin Franklin recorded his progress at the end of each day in a diary, scribbling into its blank pages his triumphs and his transgressions. I recommend a similar system. A sort of self-confessional. To make sure that such a method would be workable, I gave it a seven-day test. And to use the words of Franklin, "I soon found that I had undertaken a task of more difficulty than I had imagined."

Here, then, for what it may be worth as an encouraging

example, is my seven-day diary, a mixed record of success and failure:

Sunday

Devoted to KINDNESS and the elimination of INTOLERANCE

What wisdom can you find that is greater than Kindness?

—JEAN JACQUES ROUSSEAU

MORNING

9:30.   Unexpected breakfast treat—Spanish omelet and cottage-fried potatoes. Kissed my wife and said, "Am I a lucky guy!" She beamed.

10:15.   Telephone rang twice in two minutes. Wrong number both times. Same person. I said with a laugh, "Missed it again. Better luck next time." Last week I would have been annoyed.

11:00.   Smiled at church usher and whispered, "Good morning." He smiled back. After the service I said a cordial "Good morning" to five strangers. All of them greeted me with a smile. Made me feel good. I never used to bother greeting strangers.

12:30.   Driving home, I waved to a motorcycle policeman who was alongside my car. He looked at me suspiciously, then grinned and waved back. Maybe he thought I was a judge.

AFTERNOON

2:15.   Foursome of golf. Little wisp of a boy was caddying double. I relieved him of one bag, carried it myself. He gave me a toothy smile; looked at me gratefully with big brown eyes; followed me around the course like a tail-wagging puppy dog.

4:30.   Clubhouse lounge. Political discussion. I used to sound off, sometimes became unpleasantly argumentative when views were opposed to mine. New policy—keep silent, raise eyebrows, look wise. Avoid head-on clash with some such cliché as "That's what makes horse races." Hope this new attitude won't make me a Casper Milquetoast.

EVENING

9:15.   Reflected on progress. Conscious all day of the warm way people respond to little sparks of kindness. Must be careful not to feel smug and self-righteous. This is a real danger. Expressing kindness must come from the heart—not be contrived for self-gain!

Monday

Devoted to FORGIVENESS and the elimination of RESENTMENT

> "It is only one step from Toleration to For-
> giveness.
>
> —SIR ARTHUR WING PINERO

MORNING

8:00.   Picked up morning newspaper on front lawn, soaking wet. Phoned newspaper delivery man and complained indignantly. "Mr. Legler," he said, "I delivered your paper myself at six-thirty this morning. Your lawn was dry." Then I realized. I had turned on automatic sprinklers for 7:30. Apologized. Felt ashamed. Off to a bad start.

10:15.   Postman returned several important letters to my office which had been mailed by part-time secretary without stamps. Where does *forgiveness* leave off and *discipline* begin? Decided to admonish the girl but not to reprimand her. It worked. She won't make the same mistake again.

AFTERNOON

2:30.   Wife and I relieved because our house guest, after a long week, decided to fly back to New York. He phoned from local airport, "My plane flight was canceled. Can't leave till tomorrow." I swallowed my annoyance and drove to airport to pick up our non-departing guest. Greeted him with a broad grin and friendly slap on back. Said jokingly, "I thought we'd got rid of you!" He said, "No such luck! Listen, Henry, I want to take you and Fran to dinner tonight at the most expensive restaurant in town." We had a grand evening together!

EVENING

10:30.   Counted up seven little acts of forgiveness. Pretty good score for one day. A week ago I would have gone to bed, nursing resentments.

Tuesday
Devoted to HUMILITY and the elimination of CONCEIT
There is nothing so becoming a man as modest Humility.
—WILLIAM SHAKESPEARE
MORNING

10:30.   Insurance salesman made emphatic statement to me which I knew was incorrect. My first inclination was to contradict him, to point out the absurdity of his remark. Then I remembered "This is Humility Day!" So I said, "That's very interesting. I wonder if you would let me know the source of those figures." He said, "Sure! Glad to!" An hour later he called me on the phone. "Say, I was wrong about those figures. Way off base! Sorry." Made a friend instead of an enemy.

AFTERNOON

1:30.   Instructed our printer to set manuscript in type. He offered several suggestions. I shook my head impatiently. "Will you please set it like I want it!" Suddenly I realized I sounded like a conceited slob. Asked his advice and used his excellent ideas.

3:45.   Caught myself several times making positive assertions. In fact, I have always taken pride in my strong opinions. Considered it a sign of strength. Now I realized it is a sign of weakness, arrogance, conceit. Starting today, will respect other people's opinions.

EVENING

9:30.   For the first time in my life, I have been aware all day of the importance of *humility*. And the lessons of yesterday and Sunday have not been shunted aside. I am showing more consideration toward others. Hope it continues!

Wednesday

Devoted to SELF-CONFIDENCE and the elimination of SELF-PITY

> *Only the self-confident can hold their peace*
> *in the midst of clamor.*
> —HELENE MULLINS

MORNING

7:30.   Stayed awake most of the night worrying whether I should ask a customer two dollars or one dollar per inquiry for postcard returns. Phoned him at 9 A.M. brimming with *Self-Confidence*. Raised my asking price to four dollars. He accepted.

10:30.   Invited by Advertising Club to speak at their monthly dinner. First impulse was to refuse, politely and firmly. Hate to make speeches. Where's the *Self-Confidence?* I know my subject. How can I fail? So I said, "I'll be there! Thanks for wanting me."

12:30.   Sat down to order lunch at new Continental

Hotel. Felt lonely. Sorry for myself. Man at next table also alone. One of Florida's most prominent housing developers. Had never met him. I walked over with beaming smile. "Alone? Mind if I join you?" He waved me to sit down. "Glad to have company. I'm Jim Hunt, Coral Ridge Properties." "Yes, I know. I'm Henry Legler." Pleasant luncheon. Friendly terms with good business contact.

Thursday

Devoted to FAITH and the elimination of ANXIETY

Our Faith triumphant o'er our Fears.

—HENRY WADSWORTH LONGFELLOW

MORNING

9:30. Flew to Tallahassee. Bad weather. Fog. One engine conked out. Anxious moments. Conquered my fears. Thought of the new chapter I had just written, "New Way to Pray." Here was a chance to test it. Replaced negative thoughts with *total faith* in the Infinite Power of Good. Plane landed without further incident.

AFTERNOON

3:30. Phoned home to see if Fran was feeling better. No answer. Worried me. She wasn't well when I left. Called on Power of Infinite Good to ease my worries. Felt sense of relief. Phoned neighbor long distance. She was there. Greatly improved.

5:00. During flight home tried to rid my mind of all petty anxieties. Experienced wonderful feeling of confidence, peace of mind, security.

EVENING

11:30. Came to the conclusion that *Faith* in the Law of Good should not be used spasmodically as a curative—but constantly as a preventive. This could be the key to a whole new way of life.

Friday

Devoted to GENEROSITY and the elimination of SELFISHNESS
God blesses the Generous thought.
—JOHN GREENLEAF WHITTIER

MORNING

7:30. Woke up and pondered meaning of generosity. Does it mean giving lavish gifts? Surely not. It means being unselfish. David Dunn has caught the spirit of generosity in his inspiring book entitled, *Try Giving Yourself Away.* It means showing appreciation, being warmly gracious to other people, noticing their accomplishments instead of bragging about your own.

11:30. Answered my mail this morning with a totally new approach. Dictated warm friendly letters, written from the other person's viewpoint. It reminded me of Judy Holliday's famous letters to stockholders in *The Solid Gold Cadillac,* a comedy that taught a great lesson in human relations.

AFTERNOON

3:30. Mailman entered my office same moment the coffee service arrived. I said, "Joe, take yourself off your feet for five minutes and have a cup of coffee with me." Joe was pleasantly surprised. He accepted.

EVENING

10:30. I discovered today that little acts of good will in our family life, in our daily work and even in our fleeting contacts with strangers can bring a rich reward of happiness. As my good friend Leon Shimkin says, "Life is not *give and take;* it's *give and get.*"

Saturday

Devoted to MODERATION and the elimination of SELF-INDULGENCE

Moderation is the noblest gift of Heaven.

—EURIPIDES

MORNING

11:45. Played nine-hole par-3 golf course. Rest of foursome wanted to shoot another round. I said, "Sorry, I've had it." Determined to practice moderation in everything I do.

12:30. Bottle of beer with lunch. Friend had three martinis. Says that's his limit. He is beginning to look puffy around the jowls. Didn't dare mention moderation. After all, drinking is a personal problem.

AFTERNOON

Driving home, I thought of seven-day method. Remembered a series of ads on "Moderation" I wrote many years ago for House of Seagram. Maybe I convinced myself then that overindulgence is unwise. In the broader sense, moderation means not overdoing anything. I frequently write until 3 A.M. Foolish, I suppose. Just as immoderate as having half a dozen highballs. Must remind my wife not to work in garden to point of exhaustion, which she frequently does.

EVENING

10:30. This is the last entry in my seven-day diary. Am I a new person? It has been a great experience. Never in my life have I tried so persistently to think good thoughts, day after day, every moment of the day. If I'm not a *new person,* I'm a *different person.* Much happier. And I honestly believe I've made other people happy. I feel alive. Full of health. More outgoing. Less self-centered. I like people better, and they seem to like me better. Why quit now after seven days and slip back into old habits. I'll abandon diary but continue this way of thinking. Yes, *I am a new person.*

Perhaps it might pay to take a good long look at yourself before you embark on your seven-day experiment. In *A Christmas Carol,* by Charles Dickens, old Scrooge gets a hard look at himself through ghosts of the past, present and future. As a result of the ugly picutre presented to him, he sets about changing his way of life. When I was a youngster in school a much less mystical approach was used by the students. At regular intervals something called a "Slam Book" was surreptitiously circulated through the classroom. It was a bound notebook, with a student's name on top of each page. It began circulating with a fresh, clean page for each student. As you were handed the Slam Book, you were supposed to write (without signing, of course) your opinion of each of your fellow students on their particular page.

By the time the book had circulated throughout the classroom, everyone had a pretty good idea of what the other students thought of him. Almost every child discovered that he had at least one secret enemy in the class, but it wasn't hard to separate the good guys from the bad guys. One page would have a predominance of phrases like "A friend in need," "A great honest Joe," while another page would have cracks like "Acts just the way he looks, U-G-L-Y!" or "Don't ever turn your back on him!"

I'm not advocating Slam Books. They were often cruel and painful experiences, especially for sensitive adolescents, and the teachers used to keep a sharp eye out and confiscate them whenever they were spotted. But there's no harm in having your own private Slam Book before you try your wings at making yourself a new person. The advantage, of course, is that nobody has to see it, so you can be as honest with yourself as you like.

Just list the virtues mentioned on a previous page: kindness, consideration, courage, honesty, humility, wisdom, love, confidence, faith, peace of mind, gratitude, diligence, generosity, truthfulness, loyalty, trust, and friendliness, and slam away at yourself. Once you've done that, you will have a pretty good idea of your weak areas and strong areas.

CHAPTER 24

How to Protect Yourselves from Becoming Baby-Sitting Grandparents

The burden becomes light which is cheerfully borne.

—OVID

Jack Powell and I used to celebrate our birthdays together. We were exactly the same age and I suppose the coincidence accounted for a bond of friendship which grew stronger with the years. Came the day of retirement and our twinship again asserted itself, for we decided to cut the string that tied us to our business responsibilities at about the same time.

I remember urging Jack and Georgia to make a clean break with suburban Westchester and start life all over again in Florida.

"Come on and join us!" I used to plead. "Trade in your oak trees for palm trees. We can't wait to get away from the snow and cold."

"Sorry," said Jack. "We love Florida, but we want to be near the kids. Remember, we have eight grandchildren!"

"They can visit you during vacations."

"No," said Georgia. "I adore those youngsters. Now that Jack has more time, we're going to be baby-sitting grandparents—and we're going to love it!"

Three years went by and infrequent letters from Jack and Georgia were filled with exuberant references to Susan and

Laury and Nancy and Bud and Tommy—with colorful descriptions of their good times together at the Bronx Zoo or at Ringling Brothers Circus.

In recent letters I seemed to detect a change of tone—ever so subtle. References to the grandchildren were just as frequent, but somehow the incidents described were always interwoven with problems.

"Susan has been at our house for three weeks. Poor kid had chicken pox and they quarantined her . . ." "I know it's just a coincidence, but every time one of the kids gets a cold or the sniffles, it seems to happen at our house—and it's very obvious that Lillian blames me. She doesn't come right out and say so, but she always questions me, 'Well, did you put on his rubbers?' Or 'Did you make him wear his jacket?' As if it were my fault!"

A recent letter from Jack described with mixed overtones of amusement and annoyance "the most horribly embarrassing thing" that "happened at the supermarket today. I took Tommy shopping with me. You know those pyramids of cans they have at the ends of the aisles. Well, Tommy, the little devil, loosened one of the cans on the rim and the whole pile came tumbling down. It was a shambles! I couldn't spank Tommy. After all, he's only five. . . . Say, I've got some good news for you. Georgia and I are going to drive to Florida—just for a couple of weeks. It'll be good to see you again."

And sure enough, in a few days, a car pulled into our drive. It was Jack and Georgia. "Stay with us," we urged. "We have a big, empty guest room just waiting for you." Later, sitting around the pool with tall, frosty highballs, it came out.

"This trip is more than a vacation," said Jack. "We're going to look around—maybe buy a house, or an apartment in one of those high-rise condominiums."

"You mean you're going to live in Florida?" I said eagerly.

"We've been thinking about it for a long time," said Jack.

"But what about the grandchildren?"

"Oh, they're anxious to have 'Nonna' and 'Pop-pop' move to Florida. They want to come down and visit us."

After the second highball, Georgia loosened up and confessed quite freely that the idea of becoming a baby-sitting grandmother was not exactly as she had anticipated.

"Please understand," said Georgia. "I love the kids—all of them. But I guess I'm just getting too old to be with them for more than a couple of hours. When they're watching television, they are as quiet as can be—but most of the time, it's a madhouse. They're constantly screaming and yelling and dashing up and down stairs. I get so nervous, I feel like the woman in those aspirin commercials."

"And," I added, "you feel guilty because you think a grandmother should be patient and loving and understanding. Georgia, I'm going to talk to you like a Dutch uncle— and I hope you won't resent what I'm going to say. You and Jack are primarily selfish. So is every human being. You wanted to be near your grandchildren because you wanted the affection they gave you. When little Susan put her baby arms around your neck and said, "I love you, Nonna," you melted. But when Susan started to whine and cry and throw herself on the floor in a tantrum, you couldn't wait to drive her back to her mother.

"You know, it's just possible that your own children took advantage of your eagerness to be a baby-sitting grandmother. You asked for it. How many times have you said on the telephone, 'Nancy, wouldn't you and Susan like to come over to Nonna's for the weekend?'

"You and Jack are in your sixties. You've earned the right to some peace and quiet. That doesn't mean you have to neglect your grandchildren. Or not see them. Just don't overdo it! Little kids are for young married people. They can take it. You can't. And we can't. Occasionally, our own grandchildren come down to Florida to stay with us. It's a big thrill for them—and for us, too. But, believe me, after two weeks, we put them aboard a jet plane with a great big sigh of relief. . . . Come on, finish your Scotch—and let's go house-hunting."

I wonder how many well-meaning grandparents have become tangled in the same web of misguided sentimentality. Craving affection, they take on the chore of baby-sitting with blind enthusiasm—not admitting, even to themselves, that they are unqualified to cope with confusion and bedlam. Too often their remedy for such behavior is a cookie jar or a bedtime story. Bribery rather than discipline. No wonder grandparents and their married children are so often at odds over child-rearing methods.

Unhappily the solution is not always so simple as Jack and Georgia found it. Moving to a distant point is not always practical or possible. And sometimes it brings an emotional hardship on grandparents which might have been avoided by sensibly and honestly coming to grips with the problem.

I speak from experience. We have a married daughter who lives in the vicinity. Her four-year-old Donna is a normal, healthy child with all the vigor, the curiosity, the talkativeness and the aggressive instincts of any little girl of her age. Two hours with Donna are stimulating. Two days with Donna are nerve-racking. Recently we baby-sat Donna for one whole week, because of circumstances which were unavoidable. When our daughter and son-in-law returned from their trip, their first question was "How did Donna behave? Was she a good girl?" "I'm going to answer your question," I said laughingly, "with that old Mother Goose rhyme. You remember it. 'There was a little girl—and she had a little curl—right in the middle of her forehead.' "

"I get it!" said my daughter. " 'When she was good, she was very, very good—and when she was bad, she was horrid!' "

"That's about it. There were times when she was sweet as pie—and other times when she was a little witch!"

"Well, thanks a million to you and mother for taking care of her. We'll try not to inflict her on you again for such a long time!"

"You do, honey chile," I said, "and they are going to carry your poor ole pappy off to an institution!"

And so, with a laugh, in which my daughter joined, I registered gently, but firmly, the fact that we were available, on a very limited time only, as baby-sitters. Most grandparents are fearful of making an honest report, and because they do not want to seem selfish or unloving, they cover up a child's bad behavior with such insincere comments as "Oh, she was just wonderful. No problem at all." This sort of remark gives a grandparent a smug feeling of self-righteousness, even martyrdom, but it can be very misleading—and result in more and longer sessions as a baby-sitter.

Of course, grandparents must be seen from the other side of the fence too—namely, from the point of view of their grandchildren and their own children.

A friend of mine described a scene she saw on the streets of New York one afternoon. A young adolescent—thin and gawky, with long hair scraggling down the back of his neck and drooping over one eye (a rather common hair style among teen-age boys today) —was walking ahead of her beside a well-groomed and very attractive elderly woman, obviously his grandmother.

Traffic on the narrow sidewalk was momentarily stopped when the grandmother met another elderly woman, obviously a long-time friend whom she had not seen in many years. They greeted each other with open and effusive pleasure, embracing and laughing. The teen-ager stood shuffling next to them, head down, hands in pockets, obviously embarrassed—but then, teen-agers are embarrassed in public at least 80 per cent of the time.

After a few moments the grandmother remembered the boy was there. "Oh, Ruth," she said. "Why, you haven't seen my grandson Johnny since he was an infant. Now I know he looks a bit stupid with that hairdo of his, but he's really quite bright. He just can't be convinced to visit a barber. Do you think I should take the scissors to him myself?"

It was said in a flippant, lighthearted way, but one look at the boy showed that he didn't take it that way. His head lowered even further, and a distinctly bitter pout twisted his mouth. My listening-in friend reports that from the glint in his eye and the flush on his face, she feared that if Grandma kept it up she might wind up under a passing bus.

Now I'm sure that the grandmother did not deliberately embarrass and hurt her grandson. No doubt she truly disapproves of his hair style and thought that she could goad him into a trim. But she either forgot or never understood the sensitivity of teen-agers—perhaps the unhappiest group in our whole population. Their wounded pride, their self-consciousness make what might be amusing to a mature person an inquisitional torture.

Even so, if the grandmother had thought it through, it is dubious that she would treat an adult friend in a similar way. Can't you picture it? The same woman is walking along with another full-grown woman and meets the same old acquaintance.

"Oh, I forgot to introduce you, Ruth. You haven't seen Jane here in thirty years, and of course you won't recognize her. She's so much fatter! I've tried to talk her into a good reducing diet or at least a decent girdle, but she insists on waddling around like a lump of Jello."

Unthinkable? Of course! But the equally unthinkable social behavior toward one's grandchildren is not infrequent. Actually a grandparent can have a constructive relationship with his or her adolescent grandchildren. Seeing them less often than his parents and not being the "enemy" that dispenses chores and punishments means that the grandparent is in a position to be a confidant and to give advice to the grandchild which might never be accepted from his parents. Teen-agers are generally calmer and easier to visit with. Grandpa can play chess or take an adultlike walk with a thirteen- or fourteen-year-old grandson or granddaughter. If grandparents can make up their minds not to preach, they can be a source of quiet advice and assistance at this difficult time of life.

Unfortunately, there is a tendency to do the opposite. Not only do many grandparents become more carping critics than the children's own parents, but they also undermine their relationships with their own grown children by rudely criticizing their child-rearing routine.

These methods have changed radically over the last twenty or thirty years. Perhaps the experts will swing the pendulum back again as they have done before. But right now your children want to do what is considered correct and modern, and they don't appreciate your sour comments on the "newfangled" ways. In fact, those comments only serve to make you seem "out of it" and oldfangled, to coin a phrase.

Keeping up with the times and current opinions is also a great help in maintaining relations with children and grandchildren. No doubt many of the youngsters of today take extreme positions. But think back. Weren't many of our own children's opinions much more extreme before they matured?

Be more tolerant of the views of youngsters. Don't laugh in their faces but listen seriously and say to yourself: "This too shall pass."

If circumstances have cast you in the role of baby-sitting grandparents, here are nine rules to follow which may ease the situation—or at least result in an improved rapport between you and your married children:

1. Don't be overindulgent.

2. Practice firm discipline.

3. Report your grandchildren's behavior with honesty and without resentment if their behavior was bad.

4. Let your married son and daughter know—and with a touch of humor, if you can muster it—that your nervous system is not as young and pliable as it used to be.

5. Hope they will understand and be sympathetic. If they are not, drop the humor.

6. Let them know you love your grandchildren and that you are happy to be a baby-sitter—*on limited occasions and for a limited time.*

7. Move far enough away so that you will not be imposed upon too often.

8. If you are stuck with the job frequently, and there is no way out of it, talk to a kindergarten teacher—and get her suggestions on how to keep little children busy, quiet and interested.

9. As a last, desperate resort, dip into your pension, hire a professional baby-sitter and go off to the neighborhood movie.

CHAPTER 25

How to Avoid
Living with Your Children

*Don't live with your children if there is any
way to avoid it.*

—THOMAS COLLINS

As you approach retirement age, you have probably thought seriously of "going to live with the kids"—a married son or daughter. Perhaps the plan will be to circulate among the homes of several children.

"We're going to spend part of the time with Jane and her family in Pittsburgh and part of the time with Dick and his wife in San Francisco. They're both anxious to have us come."

The notion has strong appeal after a long period of separation, which is normal in today's American family.

"It'll be like old times—us and the kids together again. We can baby-sit for them and watch our grandchildren grow up— and it'll be easier financially for both families, sharing the same house."

If this is your intention, consider the matter well and approach it with extreme caution. Give it a trial if you must—but leave yourself a graceful way out.

If one were to quote odds on the chances of its succeeding, the odds would be heavily on the negative side.

A situation which places two families of comparable ages,

with similar tastes and inclinations, in the same household is rarely successful. Parties to such arrangements frequently learn to hate each other in short order. How much smaller, then, are the chances for a satisfactory rapport between families of different ages, different generations, with widely divergent needs and tastes and desires—even though they may be as naturally close as parents and children?

One generation ago, in the history of the American family, the odds were somewhat more favorable. Modes and manners were more stable. Inclinations and tastes and rules of behavior adhered more closely to predictable patterns. Families didn't scatter quite so widely. But vast changes in the American mode of living have taken place since then.

The gulf which separates today's retirement generation from its sons and daughters is wider as a result. One has to be almost saintly to span it day after day, month in and month out, in the situations which arise when two families dwell under the same roof.

Consider the simple matter of privacy. How many bedrooms and bathrooms can one house have? How many living rooms and kitchens?

In a ninety-room castle, or even a twenty-room mansion, separate lives might be possible. The number of daily encounters could be satisfactorily limited.

Today's typical home has but three bedrooms and two baths, one kitchen and one living area. Collisions are frequent when two families live together. Privacy flies out the window. Doors must be kept closed too often. Intimate situations, which are inevitable and much to be encouraged among young marrieds, can become virtually impossible.

When the husband drops into his easy chair after the day's work is done, with at least his wife and perhaps his children at his side, where shall the "old folks" be? In the same scene, attempting to share in it and contribute to it? Or discreetly withdrawn—and withdrawn to where? The kitchen? Their bedroom?

Once upon a time many American homes had upstairs sitting rooms, which made graceful withdrawal possible. Today a small percentage has "family rooms" or "television rooms," but by and large retreat is possible only to the kitchen or a bedroom.

When the husband and wife entertain, have a few friends in for drinks and dinner or a round of cards, their elders again face the question: Where to be and what to do? Go to bed early? Go out to a movie or a social of their own?

What is protocol, moreover, when the oldsters wish to have a few of their friends in? Must it be off to bed or a movie for the young ones?

It is acknowledged that these are not insurmountable problems and that satisfactory adjustments to them might very well be made during limited visits. But encountered repeatedly over a period of months, they can grow into towering obstacles to normal family life.

"Now, Jane, you and Bob just go your own way and we'll go ours. Don't worry about us, and don't think you have to change the way you do things just because we're in the house. We'll keep busy with things of our own."

The theory is pretty enough, but nearly impossible of application. The areas of potential conflict are countless. Meal times. Tastes in food. Disciplining of children. Noisy activities. Television programs. Sleeping hours. Working hours. Use of the car. Entertaining at home. Going out for entertainment. Churchgoing. Ethics. Tastes in friends. Housekeeping. Cooking. Finances. Politics. Child raising. And so on, indefinitely.

Even if the men can adjust to each other, conflict between

the women is almost inevitable, though they may be mother and daughter.

The female of the species is by nature sensitive; woman's intuition, accurate or not, provides her with a built-in radar which picks up minute changes in attitude, in the atmosphere, ceaselessly recording what she interprets as slights, rudeness, thoughtlessness, selfishness, favoritism, snappishness, impatience.

"Please, Mother, I'd rather do it myself!"

This quote from a television commercial now is part of the national language—possibly because it hits home so unerringly.

A mother who will take time to recall the differences which she and her daughter experienced even before daughter went off to a home of her own can picture the possibilities for domestic explosions in a home occupied by two families.

The years since may well have magnified the differences rather than ironed them out.

The permanent presence of in-laws in any home, on the whole, requires more self-control than the typical individual of our times is capable of—and the external pressures of the times, bearing in on the family from outside—holding a job, advancing in business, meeting living costs, dealing with teenage offspring, keeping up with the Joneses, changing modes— create added tensions which cannot help but be reflected in behavior within the family.

Many students of retirement discourage not only living in with the children but even moving to the same community.

On the whole, keeping a moderate distance between yourself and young folks seems wise.

Be far enough removed from them to avoid affecting their personal lives or imposing your own opinions and attitudes on them. Be close enough that periodic visits back and forth impose no hardship and demand no unusually great expense.

One of the great delights of retirement is tasting the freedom to live where you choose—a freedom that you probably never have enjoyed before. Selecting your own special spot out of the geography of this great, spreading, many-splendored continent can be one of the most rewarding experiences of your lifetime—an enormous stimulus to your leisure years.

If you are considering your retirement locale with your children in mind, ponder this: There is much to be said for a locale which will give them a rewarding change of scenery when they come to visit, a place which will make the periodic trips to see Grandma and Gramps a delight for the grandchildren and a refreshing experience for their parents.

Offer them a warm winter climate, a beautiful seashore, a fascinating city, a pretty little farm, a picturesque village with nearby orange groves and sparkling lakes.

Let your stimulating retirement activities, your happy independence, be part of your contribution to the happiness of the young folks.

PART 5

How to Make New Friends and Keep Your Old Ones

CHAPTER 26

The Rule That's Worth
Its Weight in Gold

He that does good to another does good
also to himself.

—SENECA

To illustrate how times have changed since we were young-sters, Allen Funt recently featured a group of ten-year-old children on his "Candid Camera" television program. The first child was asked to finish the sentence beginning with the words "All work and no play . . ." The youngster looked puzzled, bit his lip and stuck his tongue in his cheek, then said, ". . . makes you pretty tired!"

A little girl was told to finish this sentence: "Birds of a feather . . ." Again a thoughtful look, followed by a con-fident answer: "Birds of a feather fly south in the winter-time!"

As child after child showed a total ignorance of the old proverbs and aphorisms which are so familiar to an older generation, I could not help but feel that something good has gone out of our modern educational system.

A great many years ago when I was in second grade, our teacher, Miss Rose Cook (I still remember her name), used to write with chalk in a big Spencerian script on our var-nished desk tops, words and maxims that were to remain in our memories forever. She provided each of the children with a bowl of corn kernels and asked them to cover carefully the chalk marks, thus indelibly forming the words in our minds.

One day Miss Cook wrote on my desk, "Do unto others," and on the desk of the child behind me she outlined, "As you would have others"; then, on the third desk, she wrote, "Do unto you." When our task was finished, she asked each of us to read aloud the Golden Rule of life:

> *"Do unto others . . . As you would*
> *have others . . . Do unto you"*

Thus, at six years of age, I was given a rule of conduct which was destined to stay with me a lifetime. As years went by and I came to realize that human motivations are not always as idealistic as the McGuffey Readers would have us believe, I thought a great deal about the Golden Rule, and one day a light dawned on me with the impact of an explosion. Those eleven words, "Do unto others as you would have others do unto you," could be paraphrased without distorting their meaning into the simple axiom:

> *"What you do to others—*
> *Others do to you"*

If this were true, then the Golden Rule is really an infallible law that can be used for one's own betterment. In simple words you can get whatever you want in life by practicing the Golden Rule. Let's see how it works:

"Smile at others—others smile at you."
"Be kind to others—others are kind to you."
"Be friendly to others—others are friendly to you."
Conversely, "Hate others—others hate you."

Is this an oversimplification? I don't think so. Try it and see. I have practiced this simple philosophy a thousand times and a thousand times it has worked miracles.

Sometimes I wonder if the Golden Rule would work in the civil-rights disturbances that are festering in a dozen American cities. Would it quench the Molotov cocktails? Would it quiet the shrieks of "Black power!" and "Kill Whitey!" ? I think it would.

> *"What you do to others—*
> *Others do to you"*

A few days ago I was driving through a neighborhood in northwest Miami where the residents were predominantly Negroes. A tall young man walking beside the road eyed me with a sullen expression. I stopped the car, beckoned him with a friendly smile, opened the door and said, "Can I give you a lift?" The man was so surprised, he said nothing, but stepped into the car and sat in the seat beside me. For a moment there was silence. Then he looked at me with a puzzled expression and said, "Why you pick me up?"

"You were going my way, you looked tired, and you looked like a nice guy."

"I appreciate it," he said. A few more moments of silence, then I glanced at him sideways and asked, "Say, what do you think of those Dolphins?"

"Funny you ask me that," he said. "My cousin, he's a linebacker on the Dolphins." And for the next mile and a half I was given an expert opinion of the capabilities and shortcomings of Miami's new professional football team.

"Here's where I'm going," he said, and I pulled over to the

curb. He gave me a broad grin and with a genuine tone of friendliness said, "Thanks for the lift!"

> *"What you do to others—*
> *Others do to you"*

This attitude has worked minor miracles for others, too. I remember an interesting conversation my wife and I had one evening with a young couple vacationing in our area. At the time the New York papers were filled with stories of a young man whose family considered him a model son. He held a steady job, was engaged to a nice young woman, was quiet, neat and clean and a steady churchgoer. His family and neighbors were shocked when, with irrefutable evidence, the young man was arrested by the police as the murderer of several young girls. He had followed them home and strangled them in their own hallways.

We were discussing the ins and outs of the lurid case when the young wife presented a rather unusual theory. "That poor boy is very sick, of course, but I'm telling you if those girls had known a few simple things about human nature they probably wouldn't have died."

"Yeah," her husband quipped, "like karate?"

"No, seriously," she continued, "all they had to think about was love."

"Love?" we asked incredulously and almost in unison.

She went on to explain. "You see, I believe that one common trait every sick person has is that they never felt loved. Often they never have been really loved or their sickness prevents them from realizing that others care for them. Now the papers say that the girl who was saved by the passing policeman told the reporters that the murderer approached her very quietly. Here, let me read this part to you."

She read from the paper on her lap: " 'Hello,' he said. 'You're so pretty. Won't you talk to me a little?'

"Now how do you like that! 'Won't you talk to me a little'! I just don't think he started out with sinister intentions. And what did every single one of those girls do? They responded with a shriek—a horrible ear-piercing shriek as though the most hideous monster of the horror films was pouncing on them. Now, I don't say it's easy, but I'm convinced that if the girls had said, despite their inner trembling, 'I'd love to talk to you. You seem very nice too. But I'm late getting home now and a hall isn't a very friendly place to stand and talk. Let me give you my phone number and maybe we can make a date soon to go somewhere pleasant and get to know each other,' instead of hands raised up to strangle a frightened scream, a scream that to that sick man meant 'I hate you, you're ugly, I reject you,' I think there's a strong likelihood that the other approach would have thrown him off balance. Now I'm not talking through my hat. I had an experience when I was only sixteen that proves my point." Without too much coaxing the young woman launched into her own tale, which even her husband had never heard.

She had come home from school one day when she was fifteen or sixteen and apparently neglected to slam the front door hard enough for the latch to catch. She went to her bedroom in the back of the apartment to drop off her books and then made her way toward the front to have a snack in the kitchen.

"Something made me start as I passed the hall closet. There was someone crouched up against it as though they had just entered the apartment on my heels and then heard me coming back front and had no place to hide. My heart pounded like a trip hammer because what I saw out of the corner of my eye did little to reassure me. A boy not much older than I stood there. He was scrawny and wild-eyed, with that hungry look so common among disturbed, unhappy people. And clutched in his hand, his knuckles pressed white against it, was a long, shiny, open pocket knife. I don't know what made me react the way I did—instinct maybe, or his lonely eyes and white knuckles—but somehow I knew that he was just as afraid as I was.

"I knew somehow that the scream mounting up in my throat had to be squelched—that if I yelled I'd be as good as dead. It was like a nightmare, but somehow I managed to find my voice. It came out strained and very high.

" 'Hi, are you the delivery boy from the cleaners? I didn't hear you ring.'

"It was nonsensical and he knew it. Delivery boys just don't walk into people's apartments. But he had a second chance now to change his mind. His grip on the knife relaxed and his expression changed to a bewildered look.

" 'I'm no delivery boy,' he said. 'I came to rob the place.'

"Somehow I managed to laugh a friendly laugh. 'Oh, that's silly,' I said. 'I have no money and nobody keeps any around the house. Look, you seem like a nice guy. You must have some real troubles to act like this.'

"I had not mentioned the knife. I managed to keep my eyes off it, too. And as I watched his face, I could see it was working. His eyes softened and he looked even younger, almost as though he were about to cry. The knife folded almost by itself and slipped into his pocket.

"I pressed on. 'Come sit in the kitchen with me and have some milk and cake. Let's see if we can figure out some way to help you.' "

After that, of course, she had easy sailing. He followed her

in like a lamb and poured out his story. He had run away
from home in Pennsylvania because he had no real home, no
real family—no one, nothing. He had led a rejected, lonely
life. And those of us listening to the story were convinced
that it was highly likely that one act of "unlove," of rejection,
might have made his eyes narrow again, might have made
him raise up that knife . . . and . . . the young woman
wouldn't be in her twenties, vacationing in Florida with her
handsome young husband and telling us her experience.

She was careful not to tell him that she thought he was
sick. But she convinced him to go down to a family agency
listed in the phone book. She gave him carfare to get there
and he left—no thank yous—he left as quietly as he had come
and she firmly locked the door behind him and called the
family agency to fill them in on their visitor.

"He was gone," she continued, "and I was alive and safe.
Furthermore, I had helped him too."

The story impressed us. "Give love," she had said. "These
are rejected people. Shock them with love. They expect
another rejection. It could mean as much as your own life—if
you want to look at it selfishly."

It works just as well on the everyday level. A man who
decides to surprise his wife when she's been out shopping, by
preparing dinner, will reap rewards later.

How many times we've seen a man whose wife is confined
in the hospital, sitting alone in a cafeteria, sadly munching an
evening meal. After years of delicious dinners, his cook is
absent. The pots and pans are still there for the using; the
spices, the canned goods and recipe books are gathering dust
on the kitchen shelves. Somehow in his loneliness there is no
desire to learn to cook now—no one to compliment or criticize the first efforts.

But the man who learned to cope with the cookbook and

clatter of the pots and pans can not only save money from his often limited income but can even invite friends in for a home-cooked meal and avoid the depression of a mass-produced cafeteria dinner.

"What you do to others—
Others do to you"

Once a long time ago I met an insurance man who practiced the Golden Rule every moment of his life. His name was Vash Young. I was about thirty years old, and I had already purchased several life-insurance policies with different companies and with a heterogeneous list of benefits. When Vash approached me I told him I was loaded with insurance policies.

"I certainly don't want to load you with any more," said Vash. "You see, I don't *sell* insurance. I just try to *help* my friends—and I would like to *help* you if I can."

"Help me? How?" I said.

"If you will let me look over your policies for a few days, I will organize them for you. I'll give you a complete analysis of all the terms and conditions, the premiums, the dividends and accumulating cash values—so you will know at a glance exactly what you have."

Vash was so disarming in his manner that I accepted his suggestion. Several days later he handed me the most thorough report I had ever seen of my assets and obligations. I was most grateful, and especially so, because there was no pressure from Vash Young to sell me more insurance.

A few weeks later I called him on the telephone. "Vash," I said, "I have been studying that report. You told me you don't *sell* insurance. How about letting me *buy* some?"

For the next thirty years, until Vash Young passed away, he was "my insurance agent." I learned a wonderful lesson from Vash and especially from the inspiring book he wrote in his later years, called, *A Fortune to Share*. Like the world's great philosophers, Vash had discovered that the Golden Rule has a double edge.

"It is one of the most beautiful compensations of life," said Ralph Waldo Emerson, "that no man can sincerely try to help another without helping himself."

I have often shocked my friends with the paradoxical statement that *the most selfish people in the world are those who are continually helping others.*

Is there anything wrong with this kind of selfishness? If we find that little deeds of kindness pay enormous dividends, must we reject these rewards as something unworthy?

If we make a gesture of friendship deliberately and hopefully, expecting friendship in return, is our motivation less than noble?

Once, long ago, in a poetic mood, I expressed this philosophy in a verse, which I presume, like most romantic poetry, requires a bit of interpretation:

> "*Upward flight of arrows,*
> *How they soar*
> *Like playful swallows far above,*
> *Climbing, till they fly*
> *Right through the door*
> *Of that enchanted land called* LOVE."

This six-line verse, if understood and practiced faithfully by married couples would prevent 90 per cent of the divorces in this world. Let me explain. The first rule of nature is *survival*. "Only the fit survive." If a marriage, or any human relationship, is to survive, the participants must feel fit, worthy, important. When a husband says to his wife, "You look as pretty as the day I married you, this is an "arrow" shooting upward—a compliment, a sign of appreciation that generates a feeling of security. To assure a continuation of such compliments, the wife might say, "Aren't you sweet, dear, to tell me that. You know, I think you're a pretty nice guy yourself!"

And so the "upward flight of arrows" is set in motion, "climbing, 'till they fly right through the door of that enchanted land called LOVE." Is such an exchange of compliments, motivated by a desire for mutual "back-scratching," something to be condemned? Or is it a realistic practice of the Golden Rule?

> *"What you do to others—*
> *Others do to you"*

Most big business concerns go out of their way to give extra service beyond that which is usually expected. Department stores and restaurants, in particular, have discovered that customers appreciate little attentions. Service-station operators wipe off your windshield, check your tires and battery with no thought of a tip or gratuity. Many receptionists in small offices have adopted the practice of serving coffee to visitors as they wait for their appointments in the lobby.

Why shouldn't everyday people go out of their way to be courteous and helpful to friends and strangers alike, realizing full well the compensations that come from such acts of kindness? You can get what you want out of life by practicing the Golden Rule. If you hunger for appreciation, you can get it by giving it. If your soul cries out for friendship, you can surround yourself with friends in the same way. For this is the law of life, and never forget it:

"What you do to others—
Others do to you"

Here are ten ways to practice the Golden Rule—and all of them are guaranteed to pay priceless dividends:

1. When you enjoy a good dinner in a restaurant, tell the waiter. Ask him to pass your compliments along to the chef. He is probably proud of his cooking, but very few people go out of their way to let him know how good his food tastes.

2. When you buy a new suit of clothes and you try on coat after coat without making a choice, compliment the sales clerk on his patience. Let him know how much you appreciate his help and expert advice.

3. When your pastor preaches a particularly fine sermon, tell him how much it meant to you. Your words of appreciation are his greatest compensation for the time and thought and effort he put into the preparation of his sermon.

4. When you enjoy the music of a pianist or organist at dinner, walk over to the dais between numbers and let the fellow know how beautifully he played your favorite melodies. He will beam with appreciation for your thoughtfulness.

5. When the cashier at the supermarket punches out your enormous stack of purchases on the register, let her know that you admire her quick and nimble fingerwork. Ask her if she plays the piano. She is tired from standing on her feet all day long—and an unexpected compliment can do much to revive her.

6. When you particularly enjoy a book or a magazine

article, write a note of appreciation to the author. You will probably receive a reply that will warm your heart.

7. When you read an article or see a cartoon in a newspaper which you feel would be of interest to a friend or acquaintance, clip it out and send it to that person. Even if you do not get an answer, you will know that it was read with interest.

8. When a new neighbor moves into a home on your street, stop in and ask if there is anything you can do to help. Ask them over to your home for a highball or a glass of iced tea. They will never forget your welcome invitation—even if they don't take you up on it at the time.

9. When your barber cuts your hair in a manner which pleases you, don't fall asleep in the chair. Examine your haircut in the mirror—and tell the barber he is a real artist. The next haircut you get, you can be sure he will go all out to please you.

10. Always look on the positive side of service—even bad service. If the waiter in the restaurant is slow, notice why. See how many customers he has and note the sweat on his brow and his frantic haste. Perhaps then when he brings your coffee a little late, a little cold, you'll find yourself saying: "This is quite a busy, hard night for you. Maybe when you have a chance you'll hot this up a little." Instead of a barked "This coffee is ice cold. The service is lousy here."

This holds true for all service. The fireman who chops your door down to save your burning house deserves a thanks for whatever he's managed to save rather than a rebuke for the damage he did. The policeman who fails to find your stolen watch is not, after all, the thief. He deserves a thanks for trying. All this will come back to you somehow in the future. The police officer may keep an extra eye on your area; the waiter will rush to give you extra little services when he's not so busy.

The trick is to put yourself in the other fellow's shoes. Your criticism or silence will only bring nervousness and hostility; your understanding and patience can only bring you better relations, better service, lifetime friends.

CHAPTER 27

Do This—
and Young People Will
Like You Instantly

We are interested in others when they are
interested in us.

—PUBLIUS SYRUS

When our youngest son was a junior at Rollins College, I telephoned him a few days previous to his birthday and said, "Bob, how would you like to spend the weekend with your mother and me at Grand Bahama Island? Sort of a birthday present to you—and to us, too."

He accepted with enthusiasm. An hour later, Bob phoned us and said, "Do you mind if Penny comes along with us? You can chaperone."

We realized that we were being a little selfish in expecting our son to spend an entire weekend with his parents, so we said, "Great! Bring her. We'll meet you at the airport in Palm Beach."

On Saturday morning, as we approached the ticket desk of Mackey Airlines, we noticed a cluster of young people, at least twelve, with Bob and Penny. Bob greeted us with a grin. "Hi, folks," he said. "I want you to meet some friends from college. This thing has sure snowballed. When I told them we were going to Grand Bahama, they said, 'Terrific idea. Let's all go!'"

I must have looked thunderstruck, for Bob quickly assured me, *sotto voce,* that "these kids are on their own, Dad. They have their tickets and they made their own reservations for the hotel in West End."

"We're supposed to chaperone the whole gang?"

Bob gave me a tolerant look. "Dad, these kids are all married. They're seniors!" College life has changed since I went to school.

In the twenty-five-minute plane ride, Mrs. Legler and I commiserated in whispers. "Well, there goes our weekend. These college youngsters don't want us tagging along."

"So what! We'll sit by the pool and enjoy ourselves. At least, for Bob's sake, let's be agreeable and show them that his parents aren't old fuddy-duddies."

The weekend at Grand Bahama turned out to be one of the most heart-warming experiences of our lifetime. Bob's friends accepted us as equals, not as elders. We were "Henry" and "Fran," not "Mr. and Mrs. Legler"—not "Uncle Henry and Aunt Fran," as it might have been a few years previous. We sat on the floor of their bedrooms, sharing their smuggled-in sandwiches and cans of cold corned beef, laughing at their off-beat stories, even telling some of our own, which must have given them a mild sense of shock. On Saturday night they insisted, against our feeble protests, that we join them in a tour of the local night clubs to watch the limbo exhibitions, to dance to the blaring music of the native combos and to drink bottle after bottle of Bahamian beer. For a little while I felt like a college student on a bender—young, gay and slightly frivolous. That rewarding weekend taught me how to bridge the gap between generations. And in doing so I erased thirty years from my age, at least for a few happy moments.

If you are traveling through your forties, fifties, or sixties at a pace that seems frighteningly fast, may I suggest, strictly for the rejuvenizing effect, the cultivation of some younger friends. If a couple, twenty-five years your junior, moves into the house next door, invite them over for dinner. Offer them a drink. Suggest a game of cards during the evening—but don't press it if they are not in the mood. Steer the conversation *their* way, not *yours*. Avoid reminiscences. And don't tell bewhiskered jokes that were "belly laughs" in your day. They may not be so funny to a younger generation. You may be kidding only yourself with this updated approach, but what's the difference if you yourself believe it? You will find that self-deception, skillfully practiced, is better than brandy for creating euphoria. The ability to fool yourself becomes, in later years, an anaesthetic that makes old age painless and palatable.

As you cultivate the companionship of younger people you will find to your surprise that your contemporaries suddenly seem much older than you are. You begin to think younger, act younger and even feel younger. You are less exposed to the complaints and irascibilities of older people. By no means abandon friends of your own age. Just refuse to adopt the mannerisms and mores of the elderly.

As James Garfield once said, *"If wrinkles must be written upon our brows, let them not be written upon the heart. The spirit should not grow old."*

Winning the friendship of younger people is an art that requires preparation and practice. The best way to begin is to forget your age. Think like a forty-year-old. Look forward instead of backward. Never talk about the past. Read current books. Study modern life in all its facets—sports, theater, pop art, fashions, business, politics, travel. Keep yourself informed so you can talk about the topics of today—in the terms and vernacular of today. Let the enthusiasm in your voice and the sparkle in your eyes belie your age.

"The business of being a likeable personality," says Lelord Kordel, author of *How to Make People Like You,* "resolves itself into being agreeable instead of disagreeable, gracious instead of rude, friendly instead of aloof, responsive, cheerful, and possessed of an easy, outgoing confidence and naturalness of manner." I can think of no better attitude to win the friendship of a younger generation.

One word of caution: Meeting youth on its own terms involves certain risks if carried to extremes. Playing three sets of tennis or thirty-six holes of golf is a senseless way to prove how young you are. I recall a venerable member of our country club whose stamina at sixty-eight never ceased to astonish his fellow golfers until one hot afternoon in late July he collapsed on the twenty-seventh tee, never to play again.

There is much talk today of eradicating the barriers that exist between races, colors and creeds. While we are purging our prejudices, why not include the barrier of age, which divides generation from generation? The building of age distinctions often goes back to childhood. When my daughter, Joanne, was in elementary school many years ago, she used to walk home with a boy who lived in our neighborhood. I noticed them one day as they trudged along the sidewalk, Edward several paces ahead, while my daughter seemed to be deliberately tagging along behind him. That evening I said, "Joanne, I saw you walking home with Edward today."

She said, "I wasn't walking *with him.* I was walking *behind him.* He won't let me walk *with him.*"

"Why not?"

"Because he's two years older, he makes me walk behind him."

How true today of people in their sixties, who feel a smug complacency when comparing themselves with thirty- or forty-year-old neighbors. The pompous mediocrity of age, looking down with intolerance on the elbowing self-conceit of youth. Bigotry masquerading as status.

If each could only realize the wondrous benefits that might come from a melding of viewpoints, from an open mind and an open heart, from patience and humility, this would be a better and a wiser world.

CHAPTER 28

How to Ask Questions
People Enjoy Answering

*Talk to a man about himself and he will
listen for hours.*

—BENJAMIN DISRAELI

I have never thought of myself as a salesman. So when I decided to open up the pages of my *Florida Home Owners' Guide* to advertisers, I hired a man who had been touted as an expert. At the end of a month his order book was still filled with blank pages.

"I just don't understand it," he told me. "I have called on more than one hundred prospects. Gave each one of them the full treatment, but didn't get a single order. They all think it is a fine book, but they say, 'The budget is already spent,' or 'See me next year.' Each one has a different excuse."

In six weeks our book was scheduled to go to press. I was worried. I kept thinking about the huge printing bill—without advertising revenue to meet it. I had just finished reading Dale Carnegie's stimulating book *How to Win Friends and Influence People*. I wondered if I could influence the people who okayed advertising contracts in the smooth and easy manner Mr. Carnegie described.

The next morning, bright and early, I called on Malcolm McDonald, Vice President in Charge of Advertising of the Florida Power and Light Company. "I can only give you a few minutes," he said. "Besides, your man called on me a few days ago. Sorry I had to tell him that we've hit the bottom of the barrel on our advertising budget."

"Yes, I know, and I appreciate the time you spent with him," I said. "I just want to ask you a couple of questions. If you looked at our book you probably saw the chapter on 'Hurricanes.' Until Cleo hit this area, I had no idea of the important role of the Power and Light Company during a bad storm. I understand you had more than a thousand linesmen working night and day to mend the lines and restore power."

"We had three thousand men on the job," said Mr. McDonald. "Called them in from all over Florida. Even borrowed crews from other utility companies in Alabama and Georgia."

"How in the world can you locate a break in the line?" I asked with genuine enthusiasm. "There must have been hundreds of power lines knocked out by falling trees, or just blown down by the wind."

So started a onesided conversation that lasted an hour and a half. I shot question after question at Malcolm McDonald—but he needed no prodding. He had spent a lifetime with the Florida Power and Light Company, and this was an opportunity for him to discourse at length on the efficiency and vast facilities of the organization. I was spellbound. It was a fascinating story and completely new to me.

As we shook hands I promised to stop in again for a chat the next time I was in Miami. "Say, Legler," said Mr. McDonald, "leave me one of your order blanks. I think we can find enough in the budget to give you a page ad."

That taught me a lesson. I had not mentioned my book. I

had merely followed Dale Carnegie's advice, *"Encourage the other fellow to talk about his interests. Be a good listener."*

During the next six weeks I sold forty-seven pages of advertising, and we went to press with our full quota of ads. I would like to correct that statement. I didn't *sell* forty-seven. All I did was ask questions about "the other fellow's business," and the signed orders dropped in my lap. I asked Hubert Heilman of the famous Heilman's Restaurant how he managed to serve the finest-tasting food in town. Was it the skill of his chef? Was it the quality of the food he purchased? Was it the seasoning? Was it the atmosphere of the restaurant? Hubert sat at my table for forty-five minutes and finally invited me to inspect his kitchens and meet his head chef, who, by the way, Mr. Heilman proudly boasted, "spends six weeks each summer at a master school for chefs, freshening up on his techniques of cookery." I should mention, of course, that Heilman's Restaurant took a full-page advertisement in our book. And so did Alcoa Aluminum Screens, North American Van Lines, the Florida National Banks and many other important companies.

At this point you are probably saying, "This is good advice for a salesman, but what has it to do with me? I'm retired! I have nothing to sell." Oh, yes you have! You want friends. You need friends. Without them, retirement can be a bitter and lonely experience. And the surest way to surround yourself with congenial companions is to talk to people about the things they treasure most.

Let me give you an example. The other day my wife and I were invited, along with a dozen other people, to a supper party aboard a sleek fifty-foot cruiser, vintage unknown. About fifteen years old, I guessed. As we churned up the Intracoastal Waterway I noticed that our host, Jay Adams, was sitting aloft on the flying bridge—all alone—piloting the boat. I climbed up and sat beside him. I knew Jay only casually, but I had heard that boats were his hobby. That was the only clue I needed.

"Diesels?" I asked for openers.

"No," he said. "A couple of Chrysler 250s. I installed them myself."

"You're kidding! *You* installed them?"

"Took me a month. I'm crazy about boats."

"How long have you owned the *Half Moon?*"

"Less than a year. You should have seen it when I bought it. A real heap."

"It's a beauty now," I said. "What did you do to it?"

"I put in all new fittings. New galley. Redesigned the main cabin. New engines, like I said. And I built this flying bridge from scratch."

"Isn't that kind of overhauling terribly expensive?"

"Oh, I do all the work myself."

I looked at my host with new respect. "Is this your first boat?" I asked.

"This is Number Six! I buy 'em, repair 'em, then sell 'em. It's my retirement hobby. Gives me something to do."

An hour later, as we heaved anchor, Jay and I were still talking about the *Half Moon.* When we said goodbye later that evening, Jay got me aside and said, "Would you and Fran care to go with Mary and me—just the four of us—on a weekend cruise down in the Keys?"

"Wonderful," I said. "Name the date!"

"Anybody who loves boats like you do," said Jay, "will be good company."

Not once during the evening had I mentioned that I loved boats, but the inference was clear. Otherwise, why would I have listened with rapt attention while Jay expounded on the

technical problems of building a flying bridge on a boat that
had no flying bridge?

There is an old saying, "To be interesting, be interested."
I would like to implement it! "To make friends, ask people
questions they enjoy answering." Always remember that the
person you are talking to is vastly more interested in his own
achievements and his own problems than he is in your
achievements and your problems. If he is an avid bridge
player and you are a golfer, he would far rather tell you, trick
by trick, about the grand slam he made than to have you tell
him about the birdie you sank from a trap. Of course, the
habit of asking questions that people enjoy answering does
not always lead to a lasting friendship, as I discovered not
long ago.

I started a conversation one day with a neighbor who had
recently moved into our community, and after discovering
that he had spent many years in the manufacture of printing
inks, I made the impulsive mistake of asking, "Tell me,
Ralph, how do they achieve the different basic colors? What
chemicals do they use?"

My question was good for forty-five minutes of textbook
chemistry. I realized then and there that Ralph was an
insufferable bore and that my ingenious method of winning
friends must be used with discrimination.

Of course, the technique of asking qustions can be rewarding, too, if your protagonist happens to have been a test
pilot, or a ship's captain, or a portrait painter, or a foreign
correspondent. When you are prospecting for new friends,
these are the rare finds that stand out like gold nuggets.

Every night at sundown I walk my poodle dog a half mile
or so. One evening I stopped to chat with an elderly man who
was pruning his hibiscus hedge. I introduced myself and he
said his name was "Walter Hinton."

"Walter Hinton?" I said. "Where have I heard that name before? It was a long time ago. Help me out!"

There was a tired smile on Mr. Hinton's face as he said, "I didn't think anybody remembered. I flew the ocean in a plane once. Got quite a lot of publicity."

"Of course!" I said. "That was nearly two years before Charles Lindbergh flew to Paris in *The Spirit of St. Louis.* I can still see the big banner headline in *The New York Times.*"

Walter Hinton beamed.

"Didn't you stop at Bermuda and the Azores?" I asked.

"You have a good memory," he said, and his voice was warm with appreciation. "Most people today have never even heard of Charles Levine and Wiley Post and Chamberlain and the other old-time fliers."

A half hour later the sun had set and I was still reminiscing with Walter Hinton about his flying exploits of nearly forty years ago.

The surest way to make friends is to talk in terms of the other person's interests. The surest way to lose friends is to talk incessantly about yourself.

This advice seems obvious, yet not one person in a thousand follows it. Most of us are so wrapped up in our own self-importance that we are seldom willing to listen to anyone for long. We don't even wait for the other fellow to finish what he is talking about, but interrupt him in the middle of a sentence.

Remember, if you want to make friends, encourage people to talk about themselves. Cultivate the priceless habit of asking questions—questions people enjoy answering.

CHAPTER 29

A Simple Formula
for Remembering Names and Faces

Remember my name and you add to my
feeling of importance.

—DALE CARNEGIE

One month after we moved into our retirement home in the village of Sea Ranch Lakes, we were invited to a cocktail party at the community beach club. It seemed like a splendid opportunity to get acquainted with our new neighbors, and as we milled around, our hostess introduced us to dozens of interesting people. Later I said to Mrs. Legler, "Do you remember the name of that doctor and his wife? They were so nice. Dr. Burton, I believe."

"It was Dr. Mertin," she said, then contradicted herself. "No, it was Dr. Turton. I remember now, because when we were introduced it sounded like Dr. Turtle!"

"That big fellow," I said. "What was his name? Stella? Wasn't that it? His wife was from Dallas. That's how I happened to remember. Stella Dallas!"

Out of that entire gathering of more than one hundred people, I suddenly realized that I had remembered only one name. A poor start for making new friends.

A few weeks later I attended a Rotary Club luncheon where the guest speaker was Robert H. Nutt, author and teacher of the famous memory system used by the sales staffs of many large corporations. As a preliminary to Mr. Nutt's talk, the chairman called out the names of 150 guests at the luncheon and each one stood up as his name was called. Whereupon Mr. Nutt proceeded to astound his audience by calling out the names of all 150, correctly, not in the same order but at random, pointing to each person as he identified him by name.

I became so intrigued by this phenomenal demonstration of memory power that I drove to the nearest bookstore the moment the luncheon was over and purchased a copy of *How to Remember Names and Faces* by Robert H. Nutt. His system was so simple and easy to apply that within a few days I found myself able to meet six or eight people at once and later call them by name with no conscious effort.

At the next beach-club party I remembered the first and last names of nearly twenty people—all total strangers. Amazingly enough, when I called them by name they were no longer strangers but friends. "Good night, Grace and Don. It's been a real pleasure talking with you. Let's plan on getting together soon." And Grace and Don, not to mention fifteen other couples, beamed with warmth and appreciation when they realized that I had remembered their names.

The simplest, most obvious and most effective way to make new friends is to call people by their first names, yet how many of us do it? More often, when we are introduced to a stranger, we talk for a few minutes and then cannot even remember his name when we say goodbye. Most of us are not willing to take the time and energy necessary to fix names indelibly in our minds.

Professor William James once said, "The deepest principle in human nature is the craving to be appreciated." Every one of us hungers for the approval of those with whom we come in contact. The quickest way to let others know that you appreciate their importance is to call them by name. Always remember, the most soothing, comforting music in the world is the sound of your own name on the lips of another person.

Now it is not my purpose to disclose the professional secrets of the experts who perform their prodigious feats of memory before audiences. Nor do I think you are interested in memorizing a series of code words and key numbers used by the authors of these techniques as a part of their system. The sole purpose of including a chapter on "Remembering Names" is to make it, perhaps, a little easier for you to acquire the warmth of new contacts and new friends in your retirement years.

So let us skip over the intensive training techniques necessary to produce a miraculous memory and just concentrate on a few simple devices that will enable you to recall the names of people you meet from time to time.

Never again will you be compelled to confess, "Your face is familiar but I just can't seem to remember your name." Nothing you might say could be more hurtful. In effect, such an apology really means, "You didn't make enough of an impression for me to remember your name."

I am sure that memory experts will criticize my formula as an oversimplification. Yet I will guarantee that if you practice these three simple rules, you will gradually begin to remember the names of people you meet and people you would like to remember:

Rule Number One: *Be sure to get the name right!* As you are introduced, if your host mumbles the name indistinctly, *now* is the time to ask him to repeat it, not later. If he says, "May I present Harry Blandings," and you think he said "Bannings" or "Brandon" or "Bandon," ask him to repeat it.

Ask him to spell it and repeat it out loud, "B-l-a-n-d-i-n-g-s—is that correct, Mr. Blandings?" Believe me, Harry will be flattered that you are so insistent on getting his name straight.

Rule Number Two: *Repeat the name over and over again as you talk to Mr. Blandings.* "Do you live here year round, Mr. Blandings?" . . . "We are planning on a little vacation in Jamaica, Mr. Blandings." . . . "By the way, are you related to George Blandings? No? George Blandings was a neighbor of mine for many years." Repetition will help to stamp the name indelibly in your memory.

Rule Number Three: *Associate the name with something familiar.* This takes concentration and imagination, but if you make a game out of it, you will find it not only amusing but a foolproof way to remember his name.

Study your new acquaintance's features. Photograph them mentally. Large nose? Blue eyes? Big ears? Cleft in his chin? Mustache? Scar? Deep lines around his mouth? Bald? White-haired?

Then let your imagination go to work. What does the name "Blandings" suggest? Go through a mental process something like this. "Mr. Blandings? Didn't you build a dream home? No, that was Cary Grant. A movie, *Mr. Blandings Builds His Dream House.* You don't look like Cary Grant, Harry Blandings. Of course, Cary and Harry rhyme. But you must be at least sixty-five and you have white hair. Maybe you would like to build a dream house, Mr. Blandings, even though you are not the Mr. Blandings that built the dream house."

If this sounds silly, it is meant to be. The sillier it is, the easier to remember. Every time you look at Mr. Blandings you will think of Cary Grant and that amusing motion picture. And you will probably say over and over to yourself, "Harry-Cary, Harry-Cary, Harry-Cary." Okay! Now you won't forget Harry Blandings!

This form of mental gymnastics is guaranteed to stamp a name vividly in your memory. Some names lend themselves to pictorial association more easily than others. The system is simple. Use it only on the names of people you would like to remember, people whose friendship you would like to cultivate. Don't bother trying to remember the names of dull people. Why tax your memory?

I have selected at random a few names from the telephone book to illustrate the formula. Suppose you were to be introduced to these people at a party, and they impressed you enough to prompt you to make a real effort to remember their names. Here is the mental process you might go through to make each one unforgettable. Let your imagination run wild. The more ridiculous the association, the easier to remember. You have just met:

Jim Dressing. Picture Jim sitting on the floor, stark naked, pulling up his pants. He puts on a shirt, socks, shoes. He is *dressing!* Imagine, Jim Dressing came to the party undressed, and now he is dressing—right there in front of everybody. Jim Dressing. How shocking can you get, Jim Dressing?

Godfrey Betz. Imagine Godfrey as Arthur Godfrey with a huge roll of hundred-dollar bills in his hand, peeling them off one by one, throwing them on the floor. Godfrey Betz on the races. Godfrey Betz on the crap game. Godfrey Betz on the ball game. Godfrey Betz on anything. And he always wins, even though the odds are against him. That's why Godfrey Betz. Godfrey Betz that you won't forget his name. And you won't if you repeat Godfrey Betz often enough!

Clarence Snider. What a silly man! Clarence Snider, with a bottle of Snider's catsup in his hand. And he is pouring that Snider's catsup over his head. The gooey red catsup is matted in Snider's hair, running down over Snider's ears, dripping onto Snider's coat. What are you trying to do, Clarence Snider? Advertise Snider's catsup? Only a man with a ridiculous name like Clarence would do such a thing. Now you are pouring Snider's catsup on my head, Clarence Snider. Why don't you pour Snider's on a hamburger, where it belongs. Believe me, I'll never forget you, Clarence Snider!

Tom Mesick. What was the name, please? Tom Mesick? Did you say "Me sick"? You do look sick! Is that all you can say, "Me sick, me sick, me sick"? Shall I call a doctor, Tom? Why don't you go to the bathroom and throw up, Tom Mesick? Maybe you would feel better. Stop groaning, Tom Mesick. Stop saying, "Me sick." You're not an Indian, because an Indian has a red face and you have a green face. Because you're sick, Tom Mesick. I'm beginning to feel a little sick myself. Me sick? What am I saying!

Fred Musselman. So your name is Musselman? You don't look that strong, Fred Musselman. Prove it. Take off your coat, Musselman, and show us those bulging muscles. Wow! You *are* a Musselman, Fred Musselman! Let me feel your muscles, Mr. Musselman! By golly. You're strong. You could lift 1,000 pounds. Ever think of joining the circus? You would be a great Musselman, Fred. And everybody would remember that your name is Fred Musselman!

Harry Copple. When you are introduced to Harry Copple, vividly picture him in a policeman's uniform. He's a cop. Harry the Copple get you! Drive your car over twenty-five miles an hour, and Harry the Copple arrest you. Park beside a hydrant, and Harry the Copple arrest you. No matter what you do, Harry the Copple throw you in jail. Watch out for

Harry. Because Harry the Copple arrest you for anything you do. And you'll never forget a man like that!

Charlie Sella. What a slick salesman! You should see Charlie Sella house! Or Charlie Sella car! He's the world's greatest salesman. Just watch Charlie Sella diamond necklace. Or Charlie Sella big office building. When you have seen Charlie Sella proposition, you won't forget him.

Richard Dunkleberg. May I call you Dick? It is easy to remember your name, Dick Dunkleberg. D.D. If I were your nephew, I would call you Uncle Dunkleberg, Dick Dunkleberg. Do you dunk your doughnuts in coffee, Uncle Dunkleberg? I'll certainly remember you every time I drink coffee, Dick Dunkleberg.

It's a simple formula and remarkably effective. Just remember the three rules that help you to remember names:

1. Be sure to spell out the name correctly!

2. Repeat it over and over!

3. Associate the name with something familiar or something ridiculous.

Just for the fun of it, here are ten names picked at random. Practice the above formula with these names. You will be amazed how vividly the names will print themselves in your memory.

EDWARD BOWER

WALTER ROBBIN

ARTHUR FOXX

CLYDE WHITEHOUSE

DAISY FIELD

MAJOR AIKEN

HARRY MANTLE

ROBERT SAVAGE

RUSSELL COFFIN

NORMAN KING

CHAPTER 30

Thirty-four Ways to
Make Your Wife Love You

How do I love thee? Let me count the ways.
—ELIZABETH BARRETT BROWNING

I would like to propose an amendment to the marraige vows which, in my opinion, would have a profound effect on lowering the present divorce rate.

Whether the ceremony is performed by a clergyman, a priest or a rabbi, this, in essence, is the pledge asked of the bride and the bridegroom just before they are pronounced man and wife:

> "Do you, Katherine, take Kenneth to be your lawfully wedded husband, to have and to hold from this day forward, for better, for worse, for richer, for poorer, in sickness and in health, to love, to honor and to cherish, as long as you both shall live?"

With restrained reverence and a sincerity becoming the seriousness of this great moment in their lives, both Katherine and Kenneth say, "I do." Yet as time goes by the sacred vows are too often forgotten, as misunderstandings, bickerings, heartaches, tears, bitternesses and jealousies creep in, eventually to break down what promised to be a happy marriage. Perhaps my suggested amendment would also be forgotten.

At least it might serve to point up one of the primary causes of conflict in marital life.

With deep respect for the authors of the marriage vows, I suggest eliminating the words "to cherish," since this solemn pledge is amply covered by the words "to love." Instead, I would substitute the phrase "and never to criticize."

Imagine the stunning effect of those four words, *and never to criticize,* uttered with sanctity and with dignity by the pastors and the priests and the rabbis in ten thousand churches and temples across the nation.

> "Do you, Katherine, take Kenneth to be your lawfully wedded husband, to have and to hold from this day forward, for better, for worse, for richer, for poorer, in sickness and in health, to love, to honor, *and never to criticize,* as long as you both shall live?"

A study of *Psychological Factors in Marital Happiness,* by Lewis M. Terman, lists the grievances husbands and wives each had concerning their mate. And high among them, for both sexes, was the complaint, "My wife constantly criticizes me!" "My husband constantly criticizes me!" Sometimes it was expressed as "nagging," or "complaining," or "not showing affection."

Dorothy Dix, for many years a leading authority on the causes of marital unhappiness, once declared that "more than fifty per cent of all marriages are failures," and she gave as a primary reason "criticism—futile, heartbreaking criticism." "It is amazing but true," said Dorothy Dix, "that practically the only people who ever say mean, insulting-sounding things to us are those of our own households."

The late Dale Carnegie made a similar comment in his famous book *How to Win Friends and Influence People.* Mr.

Carnegie said, "Many men who would not dream of speaking sharply to a customer, or even to their partners in business, think nothing of barking at their wives. Yet, for their personal happiness, marriage is far more important to them, far more vital, than business. . . . It is only the members of our own family, those who are nearest and dearest to us, that we dare insult for trivial faults."

Criticism is the cancer that destroys love. It ruffles pride. Rouses resentment. Puts a person on the defensive. If this is true in the early years of marriage, think how much more corrosive criticism can be in the years of retirement. The husband, suddenly deprived of his business importance, is apt to be more sensitive to criticism than he normally would be. The wife, suddenly confronted with an "intruder" in her household, is apt to be more critical of her husband's attitudes and mannerisms. Trifles become tremendous. Irritations become an allergy. Gentle reminders give way to venomous nagging. And if the source of the trouble is an everyday occurrence, recrimination becomes chronic. The fact that the offense is petty makes it more difficult to find a rational solution. The result can be a purgatory of bickering, agonizing to their friends and degrading to themselves.

There are several retired couples whose company I deliberately avoid because of their petulant gibes. The wife will interrupt her husband to say, "Good heavens, you're not going to tell that old story again!" And the husband, with mock politeness, will retort, "My dear, will you please keep that loud-speaker of yours turned off for about three minutes —if possible." Or the wife will say, as she climbs into the back seat of their automobile, "If Harry is going to drive, you had better fasten your seat belts." And Harry will sing out, "O.K., dear, tell 'em how you got that dent in the front fender!"

This sort of pernicious repartee is all too common among married couples in their middle sixties. Their sarcasms are tempered with a perverted sense of humor, like a fencing foil with a button on the tip. Each thrust can sting, yet cannot cause a mortal wound. All too clearly their dueling says, "It's too late for a divorce, so we're making the best of it!" (Or the worst of it!)

For some couples, a benign sense of humor provides an outlet. "But humor must be handled with care, or it explodes," cautions Robert O. Blood, Jr., in his understanding book *Marriage*. "When the joker's motivation is hostile, humor easily turns into sarcasm more barbed than open criticism. Moreover," says Mr. Blood, "an insecure spouse may not be able to take even the mildest ribbing. Successful use of humor to reduce tension depends on whether the couple can laugh *together* about their 'terrible little problem,' or whether the problem spouse feels he is being laughed *at.*"

Do you recall the delightful television series starring Jackie Gleason and Audrey Meadows a few years ago? It was called "The Honeymooners," and almost invariably, in the final fade-out, the fat bus driver, Ralph Kramden, would acknowledge his false pride by embracing his wife, Alice. And as they laughed heartily together, he would say affectionately, "Baby, you're *the greatest.*" What a wonderful lesson for married people of all ages!

I know a married couple with a rare sense of humor who solved their differences by a simple device that avoided a head-on clash. They discovered that criticism usually gives way to nagging. So by mutual agreement they hung a card on the back of the closet door marked, GRIEVANCES—HIS AND HERS. Under the card they attached a pencil that dangled on a chain, and whenever one or the other developed an annoying habit, the spouse would enter his complaint, tactfully and politely. At the end of the first week, the card looked like this:

Grievances

HIS

Would you mind, sweetie, not using my safety razor?

Please don't wrap garbage in the sport section until I'm finished with it. The paper, I mean, not the garbage!

HERS

Please put cap on toothpaste!

Drop soiled shorts in the laundry basket, dear. *Not on the bathroom floor!*

You need a haircut, darling! One more week and they'll be calling you "Hippie."

The system worked. They laughed together at their grievances and, as a result, each made a sincere effort to please the other.

"Trivialities are the cause of most unhappy marriages," says Judge Joseph Sabbath of Chicago, who has reviewed some 40,000 marital disputes and reconciled 2,000 couples. "A simple thing such as a wife's waving goodbye to her husband when he goes to work in the morning would avert a good many divorces."

Little attentions are even more important to a woman— such trifles as remembering a birthday with a bunch of flowers, or a simple little gift—even an unexpected greeting card. How long has it been since you telephoned your wife in the middle of the day and said, "No reason for calling, dear. Just wanted to let you know I'm thinking about you."

Too many men underestimate the value of these small, everyday attentions. About three years ago I made a heroic effort to please my wife with an unexpected gesture—and it backfired in a most amusing way. One morning about 7 A.M. I left my house early to get in a little extra work that had piled up in my retirement office. My wife was still sleeping, so I scrawled a note and put it on the kitchen table under the memo pad. Just for the fun of it, I wrote it in rhyme, the kind of doggerel that had poured off my pen in some 5,000 radio commercials of a bygone day. As near as I can remember, this was the note:

> Fran dear—
> Though I boiled my own eggs and
> I fried my own bacon,
> I want you to know that
> I don't feel forsaken!
> > I love you—H.

At nine o'clock my telephone rang. "That was the cutest note! Do you mind if I show it to the girls? I'm having them over for bridge today."

The next morning I departed at eight o'clock. Again, my wife was asleep, so I scratched out another jingle and left it on the kitchen table. This was a real challenge. I had to top yesterday's effort. And thus began a series of early-morning "love letters," which, if not as idyllic as the love letters of Robert Browning to his wife, Elizabeth Barrett Browning, were appreciated very much, I feel sure.

I mentioned earlier that the gesture backfired. You see, my wife soon discovered that if she got up to make my breakfast, there was no occasion for a note. What a wonderful excuse for sleeping late! But my sentimental jingles paid dividends in a hundred ways. Our dinners began to improve. And our dispositions. Gradually a new bond of affection was born between us. Today, my notes, totaling more than one thousand, are as integral a part of the morning ritual as brushing my teeth.

Two thousand years ago Marcus Aurelius, stoic philosopher of ancient Rome, said, "Very little is needed to make a happy life." Today his words could be paraphrased. "Very little is needed to make a happy *wife.*"

Once again, to quote Dorothy Dix, "Although a contented wife and a happy home mean more to a man than a million dollars, not one husband in a hundred ever gives serious thought or honest effort to make his marriage a success. Women can never understand why their husbands refuse to handle them diplomatically, when it would be money in their pockets to use the velvet glove instead of the strong-arm method."

There is a simple prescription for a marital headache that works better than aspirin. I wish I could put it up in capsule form. I would give it away *free* in carload lots and advertise it like this:

A Sure Cure for Sick Marriages
"LEGLER'S CHOCOLATE-COATED COMPLIMENTS"
Guaranteed To Be Sincere—
For Best Results—Use Often

Please do not be misled by the expression "chocolate-coated." It does not mean flattery. It only means: *Say Something Nice.*

If your wife cooks a tasty dinner, tell her how good it is. She may get tired of cooking dinners, but she will never get tired of sincere compliments. Honest appreciation is one of life's greatest rewards—to the *giver* as well as to the *receiver.*

For a husband or a wife to "say something nice" is another way to say "I love you."

No matter how bruised and battered a marriage has become, it can be repaired and refurbished, repainted and polished and oiled until it runs like new with this simple three-word formula—SAY SOMETHING NICE. If you have forgotten how, try these on for size:

34 WAYS TO SAY "I LOVE YOU"
FOR THE HUSBAND

1. "I'm not kidding—that dress does something for you."

2. "I didn't think I was hungry—but this dinner sure tastes good."

3. "You made it yourself? I don't believe it! Why, it's simply beautiful!"

4. "I like that perfume. What's the name of it?"

5. "Dye your hair if you like, but frankly, I think those gray streaks give you a very distinguished look."

6. "Thanks, honey, for cleaning out my closet. I'll try to keep it neater."

7. "I phoned because it looks as if I'll be a half hour later than I thought. I didn't want to worry you."

8. "You know something—I'm lucky I married you."

9. "I just happened to see it in that gift-store window, and I thought you'd like it."

10. "What do you say we go out for dinner tonight—just the two of us?"

11. "Hey! My favorite dessert! Thanks for remembering!"

12. "You were the prettiest gal at the party tonight!"

13. "Believe me, the more I see of other women, the more I appreciate you."

14. "Have you been dieting? You look thinner!"

15. "Those new draperies are pretty. You have good taste, dear."

16. "I'll be glad to help you with the shopping—if you want me to."

17. "By the way, did I ever think to tell you that I love you?"

FOR THE WIFE

1. "I never feel nervous when you're driving."

2. "If you say so, it's O.K. with me. I trust your judgment."

3. "You handled that beautifully. I would have lost my temper."

4. "Congratulations on that grand slam. You played a terrific game tonight."

5. "You look as young today as you did ten years ago."

6. "I need your advice. What do you think I ought to do?"

7. "That sports coat looks good on you. Makes you look younger."

8. "I don't care what the neighbors say. I'm much more interested in *your* opinion."

9. "Don't worry, dear. We can get along on less if we have to."

10. "You know something? I'd love to play golf with you sometime—if you'll put up with me."

11. "You were the nicest-looking man at the party tonight."

12. "Switch it to Channel Seven if you like. I know that's your favorite program."

13. "You didn't think I'd forget your birthday, did you?"

14. "I wish you would go into politics, dear. Believe me, I'd vote for you!"

15. "You were so right when you warned me about Aunt Janie! I had a letter from her today, and she had the nerve to ask me if . . ."

16. "Take it easy, honey! I want you around the campus for a long, long time."

17. "You know something? You're a nice guy!"

Getting started is probably the hardest part of all. If up until recently your marriage was reasonably congenial, it may only be a problem of going back to good habits and discarding bad ones. But all too many couples have been at it for years. A long-waged war of words has set in and is now reaching its vitriolic climax. If no new grievances have appeared, forty-year-old grudges are still a subject of daily battling.

A young friend of mine described a weekend she and her husband spent at a summer cottage with her parents. Quarters were close, the weather was mostly rainy, and by the time they returned home they felt "as if we had spent a month in an insane asylum."

"Mother and Dad carped at each other a lot when I was growing up," she confided, "and it was awful." They are both swell people, *by themselves.* The sad thing is that deep down they really love each other, I think, but neither one will end the battle. They have everything in common; enough money set aside to live better than comfortably; they travel and have a summer place and a nice city apartment. But they seem to be always miserable. It's the spite and criticism that goes on all the time. Dad carves the roast, and Mom can't resist comment on what a rotten carver he is. Then she launches into the story of the time when he ruined a beautiful turkey in front of some very important guests. That's twenty-five years ago! And she mentions it at least once a week when he carves. He used to keep quiet, but now he uses his new approach. 'That's right!' he says in a pseudo-sarcastic tone. 'I'm nothing but a failure!'

"A failure!" my friend continued. "Why, he sent three kids through college and Mom never had to work a day in her life. She always had help in the house and he managed to keep things going even during the worst depression years.

"When he took us out for a ride, *he* started it. For a change she didn't make any remarks, and you'd think he missed it! Or maybe he figured he'd beat her to the punch. 'Well,' he said, 'I suppose your mother told you that you were in danger. I've a touch of Parkinson's, you know, and she thinks it's damaged my IQ!'

"At that point Mother happily reminded him of the night ten years ago when he ran over a cat, and the ticket he'd gotten twenty-nine years before for going the wrong way on a one-way street. The fact that he had been driving for forty years without a real accident was never mentioned, needless to say."

This couple is, of course, an extreme example. But I suspect that many others exist who carp at each other in a similar vein. All of their disappointments and frustrations are taken out on one another, instead of joining together to overcome obstacles.

The hardest task is reversing the situation. Somebody has to start, and although both may secretly long to, pride and stubbornness keep the cancer growing. If you are a partner in such a situation, the only way to change it is, secretly, to begin. If you announce your intentions, a new round of brickbats can begin flying in both directions.

Spend a "normal" day with your spouse and at the end of that day make up a list of the starting points of each bitter exchange. It might look something like this:

SHE: So it's ten o'clock! You slept late as usual.

HE: It's about time, isn't it? For twenty years I left the house at the crack of dawn with you soundly snoring.

SHE: *Me* snore!

And on and on!

Later:

HE: Well, it's about lunchtime and it's Tuesday. Ten dollars says there's chicken chow mein for lunch, unless I'm wrong and it's Wednesday, then it's tunafish salad. . . . Ah, well, variety is the spice of life!

SHE: Be glad I make anything! How many times since we're married have you taken me out to lunch?

And on and on!

Now make a determined effort to change the course of these daily bouts the very next day. Perhaps it might work out like this:

SHE: Hi, honey! I'm about to have a second cup of coffee. How's about joining me and hearing the ten-o'clock news?

HE: ????

Later:

SHE: Surprise, honey! I'm getting bored with my own cooking. I've something new for lunch—it's called shrimp à la casa.

HE: Great! Maybe tomorrow we could go to that new deli for a lunch bite and stroll over to that opening at the museum . . .

Of course, it may not work out quite that well the first time. But keep trying. Just refuse to be irritated. Remember the old Chinese saying: "If a man plants melons he will reap melons; if he sows beans, he will reap beans." Look around at your friends who are widows and widowers and feel lucky. Somewhere back in the past there was a marriage, and things you loved dearly about your particular spouse. Was it the sense of humor, the warmth, the intelligence? Or some intangible? You can help your mate to resurrect that quality by resurrecting your own charms. Start with yourself and watch the other person respond. King Vidor once said, "The quickest way to correct the other fellow's attitude is to correct your own." Try it. It works.

It is almost impossible to carp and scold at someone who responds with a smile. Most bitterness is a simple defense mechanism. It's a way of saying: "I expect you to give me the business first, so I'm going to beat you to it." If you can be the one who ends this miserable situation, you'll never be sorry. Your friends will stop avoiding your company; your grown children will visit more often. The only place where people enjoy watching a fight is at a prizefight ring. Otherwise they feel embarrassed and look for the nearest exit, often never to return.

Carping and backbiting are the worst faults, but even too much advice can be damaging. It says in effect: "I don't think you are much of a decision-maker; I'm watching you every inch of the way to prevent you from messing things up."

There's an old story that covers that nicely. Robertson, a wealthy merchant, was on his deathbed calling for his wife. When she came to his bedside he told her, "Jeanie, I have no will. You must write down everything I tell you."

When his wife returned with paper and pencil, Robertson began dictating, in a weak and trembling voice: "First of all, the business goes to Robert Junior."

"Oh, no!" his wife objected loudly. "Robert is weak; he's too crazy about women and gambling. He'd run the business to the ground in a month. Leave it instead to Charles. He has a business head."

"Good—write down Charles, then," said the dying man. "Our house in the country. Without me you won't want to go there any more. I want to leave it to Mary."

"Mary!" argued his wife. "Mary has enough money to go away every summer to the best hotels. Give the house to Diana; she has three children and no money."

"Okay, okay," her husband said resignedly. "Now for the car—I think Jack should get that."

"Jack has a car," the wife protested. "Kenneth should get it. He's old enough now."

At this, a look of anger finally came over the dying man's face. With his last strength, he sat up tall in bed and shouted loudly at his wife, "Listen, Jeanie! Who's dying around here—you or I?"

If you were working on a job, no matter how much you disagreed with your boss's decisions, you would never dream of correcting him all day. That's one of the things that married people always seem to forget. *Give each other more tolerance, politeness and good treatment than you give to strangers—not less!* Follow that rule and your marriage may begin to look as though it were made in heaven.

PART 6

How to Face Up
to the Inevitable with
Calmness and Courage

CHAPTER 31

The Greatest Love Letter You Could Ever Write to Your Wife

When good men die, their goodness does not perish, but lives though they are gone.
—EURIPIDES

When we offer condolences to the widow of a friend who has passed on, how often we find ourselves saying, "Let me know if there is something I can do."

It is an easy gesture that satisfies our conscience, for we assume that most widows have a close relative or an executor of the estate standing by to help her with the probating of the will, the collecting of the life insurance and all the other legal matters that need straightening out before she can gain the use of her property.

So a week after Bill Adams' funeral I was somewhat surprised when his widow, Jan, stopped in at my office and said, trying bravely to hold back her tears, "I'm in a mess! I need your advice."

"Well, you know, Jan, I'm not a lawyer," I said, "but I'll be glad to help you any way I can. Tell me, what's the trouble?"

"Bill didn't leave a will. At least, I can't find it, and I've searched everywhere."

"Did he ever mention a will to you?"

"Never! He hated to talk about such things."

"What about insurance?"

"He had a few policies. About thirty thousand dollars' worth, I think. But a couple of years ago he borrowed five thousand dollars on them."

"Where are the policies?"

"In his lock box. I went to the bank this morning, and they told me I couldn't open it. They had to seal it. Bill even kept some of my jewelry in the safety-deposit box—and a few securities I own."

"I guess that's the law. You'll get them all eventually, after you go through probate court."

"Yes, but meanwhile I'm in terrible shape. The mortgage on the house is due, and the payment on the car."

"What about Bill's pension?"

"His check came the day after he died. The bank wouldn't cash it. They wouldn't even cash his Social Security check. I know Bill had quite a good balance in his checking account. But it wasn't a joint account and I can't touch it."

"Have you an account of your own?"

"No. Bill gave me an allowance in cash to buy the groceries and things like that."

"How much have you?"

"I've got exactly forty-seven dollars. . . . I just don't know what to do."

Jan reached into her handbag for a handkerchief and started to sob quietly.

During the next few days I learned more about estates and taxes and probates than I had known in my lifetime. I introduced Jan to an attorney whose office was just down the hall from mine, and he said, among other things, that Jan could not have drawn money from the bank, even it it had been a joint account which included funds of her own. Nor could she have removed personal valuables from the safety-deposit box.

"But why?" I asked.

"These are legal safeguards," said my lawyer friend, "to make sure that creditors and tax collectors get their share before the heirs divide up what's left. All the assets remain tied up," he said, "until the executor appointed by the court presents to the bank the tax waivers and other documents.

"The executor collects the assets, pays the creditors and funeral expenses, and distributes the assets to the legal heirs. Then he has to file an accounting in the probate court for its approval."

"But," I protested, "all that legal rigmarole is going to take time."

"Unfortunately yes," said the lawyer. "It may take several months before the estate is settled."

"How do they expect Mrs. Adams to live in the meantime?"

"Well, I think we can get the insurance policies released. If there is going to be any real delay, the executor can ask the court for a 'widow's allowance' to pay her living costs until the estate is settled."

He turned to Mrs. Adams. "I want to warn you, Jan," he said, "against taking any short cuts to get cash. For instance, you suggested selling your color television and stereo set to a neighbor who had offered you a thousand dollars for it. If the court appraiser hears about such a thing, he could tie up your estate for weeks, until he had satisfied himself that you were not trying to cheat the tax collector."

Eventually Jan Adams received her inheritance, but only after a grueling period of frustrations and heartaches. Her experience taught me a lesson. I had always prided myself on the careful records I kept of my personal affairs. My will was up to date. My life-insurance premiums were paid the day I received them. The check for my mortgage was invariably made out on the due date. What securities I owned were in the safety-deposit box. Yes, my house was in order.

But the eye-opening experience I had shared with Jan Adams shook my faith. I began to be aware of the legal booby-traps that many well-intentioned husbands unwittingly set for their widows. And I determined to have a second look at the legacy I would be leaving my wife and my children.

I talked with an estate lawyer, a trust officer of my bank, my insurance agent and a tax accountant. And I made many adjustments which I felt would smooth the way toward a satisfactory settlement of my modest estate.

Once I had heard a lawyer say, "It's a pity a husband who has passed on cannot return for twenty minutes, just to answer questions." I decided to do the next best thing—to write a detailed letter of final instructions and to leave it with other valuable papers where it would be found by my wife after I had departed.

On second thought, this seemed unnecessarily dramatic, sentimental and somewhat morbid. But I wrote it neverthe-less—and then relented. I decided that it made much better sense to hand the letter to my wife, tell her to read it carefully and to ask me any questions that were not clearly answered.

The letter made a profound impression on my wife. She is inclined to be oversentimental and I could see her eyes misting up as she read. When she had finished the last page, I said, "Why don't you go over it again later. In fact, I'd like to suggest that you read it several times."

Fran put her arms around me. "You know something," she

said. "You're the most wonderful husband in the world. And I hope I predecease you."

I decided later, with my wife's permission, to reproduce the letter in this book as a helpful pattern for other husbands to follow. Some of the details are purely personal. Most of the letter covers basic things that every wife should know before she is plunged unexpectedly into the problems of being a widow. This is the letter:

FRAN DEAR:

I hope it will be a long time before you will need the instructions I have outlined here. If some of the information seems elementary, it is only because I am trying to answer all the questions you might possibly ask when I am no longer around to answer them.

First of all, I want you to be assured that you can continue to live in our house, which I know you love so much—I hope for the rest of your life. You have said many times, "I never want to live anywhere else; I want to go out of here 'feet first.'" There will be enough income to make this possible.

Most of your income will come from my life insurance. As you may remember, good old Vash Young, God rest his soul, first convinced me that I should have all of my policies in the form of a trust. The money will be doled out to you every month for the rest of your life. I have attached to this letter a complete list of policies, describing exactly how much you can expect each month, and from which companies. Our insurance man, Larry Godden, is thoroughly familiar with all the details. In fact, he has a copy of the memorandum I have prepared and he will follow through to make sure you receive what is coming to you. Larry's phone number and address are in the memo.

If anything should happen to you, the insurance trust will automatically go to our four children, in equal shares—not in a lump sum, but still on a monthly basis. All these details are spelled out in simple, understandable language in the "Insurance Memorandum," and I think we should go over them carefully together, so you can ask me any questions.

The insurance policies are in a big leather envelope in the safe in my closet. You know the combination. In case you should forget it, it is written on the back of the safe on a white sticker, the side that faces the wall.

The balance of your income will be a continuation of my company pension. You will receive only half of the amount I received each month, but it will continue for the next ten years. Between this and the insurance payments and your Social Security, you should have ample. It won't be as much as we have enjoyed, and you won't be able to sign my American Express credit card at the fancy LeDome Restaurant, but you won't have to scrimp.

Our house is in your name. There is still a small unpaid mortgage, but this you can pay out of a special company group insurance policy that will pay you a sizable sum in cash immediately (see memorandum). This is entirely separate and apart from the other life-insurance policies. You can use the balance for funeral expenses, lawyers' fees, inheritance tax, etc. You might even have enough left over to take a trip to Hawaii. The mortgage papers, tax receipts and everything pertaining to the house are in a brown envelope in the safe.

And speaking of taxes, the income from the insurance and the pension should be ample to pay them. In fact I have attached to this letter another memo marked "Suggested Budget" that covers everything I can think of. Study it carefully and make any revisions you think are necessary. Then let's go over it together.

As for my stocks, the certificates are all in my lock box at the bank, along with a list, description, purchase price, current value, and dividend record. The key is in the safe. You may not be able to open the box until the probate court permits you to, but any delay will not cause you a problem, since most of the stocks are to be inherited by the children in equal shares. That's all covered in my will, with which you are thoroughly familiar. My will, by the way, is also in the safe. You, of course, are the Executor, or Executrix.

Also in the safe you will find—neatly arranged, I hope (you taught me to 'BE NEAT')—a list of other assets, title to cars, automobile insurance papers, homeowners insurance policy, and what they call vital records, birth certificates, marriage records, copies of Internal Revenue reports for the past five years and complete information about my two bank accounts.

Bob has full information about every phase of my little publishing company, and since he is going to take it over completely, that is his responsibility. I have also written him a long letter and plan to go over it with him—just in case.

Our attorney, whom we both know and admire, has a copy of all the supplementary documents, and even a copy of this letter. He will help you handle all the details. I've listed the various advisors you may want to contact, with their names and phone numbers—my accountant, insurance agent, tax counsellor and the V.P. at the bank who is thoroughly familiar with my transactions.

And just in case you should need quick ready cash for immediate needs, I am putting $1,000 (in fifty-dollar bills) in an envelope in the safe, marked with your name. It's for current household expenses, or local bills that may be outstanding.

If I have overlooked any details, we can talk them over and I will revise this letter, or attach a supplementary memo.

I hope things will be easy for you. That's the whole purpose of this plan really, to protect you. The kids are grown.

They have their own lives and families. Whatever modest amount I leave to each of them will be, I hope, a welcome windfall.

Just one more point. I hate to mention funeral arrangements, but here goes! Cremation, please. No burial. No headstone. No marble statue of an angel. And *positively* no open casket! Let them sprinkle my ashes on the Intracoastal, where I can watch the Chris-Crafts go by.

If there must be a funeral, let it be small. Private. A family affair. Perhaps a few friends. No flowers. Let them donate a check to the Cancer Fund.

One last request. It'll cost twenty bucks, but do it just to satisfy a sentimental whim. I haven't been to church in years, but have an organist play, softly, that old Mary Baker Eddy hymn that used to be my favorite:

> *O'er waiting harpstrings of the mind*
> *There sweeps a strain,*
> *Low, sad and sweet,*
> *Whose measures bind the power of pain,*
> *And wake a white-winged angel throng*
> *Of thoughts, illumed by faith*
> *And breathed in raptured song,*
> *With love perfumed.*
>
> *Thus, Truth engrounds me on the rock*
> *Upon life's shore,*
> *'Gainst which the winds and waves can shock,*
> *Oh, nevermore.*
> *From tired joy and grief afar,*
> *And nearer Thee,*
> *Father, where Thine own children are,*
> *I long to be.*

* * *

Leaving instructions and providing a regular income are most important. Not all women are capable under strain to deal with sharpshooters or even with the normal problems of settling an estate.

A wife called in the doctor to tend to her sick husband, an underpaid machinist. The doctor, noting the seriousness of the man's illness and the shabbiness of the surroundings, turned callously to the wife and said, "This case is a difficult one and will take a great deal of my time. I can see you probably won't be able to pay me."

"Please, doctor," cried the distraught woman, "save my husband and we'll pay you even if we have to sell all of our belongings."

"What if I don't cure him?" persisted the physician. "Will you still pay me?"

"I'll pay you no matter what happens—if you kill him or cure him," cried the woman.

A few weeks later, the man died and shortly after the doctor sent a bill for $200 as his fee. The grief-stricken widow informed him that she could not pay, and the doctor took the case to small-claims court.

The judge realized what had happened. "Tell me again," he asked the doctor, "exactly what were the terms of verbal contract with this woman?"

"I was to get paid for treating her husband regardless of whether I cured him or killed him."

"Did you cure him?" asked the judge.

"No," admitted the doctor.

"Did you kill him?"

"Of course not," snapped the doctor tartly.

"Then since you neither killed him nor cured him, what right have you to the money?"

Let's assume that you have prepared your wife financially for your sad demise. There is one ingredient missing still that could make all the good effects of your preparations crumble.

Many women have no financial problems when they are widowed—and yet, after several months of widowhood they remain despondent.

The reason for their depression is most often boredom. You may have been your wife's only responsibility. Your interests were her only interests, your opinions her opinions. And if you are gone? What then? Who will tell her what to think and how to face the empty days and nights ahead?

Now is the time to make sure that she has some interests that are hers alone. And don't expect her to do it all by herself.

One of the best ways to prepare your wife to be a widow is to give up some of your selfishness. Encourage her to have her own likes, her own opinions. If you satisfy your ego now by cultivating a perpetual agreer, if she goes wherever you want to go and does what you want to do, you are guaranteeing that she will some day be a miserable widow, a perpetual griever.

One last word on the legal side. There has been much said and written on the question of wills, especially since the publication of the best-selling book *How to Avoid Probate*. One cartoon in *The New Yorker* showed a middle-aged couple reading the book. The husband is saying something like "I know how to avoid it. Spend your money!"

Many people consider wills old-fashioned. They provide for their mates through insurance policies and have come to the conclusion that if they are going to leave their money to their children, they would rather spend it on them while they're alive to see the joy and while their children are still young enough to reap full enjoyment from it. Most of us don't have that much money to worry about in the first place.

But if you have a bit to spread around, and you insist on holding it to be disposed of after you're gone, then remember one thing: This is one time when you can exercise honest and good judgment. You don't have to worry about pleasing everybody, because they can't do anything to you once you're gone.

CHAPTER 32

How to Conquer
the Fear of Death

Depart then without fear out of this world
even as you came into it.
—MICHEL DE MONTAIGNE

I detest funerals. Ever since I can remember I have shunned the thought of death. Rarely in my lifetime have I spoken the words "He died." It was always "He passed away." Once, not too many years ago, the police posted a yellow-and-black sign, DEAD END, at the corner of the street where I lived. In the middle of the night I took a spade, dug it up, toted it in my car two miles and threw it in the murky depths of Long Island Sound. It was never replaced, to my relief.

Not until late in life did I overcome my superstitious fear. I had an intimate contact with death which was so over-powering in its emotional impact that it changed completely and irrevocably my prejudicial attitude.

Kenny Clemson was my good friend and neighbor. About the same age, with similar tastes and talents, we were inseparable. When I trudged eighteen holes on rare occasions, and always with Kenny, it was usually because he had urged me to "get off my duff." "That carcass of yours," Kenny would say, "is going to get fouled up with rust if you don't exercise it."

Often when we walked along the beach together we would

philosophize on life—disagreeing heatedly on most subjects but always retaining a stout respect for each other's views and opinions.

One morning about eleven o'clock Kenny called me on the phone. "Can you meet me down at Murphy's Lounge," he said, "in about ten minutes? It's rather important." I sensed an urgency in his voice and, despite the time of day, I refrained from answering with a wisecrack. "I'll be there," I said.

Kenny signaled the waiter and held up two fingers. "Two martinis," he said, "and make 'em double!"

"Are you kidding? At eleven A.M.?"

"You'll need it!" said Kenny. "God knows I do!"

I looked at him quizzically, waiting for an explanation.

"Remember that gripping pain I had on the sixteenth tee? I thought I had twisted a muscle. I didn't tell you—but I went to a doctor. Several times, in fact. X rays and a lot of tests. . . . Well, I got the news this morning. He pulled no punches—but let me have it straight."

"What do you mean?" I said, shocked.

"You guessed it," said Kenny, in a hollow, choking voice. "Sure they can give me radium treatments. You know the routine. But who's kidding who? I'm a . . . terminal!" He clenched his teeth to stifle a sob.

"Oh, no!" I said, sick with the agony of sudden realization.

Four months went by. Painful, unendurable months for Kenny. Sad and frustrating months for me. The golf days were over. Even the walks on the beach. The philosophical talks we used to enjoy now became a jaundiced protest against the rotten unfairness of fate. For a while we took drives together in my car—aimless drives to nowhere in particular. I wanted so much to help—if only psychologically.

Kenny faced his situation with a stoic absence of self-pity. I suppose Nature gives us the courage to stand up to the inevitable. Moments when I was alone I tried praying to myself—quietly, fervently. For what? I don't know. It seemed so futile, so cruel, so unnecessary.

One night I skimmed through a book—a challenging book by Joshua Loth Liebman, called *Peace of Mind.* I seemed to remember vaguely that the author himself had passed away some twenty years ago. One page caught my eye and held me spellbound. I read it again and again.

The next morning I picked up Kenny and we went for our usual drive. I parked the car under the shade of a towering tree and said, "Kenny, do you mind if I read you something? I found it in a book last night. It impressed me tremendously and I think it may help you."

"You know I'm not a religious guy," said Kenny.

"This isn't religion," I said. "It's just—well, I wouldn't know how to describe it. Let me read it out loud."

I often feel that death is not the enemy of life, but its friend, for it is the knowledge that our years are limited which makes them so precious. It is the truth that time is but lent to us which makes us, at our best, look upon our years as a trust handed into our temporary keeping. We are like children privileged to spend a day in a great park, a park filled with many gardens and playgrounds and azure-tinted lakes with white boats sailing upon the tranquil waves. True, the day allotted to each one of us is not the same in length, in light, in beauty. Some children of earth are privileged to spend a long and sunlit day in the garden of the earth. For others the day is shorter, cloudier, and dusk descends more quickly as in a winter's tale. But whether our life is a long summery day or a shorter wintry afternoon, we know that inevitably there are storms and squalls which overcast even the bluest heaven and there are sunlit rays which pierce the darkest autumn sky. The day that we are privileged to spend in the great park of life is not the same for all human beings, but there is enough beauty and joy and gaiety in the hours if we will but treasure them. Then for each one of us the moment comes when the great nurse, death, takes man, the child, by the hand and quietly says, 'It is time to go home. Night is coming. It is your bedtime, child of earth. Come; you're tired. Lie down at last in the quiet of the nursery and sleep. Sleep well. The day is gone. Stars shine in the canopy of eternity.

Kenny was silent for almost a minute. I saw something glinting on his cheek—a tear, I suppose. "May I have that?" he said.

As weeks passed our talks and drives were necessarily abandoned. Time was running out for Kenny. I stood at his bedside a few days before he lapsed into a quiet coma.

"It helped," he said. "I've read it a hundred times." Then he forced a wan smile and said in a voice that was scarcely audible, just a whisper, "It's time to go home. Night is coming."

And that was the last conversation we ever had. I am no longer afraid to mention the word "death." Sooner or later every living person on earth must face it, each in his own way—some with prayers, some with sedatives, some with an inspirational poem, or sermon, or hymn that makes the transition a little easier to bear.

It may help to remember that one's attitude toward life has a great deal to do with one's attitude toward death.

A century or less ago, people were old at a much earlier

age. A man in his forties was considered an old man, and what he had accomplished in his twenties and thirties pretty much determined his attitude toward death. That is to say, if he looked back on a fruitless or wasted life, he might tend all the more to dread death's knock.

Even religion doesn't help those who have led selfish lives. Often they reject religion for fear of a dreaded hereafter. Fear of death is a common human emotion. A tale as old as Methuselah testifies to that.

Two brothers were preparing to die. Both were old and infirm and knew that their time was near at hand. They made a mutual promise. Whichever one died first would come back to the other in a dream and tell him what life after death was like.

Eventually one of the brothers died. True to his word, he appeared a few nights later in the dream of his surviving brother.

"So tell me, brother," said the surviving dreamer, "what is it like to die?"

"Why, it's lovely," the dream-image replied. "It's like floating in a beautiful warm bath with flowers on all sides of you. And heaven is like that too. But let me tell you one little thing, brother. If Saint Peter were to ask me to return to life, I'd turn him down!"

"Because it's so wonderful to be dead?" asked the dreamer.

"No! Because I'm still so scared of dying, I wouldn't want to go through it another time!"

An unhappy, conscience-stricken person usually fears death for another reason. He is concerned over what others may say about him when he's gone. His worries are groundless, for today in our culture there is a certain reverence shown toward the dead.

A chronic drunkard died. When they lowered his body into the ground not one of the people standing by found it in his heart to say a few kind words. But as the last shovelful of earth was spooned over the coffin, one aged gentleman could contain himself no longer. "Hold that a minute," he cried out. "We can't let him go on his long journey without a good word from one of us. Believe me, he wasn't as big a lush as you all think. Why, he has a son living in New York who drinks twice as much as he ever did and makes a bigger noise about it."

The assembly around the grave sighed in relief. "Ah, yes, he was a virtuous man after all," one said aloud.

Most people have little warning of the exact moment of death, but where a long illness is involved, they often have a clear suspicion that the end is inevitable. At that point they can either whimper about their bad luck or try to alleviate the grief of those around them.

A famous clown lay dying. His manager and relatives at his bedside listened to him making fun of everything and everyone.

"Haven't you done enough wisecracking in your life without doing it on your deathbed?" one relative complained. "Aren't you afraid of Hell?"

"Never fear," said the clown. "I'll joke my way out of there, too. When the Devil asks me my name I'll give him the wrong one. And when he tells me it's the wrong one, I'll ask him why he asked me my name if he already knew it."

Even when members of the burial society arrived to receive any last requests for the funeral, he said to them with his last dying breath, "Remember now, when you lift me into my coffin, be sure not to hold me under my armpits. I'm terribly ticklish."

It seems to me that since death is inevitable anyway, it is much easier to take it in its stride.

Walt Whitman, a notably happy man, wrote this poem about death:

> *Come, lovely and soothing death,*
> *Undulate round the world, serenely arriving,*
>
> *In the day, in the night, to all, to each,*
> *Sooner or later, delicate death.*

And for those who have learned to put their trust in a Heavenly Father, there is a beautiful and inspiring hymn, written one hundred years ago by Henry Francis Lyte, an English clergyman who was near the end of life's journey as he composed it. Most of us have sung it in church with a hymnal in our hands. I reproduce it here because it has brought comfort and courage to millions:

> *Abide with me; fast falls the eventide;*
> *The darkness deepens; Lord, with me abide;*
> *When other helpers fail, and comforts flee,*
> *Help of the helpless, oh abide with me.*
>
> *Swift to its close ebbs out life's little day;*
> *Earth's joys grow dim, its glories pass away;*
> *Change and decay in all around I see;*
> *O Thou who changest not, abide with me.*
>
> *I need Thy presence every passing hour;*
> *What but Thy grace can foil the tempter's power?*
> *Who like Thyself my guide and stay can be?*
> *Through cloud and sunshine, Lord, abide with me.*

I fear no foe with Thee at hand to bless;
Ills have no weight, and tears no bitterness;
Where is death's sting? where, grave, thy victory?
I triumph still, if Thou abide with me.

Hold then Thy cross before my closing eyes;
Shine through the gloom, and point me to the skies;
Heaven's morning breaks, and earth's vain shadows flee;
In life, in death, O Lord, abide with me.

CHAPTER 33

How to Heal a Heartache
Without Leaving Scars

*There is no grief which time does not lessen
and soften.*

—CICERO

It is strange how our lives can be warped by an experience in childhood. I was only ten years old when Aunt Minnie telephoned my mother, long distance, to announce the demise of Uncle Alfred. I could tell that something terrible had happened from the way my mother carried on.

"What! Oh, my God! I can't believe it! When did it happen? He did what? Bichloride of mercury? Mistook it for aspirin? Oh, Minnie, you poor dear. Yes, yes, dear. We'll catch the next train."

I was too young to be given the details, and until my parents returned from the funeral I was shunted off to a neighbor's home for safe-keeping. I shed no tears for Uncle Alfred because I vaguely remembered him as a grumpy old man with a red, blotchy nose and a stale breath that smelled of whiskey.

For a while I suspected that Aunt Minnie had purposely switched bottles in the medicine cabinet, and I didn't blame her. This theory was gradually dispelled by bits and snatches of conversation I overheard during the next few months between my mother and father.

"Aunt Minnie is taking it pretty hard," said mother.

"That's only natural."

"Not the way she's acting."

"What do you mean?"

"She goes to the cemetery every morning and sits beside Uncle Alfred's coffin."

"How gruesome!"

"Imagine! She sits in that cold, dark mausoleum all day long, sobbing and weeping."

"How do you know?"

"Cousin Hilda wrote me. She's terribly worried about Minnie."

It was nearly two years later that I learned, again through eavesdropping, that Aunt Minnie had been taken to a nursing home to spend the rest of her days—"committed" was the word they used.

That was a long time ago, yet ever since, throughout most of my life, I have resisted any outward display of emotions. When called upon to console a friend over the loss of a loved one, I have employed all kinds of conversational devices to divert the mind of the bereaved one and shield him from his grief.

In recent years I have realized that my disinclination to face the tragic realities of life is a psychological fallacy. I have proceeded on the assumption that emotionalism is something to be avoided—repressed and bottled up like the steam in a pressure cooker. This is wrong—just as wrong as Aunt Minnie's continuing paroxysms of grief.

Psychiatrists have learned through exhaustive research that a normal grief pattern is essential to a healthy-minded adjustment to life and that the denial and repression of our sorrow may well prove to be the breeding ground of a delayed mental disturbance—or possibly a physical illness.

So if you feel like crying, cry. Nature has given us tear ducts for a purpose and we should not be ashamed to use them. The unrestrained sorrow you feel in the early days that follow the loss of a lifetime mate may well be the instrument of your later healing.

Loyal friends can help by acting as a sounding board for your grief. Those among them who have experienced the same sad moments of aloneness will understand the need you feel to talk about your loss, to dwell upon your sorrow and to rehearse, again and again, the virtues of the departed one.

Perhaps your most difficult moments will be those when you decide to dispose of the personal belongings and clothing of the one who no longer needs them. Each familiar garment or gadget you touch will open the flood gates of your memory and you will find your grief almost unendurable. Don't let sentiment tempt you to retain these material things as keepsakes or mementos. They can only be symbols of sorrow. Get rid of them as quickly as possible. Sell them—or give them where they can help others. The Salvation Army, the American Legion, a church or charitable organization will gladly take them off your hands.

The day will come, sooner or later, when you will accept the bitter realization that you are destined to go on living. Grief will be less poignant and you will gradually find that you can face your friends with a cheerful front that conceals the aching void in your heart.

You may experience moments of envy and bitterness as you realize how little your loss has affected the old familiar life patterns of those around you. This is the time to resist self-pity with all the discipline you can command.

As weeks go by, you will begin to feel the need for some new area of life interest which will serve as a substitute for the pattern that death has destroyed. It won't be easy—and progress toward a normal recovery will be slow—painfully slow.

Don't be too hasty about changing your way of life. Don't sell your home until you are ready to start out all over again. You will gradually find that life as a widow, or a widower, is quite different from the companionship you have known during your married years. Suddenly you are "the extra wheel" at parties or evenings spent with married friends. And you may find, too, that the memories of past associations will be a constant reminder of your "aloneness."

If you can afford it, and if your health and mental state permit, take a trip or an ocean voyage. A few weeks in Hawaii or the Virgin Islands or in Acapulco may be the tonic you will need to regenerate a zest for living. On the other hand, widows and widowers have both told me that the loneliest place in the world is the deck chair of an ocean liner, or the sumptuous dining room of a resort hotel.

Making new friends is probably the best way to accomplish your readjustment to life. Even if you are in your sixties or seventies, you will find, under proper circumstances, it is easy to cultivate new companionships. Your church is probably the best place to meet people of your own age and interests. Florida, California and Arizona are havens for retired people —with planned communities offering scores of activities and clubs and organizations designed for bringing lonely people together.

Right in your own neighborhood you will find, if you seek them out, many men's and women's clubs and organizations engaged in various projects. Working part time for the Red

Cross or the Community Chest, United Fund or various other charitable organizations will take your mind off yourself and your worries. Most of them are forever in need of volunteers and you will be warmly welcomed.

Some years ago a widow in Fort Lauderdale, Alice D. Richards, wrote an inspiring message entitled "The Road Ahead," offering solace, advice and comfort to other women like herself who had been suddenly plunged into the dark abyss of widowhood.

So sound, so helpful, so comforting were the words and thoughts contained in Mrs. Richards' little pamphlet that ministers, priests and rabbis all over America began writing to her requesting copies for distribution to widows in their own congregations. The pamphlet, reprinted many times in the past few years, has helped thousands through the difficult period of readjustment following the loss of a loved one.

As a sort of benediction to this chapter, I would like to quote, with Mrs. Richards' generous permission, the last few paragraphs from "The Road Ahead":

> "Dark as your picture now appears, be assured there is a well-defined life pattern ahead of you just as there was form, design and meaning to the past. New doors forever open as old doors close. As people, places, things and circumstances accomplish their missions in our lives, we move on to new experiences, acquaintances and friendships.

> "Priceless memories should be cherished but it is well to develop and nurture a hopeful attitude toward the future, knowing there is compensation in all things.

> "It has been wisely observed that 'for TODAY, we can be unafraid of life or death. For TODAY, we can enjoy the beauti-

ful and believe the best.' All life's problems need not be solved today. It is well to live one day at a time—*this* day—today. The strength and fortitude to do so are miraculously given us each new morning.

"Little as you now anticipate it, in due time, new interests, new life, new friends and possibly one day new love await YOU—on the road ahead."

These hopeful words can come to pass if you take heed of a few simple rules, many of which were mentioned in the chapters on "How to Prepare Your Wife to Be a Widow" and "How to Conquer the Fear of Death."

1. Psychologists tell us frankly that much of our grief over the loss of a loved one stems from our own fear of death. Their death reminds us of the imminence of our own. So, first of all, follow the advice in the chapter on fear of death and minimize your terror. In this way, the death of a loved one will not reopen your own fears about your own passing.

2. *For men:* Make sure that you are not left in a state of infantile helplessness. Know how to cook, sew on your buttons, tidy up your own premises. You may never learn how to do it as well as someone who has done it all his life, but you are capable of not only doing an adequate job but of taking pride in your accomplishment. There is nothing effeminate about such know-how. In fact, there is nothing more effeminate than a poor, whimpering soul who is grief-stricken primarily because he doesn't even know how to pour himself a cup of coffee.

3. *For women:* Make sure you have several interests of your own outside of keeping house for your husband. Remind yourself firmly that cooking for another person may be creative and fun, but cooking for oneself is far less satisfying.

Expand your interests to include many spheres and you'll have friends and fun even if you're widowed. You don't want to be in the position of the grief-stricken widow who received $50,000 insurance and said: "What a sad world! Now that we finally are rich, Herbert goes and dies!"

4. In the changing pattern of your life, you may find new horizons waiting to be explored—activities which you had previously forsaken out of respect for the whims or prejudices of your loved one. Perhaps you loved square dancing, yet never attended a square dance because your mate thought it was too strenuous or too juvenile. Now you can do it! Did you love bowling once but your mate thought it was a dull game? Join the bowling team now. In other words, there's no reason for feeling guilty about doing things your mate hated to do. If they're people worth grieving for, then they'd be the first to say, "Perk up, honey, and do all the things you gave up doing in order to spend the time with me."

5. Do what you would advise others to do. No doubt everyone at one time or another has advised a grief-stricken friend. When you gave that advice you believed it was wholeheartedly correct. Now, take your own advice—whatever it was—and I'm sure you didn't advise your friend to give up on life.

6. Lastly, have a thorough discussion with your wife (or husband) in detail about what each of you would do if left alone in the world. It may sound maudlin, but it can contribute much toward a sensible outlook if and when that day does come.

PART 7

How to Give Your Life
a New Purpose
and a New Meaning

CHAPTER 34

How Nine People
Discovered Ways of Staying Young

*The grand essentials to happiness in life
are something to do, something to love,
and something to hope for.*

— JOSEPH ADDISON

"I've Got a Secret"

Whenever I see a certain television program, I think it applies to me. For "I've Got a Secret," and my greatest satisfaction comes from keeping it to myself.

For several years I have been playing the piano at a very attractive and somewhat expensive local restaurant. My repertoire includes the usual familiar melodies that awaken pleasant memories among our middle-aged and elderly clientele—and they seem to enjoy it immensely, for their faces are wreathed in smiles and they nod with approval when I play their favorite numbers. Once in a while a guest will shake my hand as he leaves, and to my very real embarrassment I find that he has palmed a tightly folded bill as a token of appreciation for my efforts. Which brings me to my secret.

I forgot to mention that, each evening, as a change of pace from the old familiar melodies, I let my fingers ripple over the keys in a rendition of Bach or Beethoven's Ninth Symphony, or some other classical masterpiece. The room becomes still—and when I finish there is a burst of applause that warms the heart of this seventy-five-year old white-haired ex-musician.

Why do I call myself an "ex-musician"? Just a sentimental expression. You see, there was a time in my life when I played the piano all alone on the stage at Carnegie Hall with an audience that paid admission—not for a table-d'hôte dinner but just to hear my concert. My name was well known in Milan, Rome, Madrid, London, but today—well, I'm just billed as "Ralph's Dinner Music."

—R.D.J.

"There's Many a Slip Twixt the Chin and the Lip"

I guess you could call me a "third-generation barber." My father and grandfather before me were experts in their chosen trade, or profession, as we call it. I spent forty years of my life back of a barber chair—first down on Wall Street, later at the Waldorf-Astoria—and I proudly numbered among my customers some of the most important New Yorkers of their day—Jimmy Walker, Grover Whalen, Fiorello La Guardia, to mention just a few.

The years began to take their toll in stiffened fingers—and, to my dismay, the razor would sometimes nick a chin or a lip and I would feel the disgrace of having to stop the flow of blood with a styptic pencil.

Came the day when I decided it was time to retire—and I put away my instruments with a reluctant sigh. My wife and I moved to a little town near Trenton, New Jersey, and I really began to feel my age. It was my good wife, Clara, who saved the day. "George," she said, "why don't you drive over to the big orphan asylum near the county line? I'll bet a lot of those kids need haircuts." A week later I made a deal with the superintendent—a "wholesale rate" for 200 haircuts a month. They supplied the chair and the equipment. No shaves, of course. My straight-razor days were over.

I used to think that my life was finished when I left the Waldorf—but I didn't know what happiness was in those days. I never had any children of my own—and it's a pretty nice feeling to have 200 youngsters calling me "Pop."

"Hey, Pop," they tell me, "none of that crewcut stuff! Cut it long, like Illya Kuryakin."

"Illya who?"

"Are you kiddin' ? You know, the guy in 'The Man from UNCLE.' "

If I were twenty years younger, I would adopt one of those kids, just to make sure there'd be a fourth-generation barber in our family.

—G.P.

"They Gave Me Six Months to Live—but I Outsmarted Them"

Seventeen years ago—to use a cliché—I was at death's door. The doctors said I had an advanced case of diabetes, complicated by other ailments, and they implied that I would do well to put my affairs in order. What they didn't reckon with was my determination and will to live.

I went to a library, read all the literature I could find on diabetes and began a new regimen of self-care that followed precisely the most modern medical advice. I quit my job and moved to Florida. As my health improved I became intensely interested in every phase of diabetes—its causes and how to treat it. I talked with specialists, asked a thousand questions and over a period of time became well informed on the subject.

I met others suffering from the same illness and gradually discovered that I could encourage them with my newly acquired knowledge. Now it's seven years later and a lot has happened in the meantime. I founded a Diabetes Society which became affiliated with the County Medical Association —and even though I am not an M.D. and do not expect to be one, I am recognized as an authority on the subject.

Each year I organize and promote a Diabetes Health Fair in a local auditorium, attended by hundreds of patients and sponsored by the County Health Department, the Medical Associations, the local hospitals and the city newspaper. My phone is ringing constantly—twenty, thirty times a day. My health has improved to a point where, with proper care, I expect to live out my normal span of life. It is a wonderful feeling to know that I was able to outsmart the pessimistic predictions—but even more satisfying to be able to help others who are suffering from the same ailment that almost did me in.

—J.H.C.

"I Lied Ten Years Off My Age"

On my sixtieth birthday, the members of my lodge gave me a big dinner party and a cake with sixty candles. I was proud of my age, perhaps because I looked ten years younger. Now that I've hit seventy-two, I'm not so sure I like the idea of celebrating birthdays. Especially since I overheard two teen-agers refer to me as "that old geezer."

So when I moved out to Tucson to give my seventy-two-year-old carcass some warmth and sunshine, I made a big decision. Nobody knows me. There were no long-time neighbors and well-meaning friends to remind me constantly of my three-score years and ten. I vowed that I would deliberately, dishonestly and craftily subtract ten years from my age. Everyone knows that women lie about their age. Why not men? To everyone I met who asked me, I was just sixty-two years old. "Retired early and fit as a fiddle!" The only exception who knows the truth is the local administrator of the Health, Education and Welfare Department. You don't catch me endangering my Social Security.

Funny thing about being sixty-two. I have begun to feel a lot younger than my contemporaries. In fact, when they refuse to play me a third game of shuffleboard, I feel a little sorry for them. But after all they are just a bunch of "old geezers."

—T.H.

"I Was Leading a Dog's Life—Now I'm Leading a Dog!"

Six months after I retired I was the loneliest man in the world. I had lost my wife in an automoible accident several years previous, and now for sure I had nothing to live for. No job. No friends. No interests. No hobbies to keep me busy.

All I had was a modest pension and my Social Security check. Enough for food, clothing and a roof over my head. At least, I was in good health and I suppose I should have been thankful for that. It was a pretty dreary existence—until that lucky day when I happened to pass a pet store and heard a cage full of puppies yipping and squealing inside the open door. Out of curiosity I stepped in and put my hand up against the chicken wire to stroke one of the dogs on the tip of his nose. He stood up on his hind legs, wagged his tail, licked my fingers—and pleaded with me to take him home.

I remember especially his big yellow eyes—strangely luminous and intelligent. His coat was a slick sealskin gray. I had never seen a dog of his breed—a Weimeraner they called him. I turned to the proprietor of the store and said, "What do you want for this pup?"

"That's a very rare breed," he said, "and expensive. Two hundred and fifty dollars."

"What!" I said. "You must be kidding!"

The next day I passed the pet store and couldn't resist the impulse to stop in. The little Weimeraner ("vy-mer-anner," they called him) recognized me and almost jumped through the chicken wire in his eagerness to lick my hand. In my loneliness I felt I had really found a friend.

"Will you take two hundred dollars for him?" I said to the proprietor. "It's all I have."

He agreed and fifteen minutes later I walked the little fellow home on a leash. That first day was something to remember. "Smokey," I called him, took to his new home like a duck to water. He insisted on cuddling up at night on the foot of my bed and first thing in the morning he would paw me gently, as if to say, "Time to get up and play!"

That was five years ago. I've just turned seventy-one and Smokey has been my constant companion through these years. He's a great big fellow now—too huge to sleep curled up on my bed, and when he pulls on that leash, it takes all my strength to hold him.

But our life together is a great source of joy—to both of us, I feel sure. I moved to the country where Smokey and I can go for long walks together in the woods. He swims in a nearby lake and chases ducks, who invariably fly away with a frantic clutter of wings and squawking when he catches up with them. Strangely enough, Smokey has given me a purpose for living. He keeps me busy—and few human beings could ever show me such affection and loyalty. What else can you want in life? At least, I am no longer lonely.

—L.D.

"I Used to Start Drinking at Ten O'Clock in the Morning"

They say that a drinking problem usually stems from an emotional cause a deep resentment, a hidden inferiority, a feeling of inadequacy. I drank for another reason. I was just plain bored. Would you believe it, I never had a drink stronger than Coca-Cola before I retired. I was always too active and happy in my work to feel the need of any extra stimulation.

When my head was put on the chopping block (company policy, age sixty-five) I moved to Sarasota fully expecting to enjoy a life of leisure. I'm not a golfer. I hate the smell of fish. I can't afford a boat. So what else was there to do but sit around that comfortable bar called The Irish Pub and get a snootful of good Irish whiskey? I kidded myself that I liked to play checkers with some of the other "inmates"—but after two weeks we concluded that checkers was a waste of time, so from ten in the morning until late afternoon we would just sit in the open-sky patio and "have one—have another!"

I got to know Harry, the proprietor, pretty well and I think he knew my drinking problem was strictly an antidote for boredom.

One day Harry caught me early in the morning when I was cold sober. "Johnny," he said, "I've got troubles. I have to go to Chicago. That old divorce business. Never was settled. It'll take about a week. Would you like to do me a great big favor? Take over the joint. Run it just like I would till I get back. Tend bar. No cash problems. No purchasing. Our stock will hold out."

I was flattered. This was a responsibility I never counted on. "When do I start?" I said.

"Right now! I'm leaving for the airport in an hour. You know the price schedule on drinks. I don't think you'll have any real problem."

For the first time since I retired I had something to do. A real responsibility—and believe me, until you've been a bartender you don't know what responsibility is.

True to his word, Harry was back home in seven days. The Pub was packed with people. I was behind the bar in my green jacket and white apron, pouring drinks like crazy, mixing martinis, whiskey sours and sidecars. Harry's face broke into a broad grin. "Yes, sir, what'll you have?" I said. We shook hands like old pals.

A little while later when the trade had slacked off, I said, "Harry, I did you a favor. Now it's my turn to ask one. This has been the happiest week I've had in years. I've made a lot of new friends. And you know something? I haven't touched a drop since you left! I want a job. How about it?"

"You read my mind," said Harry. "I was afraid to ask you. You've got it—starting right now!"

So that's how I happened to become a bartender at age sixty-five. Drop in some time and I'll pour you the driest martini you ever tasted!

—J.W.

"I'm the Comic of Candlestick Park"

If there is anything worse in show biz than a ham actor, it's a ham comic. I never quite made the grade on the old

Orpheum circuit and later in the better night clubs. But I did manage to get bookings at third-rate bars and lounges around the country. Small towns. Suburban steak houses.

Finally age caught up with me and the day came when I had to make a living any way I could. I happen to have been, since I was a kid, a rabid Giant baseball fan—first back at the Polo Grounds in New York and now in San Francisco. So I got myself a job as a peanut hawker with the concessionaire at Candlestick Park. You won't believe this, but I'm playing to bigger audiences today than during my whole lifetime.

At sixty-six, I guess I have become sort of a local "character." I hawk my peanuts with a sharp, loud singsong voice— and my pitch is sprinkled with wisecracks. I get plenty of laughs and probably sell more peanuts than any vendor in the park. And you tell me what retiree, at sixty-six, on Social Security and a modest income, can afford to see his favorite ball club, the San Francisco Giants, play *every* home game of the season!

—M.B.

"I Took Up Where I Left Off Forty-five Years Ago"

I have been a bookkeeper all my life. You know the type. Meticulous. Patient. I'll spend half a day on my own checking account searching for a three-cent discrepancy, just to make the books balance.

The company where I worked put me out to pasture at age sixty with a nice pension. I was lost. Frankly, I didn't know what to do with my time. My wife wanted to move to a warmer climate, but we had lived in the same house in Yonkers for thirty-five years and it's not easy to pull up stakes.

One day I was rummaging through an old trunk in the attic and I found a stamp album that had belonged to me when I was a kid of fifteen. I hadn't seen it for many years. A strange thing happened. All the glamor and excitement I had experienced as a youngster came back to me as I examined those stamps—from the U.S.A., Great Britain, New Zealand, Helvetia, Spain and a lot of countries that no longer exist.

I decided to take up where I had left off forty-five years ago. Today I am a real stamp-collecting fiend. I devour the catalogues and have developed a hundred sources for procuring rare and current canceled stamps. Life for me suddenly has a new meaning. Second childhood? I don't think so. After all, Franklin D. Roosevelt was one of the most famous stamp collectors in the world.

—A.F.

CHAPTER 35

Twelve Reasons Why
the Rest of Your Life
Can Be the Best of Your Life

Grow old along with me!
The best is yet to be.
—ROBERT BROWNING

Reason 1. Now That You Are Looking Forward to the Day When You Can Take Life a Little Easier, You Can Become the Person You Have Always Wanted to Be.

Perhaps you have secretly dreamed of being a respected author, a public official, a teacher, a minister, a community leader. Or possibly you have imagined yourself an expert flycaster, a ballroom dancer, a wood carver, a sports authority. Or maybe you have always wanted to be just a "good guy," admired and sought after by your friends. Well, now you have the time at last. Nothing can keep you from what you want to be, if you want it badly enough.

Reason 2. You Can Live Where You Like—Without Respect to Your Job.

Assuming a certain financial independence, you can live wherever the spirit takes you: the seacoast of Florida, the shores of Maine, the hills of San Francisco, the vast spaces of the West, or a sleepy moss-hung town in the deep South. If you are young in heart and still adventurous, you may want to make your home on the slopes of Italy, or the shores of a lake in Ireland, alongside a country lane in England, or on the beaches of Tahiti. The world is waiting out there to be discovered by you—when you are sixty-five.

Reason 3. You Can Play Golf or Go Fishing Any Day the Mood Suits You.

Never again need you envy the business associate who, brazenly and in open defiance of company rules, used to take a day off in the middle of the week for a round of golf. From here on you can say, "I'll meet you on the first tee at nine o'clock Tuesday"—or Wednesday or Thursday or Friday. Your life has become a perpetual string of holidays. That old bromide "Have a nice weekend" is for the poor devils who are still office slaves. Not for you. You are free at last to fish, swim, hunt, shop, whittle—or do anything you please. You've served your time. Now let time serve you.

Reason 4. You Can Throw Away Your Alarm Clock.

After a lifetime of rude awakenings, what a blessed privilege to sleep, if you like, until noon. And even if the early morning "whooosh, whooosh, whooosh" of your neighbor's car starter should interrupt your dreams, you can turn over on your pillow with a benevolent smile of sympathy for poor old George, who has to be in his office at nine sharp. Gone out of your life forever is that nerve-jangling mechanical monster, that cacophonous despoiler of dreams—the alarm clock.

Reason 5. You Can Avoid Associations with People You May Not Like.

Call it diplomacy or call it hypocrisy, somehow you felt constrained to smile and be nice to those you loathed and

despised. Now there is no longer a need for superficial politeness. Just change the pattern of your life if it brings you in
contact with obnoxious people. You are free at last to live
where you please, to seek and to find and enjoy compatible
friends.

Reason 6. You Can Stop Worrying about Raises and Promotions.

Pension checks are not so big as pay checks, but they are a
whole lot more permanent. As for promotions—well, honestly, isn't it a relief to say goodbye forever to the competitive
struggle? If not, why do so many men refer to their business
as a rat race?

Reason 7. You Can Finish a Good Book If It Takes All Night—and Sleep Till Noon If You Please.

There's a sheer luxury in staying with an exciting novel
from start to finish—especially after a lifetime of catch-as-
catch-can reading. You are free at last to become a literary
gourmand. So glut yourself with good books and read till
your eyes are red.

Reason 8. You Can Wear Slacks and a Sport Shirt on Weekdays If It Suits Your Fancy.

Neckties be damned! Business suits are for business people.
If your job henceforth is mowing the lawn or refinishing
antique furniture, then get into uniform—slacks, open shirt,
comfortable loafer shoes. You'll be surprised how your clothing bills, your laundry bills and pressing bills will shrink.

Reason 9. You Need Never Again Find It Necessary to Play Office Politics.

Do you remember how you used to smile and sing out a
cheery good morning to old Sourpuss McGregor, the office

comptroller, who approved your expense accounts, or challenged them? Well, if you should meet him on the street today, you could give him the Royal Snub. On second thought, you would be wise to smile and sing out a cheery greeting. He's the man who signs your pension checks.

Reason 10. You Can Abandon Forever the Pretense of Keeping Up with the Joneses.

As long as human beings enjoy feeling superior to other human beings, there will be status symbols, but somehow they take on less importance in the tapering-off years. And even though you may envy the Joneses for being able to afford a three-week cruise to the Greek islands, you are probably quite content to spend a week or two at Lake Winnepesaukee, now that you are in the retirement years.

Reason 11. You Can Waste Time Outrageously Without Feeling Guilty.

You can stop and listen to the chirping of a robin or the buzzing of a bee as it flits from blossom to blossom. There are thousands of things in nature waiting to be explored—now that you have time on your hands. You can spend an entire afternoon, if you wish, at the zoo, all by yourself; or sit on a park bench, reading, musing, philosophizing, or simply drowsing away the hours. Bernard Baruch set a good example. Why not follow it?

Reason 12. You Can Build Air Castles—and Not be Disappointed When They Crumble.

By the time you have reached sixty-five, life has taught you that the ultimate reward is the dream itself—seldom the fulfillment of the dream. So be a Walter Mitty. Turn your imagination loose. Plan a sailing trip in the turquoise waters of the Caribbean. Dig in the jungle ruins of Peru for Inca gold. Rent a pink villa on the Riviera. Pipe dreams? Who cares? The fun is in the dreaming.

And if you still buy the old myths about the aging brain and believe that the twelve reasons given here "sound very nice, but elderly people just don't have the mental go-power to accomplish half of them," then do a little reading up on the latest scientific facts. For example:

1. Certain brain cells develop pigment deposits during the aging process. Formerly it was believed that this spelled deterioration and senility. Now scientists have proven that the wisdom for judging new ideas is best achieved by the pigmented brain.

2. Another fallacy that stops retired people from trying is the popular belief about unemployability. More and more firms are counting on the reliability, loyalty and consistency of older employees. They are discovering that the virtues of youth—memory, energy, dynamism—are no more important than the virtues of the mature person.

Francis Bacon, over 400 years ago, came up with an especially acute evaluation of youth and old age. He said: "Young men embrace more than they can hold; stir more than they can quiet; fly to the end, without consideration of the means and degrees; pursue principles which they have chanced upon absurdly; care not to innovate, which draws unknown inconveniences; use extreme remedies at first; and will not acknowledge or retract them.

"Men of age object too much, consult too long, adventure too little, repent too soon, and seldom drive business home to the full period, but content themselves with a mediocrity of success. Certainly it is good to compound employments of both; because the virtues of either age may correct the defects of both."

What Bacon neglected to mention, I think, is that the faults he outlined for younger people are less readily corrected than those he assigned to older people. Immaturity is stubborn and refuses to admit its faults. The self-critical attitude of most older people often results in healing the defects which Bacon mentions. While older people are ironically considered too old to work, nine times out of ten voters will pick an older person to guide their nation through perilous times. Let's face it, with the exception of John F. Kennedy, almost every leading statesman was somewhere in the neighborhood of sixty or beyond during his most critical period in history: Churchill, Roosevelt, Truman, Lincoln, Washington. Think about it!

Sir William Muloch, Chief Justice of Ontario, who lived to the age of one hundred, enjoyed a rich and rewarding life to the very end. This grand old statesman scorned the passage of time. On his ninety-fifth birthday Sir William stood before a distinguished group who had gathered in his honor and said, "The shadows of evening lengthen about me, but morning is in my heart. The testimony I bear is this: that the Castle of Enchantment is not yet behind me. It is before me still, and daily I catch glimpses of its battlements and towers. The rich spoils of memory are mine. Mine, too, are the precious things of today, books, flowers, pictures, nature and sport. . . . The best of life is always further on."

Though today Sir William's voice is stilled, his message lives on, to give comfort and hope and purpose to younger men who fear the thought of growing old.

The achievement of an inner peace—a serene contentment

in later years—is a lifetime goal that brings a reward far greater than riches. Truly, the rest of your life can be the best of your life, if you are willing to make it so. As Henry van Dyke eloquently put it:

Let me but live my life from year to year,
*   With forward face and unreluctant soul.*
*   Not hurrying to, nor turning from the goal;*
Not mourning for the things that disappear
In the dim past, nor holding back in fear
*   From what the future veils; but with a whole*
*   And happy heart, that pays its toll*
To youth and age, and travels on with cheer.
So let the way wind up the hill or down,
*   O'er rough or smooth, the journey will be joy;*
*   Still seeking what I sought when but a boy,*
New friendship, high adventure, and a crown,
*   I shall grow old, but never lose life's zest,*
*   Because the road's last turn will be the best.*

CHAPTER 36

Something to Cling to—
When You Need Faith, Hope,
Courage and Peace of Mind

*There are gems of thought that are ageless
and eternal.*

—CICERO

There has never been a time in the history of civilization when all people, irrespective of their race, creed or nationality, were more desperately in need of something to cling to—some philosophy that promises hope for a world hell-bent on its own destruction.

Constantly reminded of our impending fate by newscasters, editorial writers, preachers and politicians, we live from day to day in a jaundiced state of subconscious fears. The inner peace and tranquility for which so many of us search today seem unattainable. Yet occasionally we catch a glimmer of wisdom from words that have been written or spoken by courageous men and women—words that have the power to lift the spirit and sustain us in our moments of desperation.

Here is a carefully selected collection of inspirational quotations, culled from many sources, which may bring you a spark of comfort in those moments when you are face to face with sorrow, confusion or uncertainty. Some are simple, some are eloquent, some are prayerful. All of them have a bearing

on the conflicts, tensions and anxieties that plague our lives
today.

For Moments of Uncertainty

"As I grow older, I grow calm. . . . I do not lose my
hopes. . . . I think it probable that civilization somehow
will last as long as I care to look ahead—perhaps with smaller
numbers but perhaps also bred to splendor and greatness by
science. I think it not improbable that man, like the grub
that prepares a chamber for the winged thing it never has
seen but is to be—that man may have cosmic destinies he
does not understand. And so beyond the vision of battling
races and an impoverished earth, I catch a dreaming glimpse
of peace."

—OLIVER WENDELL HOLMES

For Moments of Discouragement

"We are not the first generation to be discouraged by the
contemporary scene. Victor Hugo reminds us that we now
think of the sixteenth century as one of history's main turning points, with the Protestant Reformation and all the rest,
but that Erasmus, who lived then, called it 'the excrement of
the ages'; that we see in the seventeenth century thrilling
discovery and adventure, opening up the new world, but that
Bossuet, in the thick of it, called it 'a wicked and paltry age';
that to us the eighteenth century represents a stirring scene
of political liberation, with the French and American Revo-
lutions and the like, but that even Rousseau in a disheartened
hour described it as 'this great rottenness amidst which we

live.' So in the sixteenth, seventeenth and eighteenth centuries the people who really fooled themselves were the skep-
tics, the cynics, while those who saw the possibilities and with
a faith that moved mountains believed in them, were realistically right. Surely, in this regard, history can repeat itself in
our century, if we only stand by the best."

—HARRY EMERSON FOSDICK

For Moments of Anxiety

"Civilization will survive and will flourish. The future will
be better than ever. We stand at the gateway of vast new
developments, widening horizons. Enormous technological
progress is on the way. Opportunities for individual achievement will be greater than ever. An era of challenging promise lies ahead.

"Atomic energy can be a greater force for good than for
evil. We have the knowledge and the power to mold the very
face of things. What we need is the will and the faith. Faith is
greater than any bomb! Faith is the most potent weapon ever
devised. Faith in action is the wellspring of America's great
strength, the source of America's great power and achievement. Do not lose faith in mankind, and in the purposes of
the Creator. Do not lose faith in the future."

—DAVID E. LILIENTHAL

For Moments of Melancholy

"If you make a habit of sincere prayer, your life will be
very noticeably and profoundly altered. Prayer stamps with
its indelible mark our actions and demeanor. A tranquility
of bearing, a facial and bodily repose, are observed in those

whose inner lives are thus enriched. Within the depths of consciousness a flame kindles. And man sees himself. He discovers his selfishness, his silly pride, his fears, his greeds, his blunders. He develops a sense of moral obligation, intellectual humility. Thus begins a journey of the soul toward the realm of grace.

"Prayer is a force as real as terrestrial gravity. As a physician, I have seen men, after all other therapy has failed, lifted out of disease and melancholy by the serene effort of prayer. It is the only power in the world that seems to overcome the so-called 'laws of nature'; the occasions on which prayer has dramatically done this have been termed 'miracles.' But a constant, quieter miracle takes place hourly in the hearts of men and women who have discovered that prayer supplies them with a steady flow of sustaining power in their daily lives.

"Too many people regard prayer as a formalized routine of words, a refuge for weaklings, or a childish petition for material things. We sadly undervalue prayer when we conceive it in these terms, just as we should underestimate rain by describing it as something that fills a birdbath in our garden. Properly understood, prayer is a mature activity indispensable to the fullest development of personality—the ultimate integration of man's highest faculties. Only in prayer do we achieve that complete and harmonious assembly of body, mind and spirit which gives the frail human reed its unshakable strength."

—ALEXIS CARREL

For Moments of Grief

"Father, I am only human. I need the touch of human companionship. Sorely I miss those I love who are with Thee.

"I pray that Thou wilt reveal to me unseen presences. Help me to know how close my loved ones are. For if they are with Thee, and Thou art with me, I know they cannot be far away.

"Make real for me that contact of spirit with spirit that will re-establish the lost fellowship for which my heart yearns.

"Give to me faith shining through my tears.

"Plant peace and hope within mine heart. Point me with joy to the great reunion.

"But until then, enable me to live happily, and worthy of those who are with Thee. In the name of Him who is the Lord of Life, I pray. Amen."

—PETER MARSHALL

For Moments of Despair

"I believe that life is given to us so we may grow in love, and I believe that God is in me as the sun is in the color and fragrance of a flower—the Light in my darkness—the Voice in my silence.

"I believe that only in broken gleams has the Sun of Truth yet shone upon men. I believe that love will finally establish the Kingdom of God on earth, and that the cornerstones of that Kingdom will be Liberty, Truth, Brotherhood and Service.

"I believe that no good shall be lost, and that all man has willed or hoped or dreamed of good shall exist forever.

"I believe in the immortality of the soul because I have within me immortal longings. I believe that the state we enter after death is wrought of our own motives, thoughts and deeds.

"I believe that in the life to come I shall have the senses I have not had here, and that my home there will be beautiful with color, music and speech of flowers and faces I love.

"Without this faith there would be little meaning in my life. I should be a 'mere pillar of darkness in the dark.' Observers in the full enjoyment of their bodily senses pity me, but it is because they do not see the golden chamber in my life where I dwell delighted; for, dark as my path may seem to them, I carry a magic light in my heart. Faith, the spiritual strong searchlight, illumines the way, and although sinister doubts lurk in the shadow, I walk unafraid toward the Enchanted Wood where the foliage is always green, where joy abides, where nightingales nest and sing, and where life and death are one in the Presence of the Lord."

—Helen Keller

For Moments of Confusion

"Go placidly amid the noise and the haste, and remember what peace there may be in silence. As far as possible, without surrender, be on good terms with all persons. Speak your truth quietly and clearly; and listen to others, even the dull and ignorant; they, too, have their story. Avoid loud and aggressive persons; they are vexatious to the spirit.

"If you compare yourself to others, you may become vain and bitter; for always there will be greater and lesser persons than yourself. Enjoy your achievements as well as your plans. Keep interested in your own career, however humble; it is a real possession in the changing fortunes of time. Exercise

caution in your business affairs; for the world is full of
trickery. But let this not blind you to what virtue there is;
many persons strive for high ideals, and everywhere life is
full of heroism.

"Be yourself. Especially do not feign affection. Neither be
cynical about love; for in the face of all aridity and dis-
enchantment, it is as perennial as the grass. Take kindly the
counsel of the years, gracefully surrendering the things of
youth. Nurture strength of spirit to shield you in sudden
misfortune. But do not distress yourself with imaginings.
Many fears are born of fatigue and loneliness. Beyond a
wholesome discipline, be gentle with yourself.

"You are a child of the universe no less than the trees and
the stars; you have a right to be here. And whether or not it is
clear to you, no doubt the universe is unfolding as it should.
Therefore, be at peace with God, whatever you conceive Him
to be, and whatever your labors and aspirations, in the noisy
confusion of life, keep peace with your soul. With all its
sham, drudgery, and broken dreams, it is still a beautiful
world. Be careful. Strive to be happy."

—Found in Old St. Paul's Church,
Baltimore, dated 1692.

(Note: The above printed manuscript, entitled "Desiderata,"
was framed on the wall of Adlai Stevenson's office at the time of
his death in 1965.)

For Moments of Disillusionment

"We go through many stages in our development. As
children and as youths we often come to expect life to give us

unblemished joy, unstained happiness. Sometimes we share the ecstatic optimism of a Browning or a Walt Whitman and declare that the whole earth is good and it is a sheer joy to be alive. Then pain intrudes upon our paradise and we become disillusioned and give way to despair. 'Life,' we say, 'is imperfect; friends are deceitful; fame is fleeting; love is fickle.'

"The way to a mature happiness is to move from the stage when we say 'yes' to all of life, through that stage when we say 'no' to all of life, and then on to the ultimate stage when we say, 'in spite of.' In spite of disappointment, sorrow, frustration, imperfection, we can make life worth living, friendship worth treasuring, love worth serving, work worth doing. This is the true human situation. Man, becoming healthy, learns to affirm himself even though he is imperfect and also to affirm his fellowmen. We come to love others because of their faults as well as their virtues. They are human, like ourselves. They are our fellowmen. This, perhaps, is the ultimate meaning of the phrase, 'Thou shalt love thy neighbor as thyself.' We begin to take ourselves and our neighbors for what all of us are.

"The courage of imperfection means, therefore, that while we shall strive always to achieve the best in our power, we shall not torment ourselves continually by seeking to make an absolute out of our relative achievements. Many human beings go through life punishing themselves more severely than anyone could possibly punish them, criticizing themselves, inwardly tearing themselves down, disparaging their own worth. Such self-flagellation shows that the individual has not grown up, that he has not become able to face himself and his conflicts and his impulses without too much disturbance about them.

"Creative growth should be the goal. When we accept the truth, we learn that failure and error are ofttimes as valuable teachers as success and achievement."

—JOSHUA LOTH LIEBMAN

For Moments of Pain

Art thou in agony, brother? Then I pray
Be comforted. Thy pain shall pass away.
Art thou elated? Ah, be not too gay;
Temper thy joy; this, too, shall pass away.
Art thou in danger? Still let reason sway,
And cling to hope; this, too, shall pass away.
Tempted art thou? In all thine anguish lay
One truth to heart; this, too, shall pass away.
Do rays of loftier glory round thee play?
Kinglike, art thou? This, too, shall pass away.
Whate'er thou art, where'er thy footsteps stray,
Heed these wise words; this, too, shall pass away.

—PAUL HAMILTON HAYNE

For Moments of Boredom

"Happiness, I have discovered, is nearly always a rebound from hard work. It is one of the follies of men to imagine that they can enjoy mere thought, or emotion, or sentiment. As well try to eat beauty! For happiness must be tricked. She loves to see men at work. She loves sweat, weariness, self-sacrifice. She will be found not in palaces but lurking in cornfields and factories and hovering over littered desks; she crowns the unconscious head of the busy child. If you look up suddenly from hard work, you will see her, but if you look too long she fades sorrowfully away.

"There is something fine in hard, physical labor. . . . One actually stops thinking. I often work long enough without any thought whatever, so far as I know, save that connected with the monotonous repetition of the labor itself—down with the spade—out with it—up with it—over with it—and repeat.

"And yet sometimes—mostly in the forenoon when I am not at all tired—I will suddenly have a sense as of the world opening around me—a sense of its beauty and its meanings—giving me a peculiar deep happiness, that is nearly complete content."

—DAVID GRAYSON